Quaker HOUSE

1969-2009: 40 Years of Front-Line Peace Witness . . .
. . .*And Just Getting Started.*
www.quakerhouse.org

YES To The Troops.
NO To The Wars.

Quaker House
& Forty Years of
Front-Line Peace Witness

Chris Mc Callum

General Editor
Chuck Fager

Quaker House
Fayetteville/Fort Bragg
North Carolina

On The Cover

A Salute and Thanks to Harvey Tharp, former Lieutenant who served in Iraq, and resigned his commission in protest of the war. He joined Iraq Veterans Against the War, and came to Fayetteville for the peace rally in March 2006, then held his own vigil outside the gates on a freezing Monday morning. To the two angry sergeants who objected to his wearing of medals and service ribbons, his reply was simple, steady and unanswerable: "I earned them."

ISBN No. 0-945177-51-8

Quaker House
223 Hillside Avenue
Fayetteville NC 28301
www.quakerhouse.org

I would like to thank Jack and Donna McCallum, Dusty, Jillian and Mona, K.K., Kent Smith, Ben and Leslie, Rhonda Williams and all the folks at the Headquarters Library in Fayetteville, Bob, Barbara and Gwen Gosney Erickson, Bonnie and David Parsons, Fayetteville Friends Meeting, the Fayetteville Office of Legal Aid of North Carolina and the nice folks at the Java Bean coffee shop in downtown Fayetteville.

– Chris McCallum

From
Some Fruits of Solitude in Reflections and Maxims
Relating to the Conduct of Human Life:

"The author does not pretend to deliver thee an exact piece; his Business not being Ostentation but Charity...But it contains Hints, that may serve thee for Texts to Preach to thy Self upon, and which comprehend Much of the Course of Human Life: Since whether thou art Parent or Child, Prince or Subject, Master or Servant, Single or Married, Publick or Private, Mean or Honorable, Rich or Poor, Prosperous or Improsperous, in Peace or Controversy, in Business or Solitude; Whatever be thy Inclination or Aversion, Practice, or Duty, thou wilt find something not unsuitably said for thy Direction & Advantage. Accept and Improve what deserves thy Notice; The rest excuse, and place to account of good Will to Thee and the whole Creation of God.

– William Penn, 1682

CONTENTS

Prelude

Call it quixotic. Or call it crazy.

June 1969: In Montreal, John Lennon and Yoko Ono released their anthem, "Give Peace A Chance." In Moscow, an international Communist conference wrangled. In Chicago, control of the Students for A Democratic Society was seized by the violent Weatherman faction. In Manhattan, what became known as the Stonewall riots marked the rise of the gay rights movement. In Vietnam, more than 500 US soldiers were killed in the ongoing War.

And on June 29, a committee of Quakers arrived in Fayetteville, North Carolina. These earnest liberals from the cultivated campus community of Chapel Hill were resolved to bring peace to America's quintessential warrior's town.

Fayetteville was home to Fort Bragg, one of the largest Army bases in the US In that summer of 1969, Fort Bragg was busy putting thousands of draftees through simulated combat exercises. These raw troops were then shipped off to Vietnam to face the real thing.

Besides the trainees learning the basics of weapons and tactics, deeper in the post's woods hundreds of Green Berets were preparing for more sophisticated and deadly secret missions behind enemy lines.

On the map, it was a journey of only eighty-plus miles. Yet culturally, Fayetteville was light years from Chapel Hill. Plus the invading Quakers were outnumbered there by a factor of thousands to one.

Nevertheless, here they came, and soon they had established their beachhead, calling it Quaker House.

Forty years later, Fort Bragg was still going strong. In 2008 it dominated the Fayetteville economy and culture more than ever, and was deeply involved in two overt wars, and numerous more secret conflicts. Peace, if it had ever come here, was only the briefest visitor. Military strategists now spoke casually of being in the early phases of what they called "The Long War."

Yet Quaker House was still here too, despite the odds and other difficulties, and notwithstanding the manifest failure to achieve its overall goal. Also like the post, Quaker House was busier than ever in its fortieth year, and had likewise been preparing for another generation or more of service.

It's not really remarkable that Fort Bragg is still active; since 1969, the American "military industrial complex" of which it is a key cog has grown steadily, war or no.

The perseverance of Quaker House is another matter. When it began, as we shall see, it was part of a nationwide organizing upsurge that produced dozens of antiwar projects near military bases. But of these, there was in 2008 only one left, the one that is the subject of this book.

What accounts for the survival of Quaker House? What has it accomplished? Have its founders and staff learned anything that could benefit others who are interested in peace work, or a close-in but critical look at military culture?

These are big questions. Let's sneak up on them, like a clandestine Green Beret team, beginning with a tale about flipping the papers . . . .

1. *Bragg Briefs* – Flipping the Papers

Early morning, a summer day in 1970. Long leaf pines covered much of the open ground on Fort Bragg with cool shadows–the day hadn't really heated up yet. The shadows were welcome. That time of year in the North Carolina Sandhills, any day can get above 95 degrees–cloudless and hot.

Fort Bragg was an open post back then, without gates or enclosing fences. Anybody could drive right onto its streets, past the rectangular red brick office buildings, the white clapboard chapels, the boxy duplexes for sergeants' families, the base schools, its library, the PX – and of course, past the long rows of barracks.

The couple in the old blue Chevy could have taken any number of routes from Fayetteville to the post. This particular morning, they got on Rowan Street in downtown and turned north onto Murchison Road which becomes Highway 210 as it leaves the city, headed northwest through rural Harnett County, before swinging back northeast to end at Smithfield, in Johnston County.

The car was a 1950's survivor that Dave Moose, a local realtor and former labor organizer who quietly supported
the antiwar movement, had loaned them. In his honor, it was called The Moose Mobile.

Even with only two passengers, space was tight in the sedan, because it was stuffed with hundreds of copies of a newspaper called *Bragg Briefs*.

The driver, a GI or maybe an ex-GI, was familiar with the post and maneuvered the car confidently up and down the quiet, narrow streets. The passenger, a sometime student at Duke University, didn't know how to drive yet, didn't even have her license even though she was in her early twenties. A stack of the newspapers covered her lap and the breeze coming through the open windows lifted her long, blond hair away from her face and let it fall back.

It was quiet in the car. The radio was turned off so they didn't attract unwanted attention. It was the driver's job to keep an eye out for the MP's who might give them trouble. After all, this wasn't a normal paper route.

This was Sunday, not a duty day, and the post was still sleeping and quiet. There was no outward sign of the tension, dissent and violence that filled the long white barracks that rolled slowly past the car windows. In the bunks inside the buildings were thousands of America's young men. Their bodies filled the stage in what was arguably the most fantastic spectacle of a spectacular era. But all that drama and horror was veiled and the post lay

3

BRAGG BRIEFS

VOL. 4 NO. 7   NOVEMBER 1971   DONATIONS

Is Fort Bragg ARMY RUNNING you DOWN? HELP!

©1971, Russ Jones

quiet, like a movie set before the arrival of the film crew and actors.

The night before, a group of guys had driven up to Mebane, nearly two hours away, to get the newspapers. A printer up there produced half of the radical papers in the US and *Bragg Briefs* was one of them. It was an underground publication by a group of soldiers at Fort Bragg called *GIs United Against the War in Vietnam*. It was volunteer run with informal headquarters at Quaker House in downtown Fayetteville. Although Quaker House was barely a year old, *GIs United*, a burgeoning women's rights movement and a political theater group—all got considerable support through the networks that intersected there. Quaker House had become the hub of youthful energy and resistance in the area. It had a staff of two then. One of them was J.C. Honeycutt.

Producing and distributing *Bragg Briefs* was a key part of the resistance Quaker House aided. It was distributed to GIs on the post for free, this time by the watchful couple in the chevy. Watching out for MPs was the driver's job, delivering papers was Honeycutt's job; she was the flipper. She folded each copy of *Bragg Briefs* tucking the pages just right to make a compact package that flew ten to fifteen feet when she flipped it out the Moose Mobile's window onto the lawns of the barracks full of sleeping soldiers. Every ten feet she flipped another paper out onto the grass, leaving over a hundred papers in front of one barracks.

"It was fun," Honeycutt said, forty years later. "There was a risk involved but not a real big risk. It was daring and there was a sort of humor in it because it was unexpected to the people coming out and finding this paper and not knowing how it got there."

Quaker House, then just a year old, had much to do with how the paper got there. In its brief existence, Quaker House had achieved a lot. It had also been through a lot. Indeed, in that summer, as J.C. Honeycutt flipped her papers, its survival hung in the balance, and not for the first, or last time.

But there never would have been a Quaker House in Fayetteville if not for Dean Holland. And by rights, it should have been called Unitarian House. But as it happened, when a young Fort Bragg soldier called out for help, the Unitarians missed their chance.

Holland and his two sisters had been raised Unitarian in Omaha, Nebraska by their parents, Richard and Mary. Dean enlisted in the Army in 1968 when he was eighteen and studied Vietnamese at the Defense Language Institute in California.

A photograph of Holland taken on maneuvers in 1968 shows a young Private wearing thick black glasses and clutching a field radio, kneeling in high grass next to some barbed wire. The enormous load of gear strapped to his back and the huge helmet dwarfing his head make him look a bit goofy and even younger than he was.

He was reassigned to the Army Medical Corps when he expressed concerns to his commanding officers about the morality of war. Soon after arriving in Fayetteville he applied to become a conscientious objector, or CO.

"When he applied, no one had ever applied for a CO discharge at Fort Bragg," said Bruce Pulliam, who was a professor of history at Methodist College in Fayetteville at the time. "[The Army] was giving him a very difficult time and so he came and asked the Unitarians if they would help him."

Pulliam attended the Fayetteville Unitarian Fellowship which, then and later, had many military connections. In fact, it met in the YMCA on Fort Bragg. The Fellowship's president was married to an Army Major, and about half the attenders were soldiers or military dependents.

One day in the winter of 1969, Holland visited the Unitarian Fellowship and asked for support from the group. Yet despite the fact the Holland was an enlisted soldier and a fellow Unitarian, "we could not reach an agreement on how we could help him as a Fellowship," Pulliam said. The President of the Fellowship announced that anyone who wanted to support the young soldier could do that on an individual basis; and that was that.

One individual did. After the service Pulliam introduced himself to Holland and gave him a ride back to his barracks. "He was just really broken-hearted...He was crying out like St. Paul," Pulliam recalled.

During the ride Holland asked Pulliam for suggestions of other places he could go for help. Pulliam recommended the Meeting of the Religious Society of Friends (or Quakers) in Chapel Hill, North Carolina. Pulliam was not raised Quaker, but his mother's family had been strong Quakers, and he had briefly attended the Meeting in Chapel Hill in 1962,

Dean Holland

before accepting a teaching position at Methodist College in Fayetteville.

He knew that pacifism had been a major Quaker conviction for the 300-plus years existence of the Religious Society of Friends, and that they–along with the Church of the Brethren and the Mennonites–were considered a "peace church." In many US wars, conscientious objectors from these three churches had been recognized by the federal government and offered alternatives to being drafted to fight. Chapel Hill was eighty-plus miles away, but it was the closest "peace church" Pulliam could think of.

Holland took Pulliam's advice and hitch-hiked up to Chapel Hill on a Sunday morning. He didn't wear his Army uniform, and with his sincere mid-western face and glasses with thick black frames he probably had no trouble getting rides. The date of this solitary pilgrimage is uncertain, but was most likely in late January.

Chapel Hill Meeting gathers in a modest, easy-to-overlook brick building, with no steeple in the Quaker fashion. It adjoins the campus of the University of North Carolina (UNC), and many attenders had university connections.

"He seemed so young," recalled Bob Gwyn, a Quaker from Texas who was a member of the Meeting and a UNC professor of communications. "He didn't look especially military," Gwyn added.

There's no record of Dean Holland's thoughts about that particular meeting, whether it was the first Quaker meeting he'd ever attended, or if he liked it. But at the end he stood up and addressed the roughly twenty people there. He told them that he was part of the antiwar movement at Fort Bragg called GIs United Against the War in Vietnam and that by speaking out he ran the risk of being arrested.

Pvt. Dean Holland, in training

Whatever impression the session made on him, Holland's plea made an impression on the Meeting. And why not? A few days earlier,

6

on January 20, a Quaker president, Richard Nixon, had been sworn in. Antiwar protesters had pelted the Nixon inaugural parade with rocks and balloons filled with ink. And Nixon was deeply distrusted by most of his putative co-religionists in Chapel Hill, regarded as a renegade, a war-monger, and a prevaricator.

Besides, the Vietnam War was then in the fourth year of heavy, ongoing combat; US casualties were piling up at the rate of 100 to 200 deaths per week. Young American men were still being drafted in to the military by the tens of thousands. Some hundreds refused, burned draft cards, and faced jail; thousands more fled to Canada; hundreds of thousands were being counseled, especially by Quakers, on legal ways of avoiding the draft.

These national protests had local counterparts. Bob Gwyn did draft counseling. And just three months earlier, on November 16, 1968, eleven UNC students had been arrested at Fort Bragg for handing out antiwar leaflets on the post. After the incident, two agents from the army's Criminal Investigation Division visited the campus, questioning student activists about whether their group was a communist front. Thus, whatever else was going on, the war remained at or near the top of the list of concerns for most Chapel Hill Friends.

On Sunday, February 6th, 1969, Chapel Hill Friends held their monthly Meeting for Business after worship. A variety of topics were considered–the treasurer reported, and the Meeting approved a strong resolution urging the Orange County Commissioners to remedy the problems with the existing ambulance service in and around Chapel Hill.

But among the mundane and quotidian pieces of business, there was also consideration of what Dean Holland had come to say not long before.

"He didn't offer any specific program," said Bob Gwyn, "but he said something that has stuck in the minds of people who have been involved with Quaker House for a long time and that is, 'Quakers should be in Fayetteville.'" At the time, the Chapel Hill Friends Meeting also had a weekly antiwar vigil. Going to Fayetteville, though, would be pushing the envelope.

"But [Holland] offered a challenge," Gwyn said. "A challenge to do something that would help individuals in the military and would aid their efforts in opposition to the war."

After his visit, Holland hitch-hiked back to Fort Bragg with little or no indication of what was going to happen as a result of speaking to this group of strangers. The Chapel Hill Friends, on the other hand, took Holland's visit very seriously. The Peace Committee agreed to consider the issue of helping individual soldiers at Fort Bragg who were struggling with matters of conscience.

As a way to do that, they decided to explore the possibility of establishing a house in Fayetteville, occupied and run by Friends, that would have regular Quaker worship services. They envisioned a place open for counseling and support for GIs who wanted to become conscientious objectors. It would be a religious witness, part of the Quaker tradition of support for the leadings each individual may feel through his personal connection with God, however they understood the divine. They also wanted the project to be a cooperative effort among multiple Quaker meetings in the state, not only for solidarity but because money was tight; Chapel Hill Meeting was struggling to meet its annual budget of $8000.

The Peace Committee shared the concern with other meetings in and near the Triangle region got positive responses. They also sought support from the American Friends Service Committee (AFSC), one of the oldest Quaker organizations in the US and well-known for its support of conscientious objectors.

Bill Jeffries was one of AFSC's Directors of Peace Education. He headed a committee based in High Point, North Carolina. When Gwyn told him what they wanted to do, Jeffries was shocked. "I thought it was preaching to Nineveh!" he said. [In the biblical book of Jonah, God commanded Jonah to preach to the wicked city of Nineveh, declaring its imminent doom. Jonah refused and ran away, had a famous epiphany in the belly of a whale, or "great fish," and then only reluctantly got on with his preaching mission, which after some initial setbacks, had remarkable success.]

Nevertheless, Jeffries believed that the project would be a powerful witness. "It didn't take a lot of convincing as far as getting AFSC support," he said.

Four months after Holland spoke to the Friends in Chapel Hill, the Peace Committee presented the concern at the Business Meeting once again. (Four months, by the way, is rather speedy for such deliberations in the Quaker fashion.) There were still many unanswered questions: who would oversee the project? Was it to be a short term or a long term thing? How exactly would the operation of the project be shared among different meetings? How much would it cost – and where would the funds come from?

In the meantime, Wood and Susie Bouldin, a married couple who attended the Durham Friends Meeting, had approached the Peace Committee to say they would be interested in taking part in the new project. So, with two volunteers to get the project started and committed support from local meetings and the most prominent Quaker social concerns organization, the Chapel Hill meeting agreed to go forward with the project. A delegation was selected to visit Fayetteville and look for a house.

2. 1969: A Friendly Visit To "Fayettenam"

When the Henry Phillips family left Massachusetts and settled in the vicinity of Albemarle in 1665, they became the first Quakers in what would later be called North Carolina. A visit by the founder of the philosophy, George Fox, seven years later helped the Religious Society of Friends flourish in the area of northeastern North Carolina and beyond. In 1698 North Carolina Yearly Meeting was established, and by the end of the 17th century, Friends briefly controlled the assembly that governed both North and South Carolina and the Governor, John Archdale, was himself a Friend.

Since many Quakers are pacifists and refuse to fight in wars, the Revolutionary War made many Quakers reluctant resisters, and the sufferings of many at the hands of the contending armies were severe. Friends also came to believe the slavery was wrong, and by 1776, North Carolina Yearly Meeting forbade its members from owning slaves.

But complying with this dictum proved hazardous, especially to the freed slaves, because local law allowed them to be recaptured by others and sold back into bondage. Carolina Quakers thus entered into a long and debilitating struggle against one of the key institutions of their society, which was backed by all the instruments of state power.

One outcome of this conflict was the growth of the storied Underground Railroad, which helped many slaves to escape north. The other, and larger, response, however, was an exodus of Quakers themselves. Thousands grew weary of this struggle, and took a similar path north and west, to re-settle in free states such as Ohio and Indiana.

The Civil War again produced many sufferings for Friends, including those who avoided or refused military service for the Confederacy. After the Civil War, the community recovered slowly, and in the process took on much of the coloration of more conventional churches in the surrounding areas. The traditional silence-based, non-pastoral worship meetings were modified to incorporate programmed elements such as hymn-singing and prepared sermons by professional pastors. In addition, in many places the Quaker pacifist heritage was discarded and even derided.

Most of the Friends meetings in North Carolina at the beginning of the twenty-first century are of this "programmed" variety. However, after World War One, a number of new unprogrammed meetings sprang up in the vicinity of area universities. Eschewing pastors and prizing silence, much more liberal in their theological and political views, Chapel Hill Meeting, and the others which supported the founding of Quaker House, were of this sort.

Now, in one of the more unlikely assaults in the state's history, a small band of liberal Quakers was preparing to take on a sizeable chunk of the American military machine, including some of its toughest, most secretive and deadly units. Fort Bragg

Quaker headstone at New Garden Friends Meeting, Greensboro NC: "A lifelong Friend but never a Pacifist."

was the home of the storied 82nd Airborne Division, the Special Forces and their Green Berets. During the Vietnam War, Fort Bragg was one of the major sites from which the Army deployed soldiers to Vietnam, with nearly two hundred thousand men training there during the war (CL).

These Friends weren't the first of their sect to come. In 1755, a Quaker mill-wright named John Newberry set up a water-wheel along Cross Creek in the Sandhills, and a settlement called Cross Creek began. Quakerism never really took root there, but the town grew and after the Revolution was renamed Fayetteville, in honor of the French Marquis de Lafayette, who had supported the victorious rebels.

In 1969, Fayetteville, was North Carolina's fifth-largest city, the biggest town in the Sandhills. The Sandhills are an in-between region, lower and flatter than the Piedmont to its northwest, with the mountains of Asheville a few hours farther inland. A hundred miles to the east was the Atlantic coast, with golf communities growing in the south, the narrow, resort-crowded Outer Banks to the north. Interstate 95, the main route from Maine to south Florida, was not yet complete, but a portion skirted Fayetteville's eastern edge. Passenger trains of the Seaboard Coast Line paralleled the highway and stopped downtown, with direct connections up to New York City or down to Florida.

Small, nearly all-white Methodist College was on the north edge of town; mostly black Fayetteville State University was closer in, the center of a historically black neighborhood and business area. Despite its conventionally southern segregated history, Fayetteville had been pushed further along the path toward integration than most other cities in the state, and perhaps much of the south. This was the result of pressure from the military, under orders to desegregate since the Truman administration in the late 1940s. The mix of old and new in racial attitudes was often jarring: the next county to the north, Harnett, had long been a Ku Klux Klan stronghold.

In 1969 Fayetteville was not quite a one-company town; numerous factories there still made tires, children's games, books, tobacco and small appliances; the Putt-Putt Miniature Golf chain was once headquartered there. Textile mills processed the cotton grown all around; a large downtown warehouse was filled with sheaves of large local tobacco leaves.

The city's commercial heritage was epitomized in the brick Market House, which has stood at the crossroads of the old downtown since 1832. The city fathers had already made its arched profile the city's icon and logo, long before they noticed that Fayetteville's black citizens resented the associations of the Market with the selling there of humans along with cattle and produce.

The rest of downtown, however, was more representative of the city's current reality: Fort Bragg, one of the nation's largest army bases, was unquestionably the main engine of its growth and support, and had been since it opened shortly after World War

The Market House, Fayetteville NC in 2008

One. The post, along with the adjoining Pope Air Force Base, took up over two hundred square miles, extending from Fayetteville's western perimeter into three adjoining counties. Upwards of 20,000 soldiers, mostly draftees, were stationed there in 1969, with many headed for year-long combat tours in Vietnam, or recently returned.

This military presence was a strong safety net for local businesspeople, because a process of de-industrialization was about to kick into gear, which would send the area's traditional industries streaming out of the country, making the GI paychecks and army contracts ever more central to the city's life.

11

The population on the post has risen or fallen according to US military involvement abroad. For example, in 1940 there were 5,400 people at Fort Bragg, but the next year the number rose to 67,000 and during the peak years of World War Two there were close to 200,000. As of the 2000 census there were close to 30,000 troops there.

When the fort was opened in 1918, the ten miles that separated it from downtown Fayetteville and the lack of transportation meant there was little contact between soldiers stationed there and local civilians. What brought the two communities together for the first time was the buildup for World War Two.

In the early decades, "The city had more people than the fort," explained Bruce Daws, Fayetteville's Historic Properties manager. With entry into World War Two, the post's population mushroomed overnight, and "as extra housing was built to accommodate the soldiers, the communities merged," Daws said. Bars began popping up in downtown, and in the Vietnam War years the "strip" was at its peak.

Hay Street, which headed west from the Market House showcased both sides of Fayetteville's reality. Before it mounted a hill into the comfortable Haymount neighborhood, Hay Street ran past several blocks of department stores: Penneys, Belk's, Sears and a local hub, the Capitol. But respectable shoppers turned back when they approached the 400 block of Hay Street, and the looming bulk of the once-elegant Prince Charles Hotel.

There the commercial array changed abruptly to one marked by sleazy bars and strip joints. The Korean Lounge, the Bunny Club, Rick's Lounge, and the Seven Dwarves, were just a few. Tattoo parlors, loan sharks, pawn shops, and stores like Tyrell's jewelry shop, selling overpriced gew-gaws accompanied the adult entertainment. The Prince Charles itself was reliably reported to be heavily patronized by call girls and their johns. This stretch was not for local residents; it was aimed squarely at soldiers unleashed, with cash in their pockets, booze in their gullets, lust in their loins, trouble in their fists and oblivion on their minds.

This strip's chronic brawling and licentiousness had made Fayetteville notorious around the state. The arrival of the city's abiding nickname, "Fayettenam," was a few years in the future, but the basis for it had been laid and reinforced long before.

Just east of the Prince Charles, Hay Street was bisected by Ray Avenue, which ran north through a white working class neighborhood of small wood frame houses. Two blocks up stood a USO center for soldiers at loose ends, and farther up was a VFW lodge. Across the street stood a nondescript two-story house, its white paint graying from time and weather, with a peaked roof, at 324.

This was the house the Quakers settled on. Gwyn and Bouldin met with Dean Holland there."Everyone thought 'What on earth are Quakers doing here? This is not our lifestyle,'" Gwyn recalled.

Uncomfortable though they may have been at first, the group was committed to meeting Holland's challenge. Before the Quakers left town that evening they had held a meeting for worship, pooled their money and paid $100 for the first month's rent, on a six-month lease on 324 Ray Avenue, which would become Quaker House. According to Bruce Pulliam, it was owned by a local man, who did not ask for a security deposit.

The house had been built around 1910 and sat on unsecured brick pillars. Inside the house the plaster was chipped and cracked. Peels of paint hung from the ceiling . The house sat just a few blocks off Hay Street on a large lot that backed up to Cross Creek. It was just a few hundred yards down the same creek that Quaker John Newberry had set up his water-wheel in 1755.

Before long, volunteer labor had made it not only habitable, but characteristic of its countercultural milieu. The front steps led up to a wooden porch outfitted with a bench, a few chairs and a hand-painted sign advertising meeting for worship and an open reading room. The entry-way was lined with stacks of *Bragg Briefs* while tacky bookcases in the reading room offered antiwar and anti-establishment paperbacks.

Most foot traffic came in through a side door, which opened directly into a living room full of chairs and couches where GIs and civilians could sit around and talk. A large portrait of Martin Luther King hung on one wall. Behind the living room was the entertainment room with books, magazines, games and a

Quaker House, 324 Ray Avenue, 1969-70.

record player. Jimi Hendrix, Cream, Jefferson Airplane and Joan Baez were in heavy rotation on the turntable, but there were also classical records and lesser-known pop groups too. The room's centerpiece was an elaborate German chess set belonging to J.C. Honeycutt. Upstairs there were two bedrooms which were for Quaker House staff.

"I did not know the committee had come to Fayetteville and rented the house until I saw the article in the paper," said Pulliam. "So I immediately went down to the house and met Susan and Wood Bouldin and I was, I think, the first person in Fayetteville to visit them." This is entirely appropriate as Pulliam would provide unwavering support for every Quaker House staffer over the next two and a half decades.

Wood Bouldin grew up in the West Virginia Bible Belt, and ran across George Fox in sixth grade while doing a project in Geography class on the state of Pennsylvania and its Quaker founders. He still admired Fox when, in college, he was introduced to the writings of Elton Trueblood; and being ready for adventure, he found himself at Duke Divinity School in 1967.

That didn't work out too well, he said. One day in early 1969 he got into a huge angry shouting match with a Methodist seminarian over the timely question of the propriety of, as he put it, "killing Commies for Christ." Bouldin was arguing the negative, to little effect. As a result of this encounter, Bouldin walked out of Duke Divinity and never looked back.

Maybe he let off steam at the apartment of a woman he was involved with, who had a housemate, another Duke student, named J.C. Honeycutt. He might even have talked it over with Honeycutt's boyfriend, a GI from Fort Bragg named Dean Holland. Anyway, he knew both of them.

Or maybe Holland introduced him to a mild-mannered but persistent academic from Chapel Hill named Bob Gwyn. Gwyn said Dean Holland had come to Chapel Hill Friends Meeting in early 1969, probably January, to announce that the Quakers should be in Fayetteville. Gwyn agreed, and was working to put some kind of project together there. A house; a Quaker house. They hoped to open it by summer; but they needed somebody to live in it and be staff.

Since Bouldin had unexpectedly found himself with considerable time on his hands, this Fayetteville idea was appealing. Before he knew it, he'd agreed, along with his wife Susan, to take on the staff role.

So Wood Bouldin became, in July 1969, the first "Director" of Quaker House. In this new post, he was paid the princely sum of $10 a month. Or maybe per week; talking about it years later, he wasn't sure anymore. The Chapel Hill Peace Committee minutes noted that donations of canned goods would be welcome for the new staff, provided they did not include meat products, as the couple were vegetarians.

As it turned out, only Susie was. With his pay he could buy hot dogs and orangeade at a drug store down by what he called the old slave market. "That was the best orangeade I ever tasted," he said nostalgically.

And active work was going on as well. "Quaker House was the center of the movement then," he said. GIs United held its meetings there. And they worked on *Bragg Briefs*. Once the copy was all typed up at Quaker House, they took it up to Duke in Durham, where they were quietly allowed to use the campus paper's equipment to prepare it for the printer.

Then came distribution, passing it out a few blocks away downtown. Occasionally Bouldin got hassled by what he called "green beanies," or Special Forces soldiers, coming out of bars full of patriotism leavened with liquid reinforcement. But he didn't feel intimidated. He also figured – they all figured – that Military Intelligence was spying on them, but so what?

From the beginning there was another kind of work too. What in more exalted language would be referred to as a ministry of presence. But more than that, he thought of it as maintaining an "alternate environment," where young men trapped in a military system they disliked could find some relief.

One part of it included talking to GIs who were thinking about filing CO claims; Bouldin had a big book of laws and regulations to consult. But mostly it involved what was called "hanging out," and lots of that went on, day and night.

Some of this was doubtless more than a little silly: Bouldin recalls earnestly talking theology and such with a young woman for many hours one day, as a result of which they created, on the spot, what they called PRUM, the Peaceful Revolution of the Universe Movement.

Yet some of this could have been therapeutic, even life-saving. Bouldin remembered one GI spent a lot of time at Quaker House that first summer. He wasn't really an activist type, Bouldin said, didn't work on *Bragg Briefs* or plan rallies. He was just more burned out.

His story was that he'd been hauled before a judge in California after several rounds of getting very stoned and raucously riding rides in Disneyland. The judge told him to take his pick: jail or the army.

He picked the army.

Bad move. He was shipped to Vietnam, and wounded by something that left his skin covered with little bumps, like he'd been pushed into a colander. Wounded by more than that, it seemed. Sent back to Fort Bragg, he often came into the house on Ray Avenue, flopped down on the floor, put on the LP record of the Iron Butterfly's "In-A-Gadda-Da-Vida," and then had flashbacks or something while the music droned and thumped. Wood Bouldin, along with other GIs who were hanging out, talked the guy through these bad spells. "There was a lot of that," Bouldin said.

In a later war they'd call it PTSD. There wasn't a useful name for it then. Wood Bouldin figured that GI was often wasted on heroin, though he followed the house rules and kept it outside somewhere, snorted or shot up before he came in.

"We worked hard to keep the place 'un-arrestable,'" Bouldin said. That meant leaving drugs somewhere else.

15

His wife left Fayetteville for Chapel Hill after the summer. Maybe she didn't take to the city so much; she would not have been the first. He followed soon afterward, but not before Dean Holland, finally out of the army, moved his stuff in.

Was Dean Holland aware of the multiple levels of incongruity involved in having Quakers in "Fayettenam" when he urged them to come? How would these spiritual offspring of the plain-speaking, simple-living, pacifist, tall-black-hat-wearing Friends fare here? In their sensible shoes, they were more suited to an oatmeal box label, or a genteel college town, than trying to find their way amid the machinery of combat and its sideshow carnival of vice fueled by alcohol and hot-tempers.

But for all their misgivings and culture shock, Holland knew something that the Quakers did not: a supportive, diverse community of fellow pacifists and antiwar activists awaited them. They might be outnumbered in Fayetteville; but they would not be alone.

The Sign at Quaker House, 324 Ray Ave.

If the authorities on Fort Bragg had wanted to round up a group of anti-military subversives in 1969, they knew right where they could find them—on post. Fort Bragg itself was the locus of antiwar organizing–before Quaker House, that is. The center of all the town's self-serving patriotism and support was roiling with anger against the war, against the Army and even against America.

The crisis of dissent within all branches of the Armed Forces during the period of 1965 to 1975 was well documented by the military at the time and by civilian historians since then. Few described this more forcefully than retired Marine Col. Robert Heinl, a military historian, writing in 1971:

> "The morale, discipline and battleworthiness of the US Armed Forces are, with a few salient exceptions, lower and worse than at anytime in this century and possibly in the history of the United States.

16

"By every conceivable indicator, our army that now remains in Vietnam is in a state approaching collapse, with individual units avoiding or having refused combat, murdering their officers and non commissioned officers, drug-ridden, and dispirited where not near mutinous.

"Elsewhere than Vietnam, the situation is nearly as serious."

How serious? Heinl saw a military force roiled by "social turbulence, pandemic drug addiction, race war, sedition, civilian scapegoating, draftee recalcitrance and malevolence, barracks theft and common crime . . . . " In this maelstrom, "By several orders of magnitude, the Army seems to be in worse trouble."

Heinl's prose may have been purple, but his overall conclusion was not really in dispute: "Nowhere, however, in the history of the Armed Forces have comparable past troubles presented themselves in such general magnitude, acuteness, or concentrated focus as today."

Fort Bragg was one of the hotbeds of GI resistance. The Army itself counted 1,907 court martials at Fort Bragg in 1968 alone. G.I s at Fort Bragg produced some of the earliest and most successful of all G.I underground publications, *Strikeback* and later *Bragg Briefs*. Private Joseph Miles and a group of buddies organized GIs United Against the War in Vietnam shortly after he was transferred to Fort Bragg in 1968 from Fort Jackson in South

Illustration from *Bragg Briefs,* February 1970.

Carolina, as punishment for antiwar organizing there.

Fort Bragg was regarded as the Siberia where Army dissenters were sent to be straightened out by the spit-and-polish atmosphere of an airborne infantry post. Dean Holland too believed he had been sent there in retaliation for working on *Last Harass*, an underground antiwar newspaper at Fort Gordon, Georgia. But, he told the Greensboro Daily Record, the Army's policy of sending agitators to Fort Bragg backfired because they all got together there.

In early 1969 GIs United filed suit in federal court seeking unfettered on-post distribution of *Bragg Briefs*. The paper was published regularly through 1971 and circulation at times exceeded 5,000. Many similar underground newspapers were being published by soldiers on bases across the country.

Over the next few years, the energy of GIs United would spawn the Haymarket Square coffeehouse in downtown Fayetteville, the Black Brigade

(an antiwar group of African American GIs at Fort Bragg) and the Fayetteville Liberation Arts Committee. All these groups, with varied goals and politics, intertwined with each other and had important roles in Quaker House's formative period.

By summer's end, Quaker House was underway. In September Susan and Wood Bouldin left Fayetteville and returned to the university for the next semester. Dean Holland was discharged from the Army as a conscientious objector and moved into one of the upstairs bedrooms at 324 Ray Avenue to take over staff duties. Occupying the other upstairs bedroom, and also a full-time Quaker House volunteer, was Edith Kaye Lindsey.

Kaye Lindsey

Unlike most of the other characters in the Quaker House story, Lindsey was a local girl. She grew up in Raeford, a small town twenty-five miles west of Fayetteville. She had graduated with honors from Pembroke (NC) State University earlier that year. There she had shown promising writing talents, and had been accepted into the prestigious creative writing program at the University of Iowa.

But her concerns about women's rights, racism and injustice in the military drew her to the new Quaker House project. The pull was strong enough that she postponed her enrolment in the Iowa writing program; besides, as her mother, Mrs. Edith Best, said, "she wanted to gain experience as a background from which to write." There was plenty of experience to be had in Fayetteville.

It was around this time that JC Honeycutt began spending time at Quaker House. Honeycutt grew up in a Methodist family on a farm near Troutman, a small town in the hills of western North Carolina. She was working towards an English degree at Duke and had a job as a secretary at Duke Hospital in Durham when she met Holland through mutual friends and they began dating.

"I guess I was probably a liberal by the time I graduated from high school and got involved in some peace actions and social justice actions in college," Honeycutt said. "What Dean was doing was something that I agreed with and was interested in." Through Quaker House she began going to marches and political actions in Fayetteville and got more involved in the women's movement.

"Dean and I were different but only in that we were from different parts of the country and he was from a more middle class upbringing than I was," Honeycutt says. "My family had middle class values, but not the income to support them." The young lovers found a lot in common and the ninety miles between their cities disappeared each weekend when they got together.

Holland sometimes hitch-hiked. To get to Durham to visit his sweetheart during the summer of 1969 perhaps he walked from the barracks out to Highway 87, Bragg Boulevard, which runs through the post north to south. It's a two-lane country road once it leaves the post. He could walk on the shoulder like he was taking a walk in the country, maybe picking a bouquet of wildflowers as a present for JC.

The young couple were absorbed with each other. "We would talk about the immediate future but not the far future," she recalled. The immediate future was more than enough to deal with–Honeycutt was just ten credits away from graduation and Holland had just been discharged from the Army. Politics and culture were polarizing America in every way and the end of a tumultuous decade of global revolution and repression was in sight. Who knew what would come next? Who cared?

It may be the privilege of young lovers to think of nothing but the immediate, and if so Honeycutt and Holland were more blameless than most.

Quaker House offered a safe place off the post where *Bragg Briefs* could be put together. GIs United held weekly meetings there, on Tuesday nights. And there's no doubt that the many bull sessions among the staff and visiting GIs helped hatch plans for other actions. But residents were also mindful of their vulnerability. "To guard against what they feel is the most likely pretext for a police raid, Quaker House staff members rigidly enforce a ban on drugs and alcohol," reported the *Greensboro Daily News* in late 1969. "We were trying to make it pretty clear that it wasn't just old fashioned piety, but that it would be very bad politically to get the house busted," Bill Jeffries said. Jeffries, the AFSC staffer and a Methodist minister, was part of the group that oversaw the fledgling project.

By mid-autumn, a new period of public protest began in Fayetteville, the likes of which had never been seen before. On the afternoon of Saturday, October 11, 1969 a hundred off-duty soldiers from Fort Bragg wearing civilian clothes led a parade of about six hundred "Patriots for Peace" down Hay Street.

College students and other civilians left their campuses and homes to join the GIs. The impressive column filled the street and the sidewalks and bristled with signs demanding an end to the war. From downtown they climbed Haymount Hill–Fayetteville's once-rich, still historic residential district–and filled Rowan Park. Dr. Howard Levy, one of the speakers to address the historic gathering, was a former Green Beret who had been jailed for refusing to train others.

The cover of *Bragg Briefs* following the march indicates that this

"Patriots For Peace" marching up Hay Street, Fayetteville, 1969.

particular issue was dedicated to the students of a local high school who were suspended for wearing black arm bands in solidarity with the antiwar protesters.

Active-duty soldiers leading an antiwar march through downtown? Organizers breaching the boundaries between civilian and military? Students defying authority inside public high schools? Fayetteville seemed like a town on the brink of revolution–how did it get to this point?

The Fayetteville march, however startling, was not an isolated event.

In 1969 one event after another kept the pot of protest boiling. Some were grim, like the bloody assault in Vietnam known as the battle of Hamburger Hill, where hundreds of GIs were killed and wounded in a ten-day assault on a hill that, once taken, proved to be of little strategic value and was soon abandoned. The public was further shocked by an issue of *Life* Magazine in June, which published photos of 241 US troops, all killed in a single week of Vietnam fighting.

Other actions were more ambiguous, yet kept the pot stirred: in May, California Governor Ronald Reagan had sent hundreds of police into what was called "Peoples Park" in Berkeley, and the resulting bloody rampage became a countercultural legend.

Even the Carolina Sandhills were affected by cultural currents. Fayetteville was about halfway between New York and Miami. Numerous journeyman musicians who couldn't afford to fly to their gigs stopped off there on the long trek back and forth, and played at a club called The Other Side, up Bragg Boulevard away from the Strip. Debbie Liebers, an adventurous teenager then, remembered seeing Joni Mitchell, Tom Rush, Spanky and Our Gang, and others, perform there. Plus there were numerous "hippies" moving into down-at-the-heels rental houses on the fringes of Haymount, where lurid color schemes predominated along with long hair and psychedelic music, and aromatic herbs and other chemicals were inhaled. Fayetteville was still an army town; but this was still 1969.

By fall, antiwar protests were heating up again nationwide. Four days after the Fayetteville march Vietnam Moratorium protests occurred all over the country. They were followed a month later by an enormous peace rally in Washington DC.

At this point, the Quaker House sponsors felt hopeful about their venture; but money remained very tight. Comprised of about a dozen representatives from the meetings that supported the project, in late November the group wrote to other Friends Meetings informing them about it and asking for support, the first broader outreach for the project.

"There may be young people in your meeting who would be interested in a period of service as residents at the House," the letter read. "It would be best for staff to have a better than superficial acquaintance of the traditions and developments of world radicalism, particularly as they relate to the American New Left, as this is the context of discourse-both pro and con."

This displays a remarkable grasp of the situation. First, it is clearly an attempt to draw from the ranks of Friends for staff people, and young Friends in particular. Secondly, the strategy of the approach, i.e., that whether or not the New Left was Friendly (read Quakerly), it was dominant and for Quaker House to be effective it had better engage it.

The first real crisis for Quaker House, however, did not come from the police. Sometime after Christmas, Dean Holland and Kaye Lindsey joined a third person, George Henry Johnson, on an impromptu trip south.

"They had been attending a rock music festival in Florida near the Hollywood area," and visiting friends, Lindsey's mother later said. On December 31, their "compact foreign car," with Johnson at the wheel, tried to pass a long line of vehicles headed north on a curve of US Highway 17 near Riceboro, Georgia, south of Savannah. The car smashed into an oncoming automobile. Holland and Lindsey were killed. Dean was 20; Kaye was 23.

On January 2nd, 1970 beneath the headline "Director's Death Clouds Future of Quaker House," the *Fayetteville Observer* reported that the project "will be closed until its board of directors...meet to consider future action." It added that "the unique home...has been the focal point of much of the antiwar sentiment in recent months."

But as devastating as their loss was, even after only six months of presence, the Overseers found it impossible to lay down the project. They requested and received pledges of financial support from the constituent meetings and as a result, Wood Bouldin returned to re-open the house at 324 Ray Avenue.

After a couple more months keeping the place open, Bouldin left Fayetteville for good, heading back to West Virginia and work with the United Mine Workers union, then to graduate school in renaissance history, and a teaching career around Philadelphia. By 2008, he had retired from teaching and was back in West Virginia.

Quaker House quickly welcomed its next staffers. "After Dean was killed I felt moved to carry on what he was doing," said JC Honeycutt. She left Duke a few credits short of her degree and moved into the back bedroom on the second floor of Quaker House. Yet it was not only Holland's influence that instigated her decision.

"A lot of what I characterize as my liberal ideas growing up came straight out of the Sunday school books," Honeycutt explained. Her upbringing in the Methodist Church included an emphasis on the social gospel. The political activism and the spiritual nature of Quaker House suited her well.

Honeycutt was joined by another staff person, Gary Horvitz, a 22 year old who had recently graduated from Duke with a degree in political science. Horvitz, originally from Iowa, grew up in Raleigh and was eligible for the draft but had filed for conscientious objector status

"The Quaker House was created to provide an alternative to Fort Bragg and all that it represents," Horvitz told the *Fayetteville Observer* in early 1970. Horvitz told the newspaper that an average of eight to ten men visited the house during January and February of 1970, expressing interest in becoming conscientious objectors.

But counseling potential pacifists was by no means the only activity there. Some useful details about what else went on were provided by Army Military Intelligence, who kept the house under frequent surveillance.

One of their reports described a meeting held at Quaker House on January 28th 1970. No fewer than four agents were conducting surveillance

22

outside the building that night and two infiltrated the meeting itself. The agents reported on such things as the planned house-painting party, a shortage of funds and complaints about haircut policies and kitchen police. The agents managed to identify 12 of the 45 people present, three of whom were dentists at Fort Bragg.

Two nights later, they were busy again, as their report recounts:

"On 30 January, 1970, from 1900 hours to 2130 hours, a foot and vehicular surveillance of activities of GI's United Against the War in Vietnam (GIUAWV) was conducted a the Quaker House, 324 Ray Avenue, Fayetteville, North Carolina, and in the downtown Fayetteville area by Special Agents . . . [from the] Fort Bragg Field Office, Region II, 111th Military Intelligence Group, Fort Bragg, North Carolina, with the following results:

"At approximately 1900 hours, an undetermined number of members of GIUAWV gathered at the Quaker House to distribute the February issue of Bragg Briefs, the GIUAWV dissident newspaper. At approximately 2000 hours, two unidentified male caucasians and one unidentified female caucasian departed the Quaker House and began to distribute Bragg Briefs on Hay Street in downtown Fayetteville. An estimated 150 copies of the newspaper were gratuitously distributed. The three individuals mentioned above were dressed in civilian clothes, and the two males appeared to be civilians because of their long hair and sideburns. The distribution continued until approximately 2045 hours at which time the three individuals returned to the Quaker House. No incidents or arrests occurred during the distribution."

The agents also copied and checked the license plates of cars parked near the house. One they identified as belonging to Specialist William Carothers, a name we shall hear again.

The work at the house went beyond producing the underground paper. As spring came on, more public protests were being planned. From Military Intelligence:

On 28 April at 1900 hours, GIs United Against the War in Vietnam (GIUAWV) held a meeting at the Quaker House, 324 Ray Avenue, Fayetteville, North Carolina. There were 35 persons present, consisting of 30 male Caucasians and five female Caucasians."

[Among them: Carothers, Horvitz and Honeycutt, along with Second

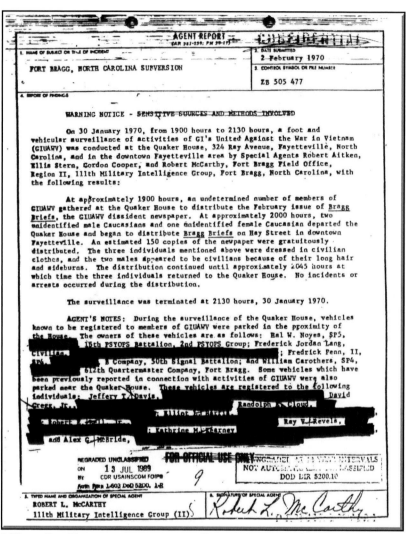

1. NAME OF SUBJECT OR TITLE OF INCIDENT	3. DATE SUBMITTED
FORT BRAGG, NORTH CAROLINA SUBVERSION	2 February 1970
	2. CONTROL SYMBOL OR FILE NUMBER
	ZB 505 477

4. REPORT OF FINDINGS

WARNING NOTICE - SENSITIVE SOURCES AND METHODS INVOLVED

On 30 January 1970, from 1900 hours to 2130 hours, a foot and vehicular surveillance of activities of GI's United Against the War in Vietnam (GIUAWV) was conducted at the Quaker House, 324 Ray Avenue, Fayetteville, North Carolina, and in the downtown Fayetteville area by Special Agents Robert Aitken, Ellis Stern, Gordon Cooper, and Robert McCarthy, Fort Bragg Field Office, Region II, 111th Military Intelligence Group, Fort Bragg, North Carolina, with the following results:

At approximately 1900 hours, an undetermined number of members of GIUAWV gathered at the Quaker House to distribute the February issue of Bragg Briefs, the GIUAWV dissident newspaper. At approximately 2000 hours, two unidentified male Caucasians and one unidentified female Caucasian departed the Quaker House and began to distribute Bragg Briefs on Hay Street in downtown Fayetteville. An estimated 150 copies of the newpaper were gratuitously distributed. The three individuals mentioned above were dressed in civilian clothes, and the two males appeared to be civilians because of their long hair and sideburns. The distribution continued until approximately 2045 hours at which time the three individuals returned to the Quaker House. No incidents or arrests occurred during the distribution.

The surveillance was terminated at 2130 hours, 30 January 1970.

AGENT'S NOTES: During the surveillance of the Quaker House, vehicles known to be registered to members of GIUAWV were parked in the proximity of the House. The owners of these vehicles are as follows: Hal W. Noyes, SP5, 15th PSYOPS Battalion, 2nd PSYOPS Group; Frederick Jordan Lang, ██████████ ; Fredrick Penn, II, ███ , ██ Company, 50th Signal Battalion; and William Carothers, SP4, 612th Quartermaster Company, Fort Bragg. Some vehicles which have been previously reported in connection with activities of GIUAWV were also parked near the Quaker House. These vehicles are registered to the following individuals: Jeffery T. Davis, ██████████████████ David Gregg, Jr., ████████████ , Randolph ██████ , ██████████ , ████████████████ , Ray V. Revels, ██████████ , ████████████ , █ Kathrine M. Kearney ██████ , and Alex G. McBride, ██████████████

5. TYPED NAME AND ORGANIZATION OF SPECIAL AGENT	6. SIGNATURE OF SPECIAL AGENT
ROBERT L. McCARTHY 111th Military Intelligence Group (II)	Robert L. McCarthy

Military Intelligence report on surveillance of Quaker House, January 30, 1970.

Lieutenant James Klimaski & Pvts John I.B. Vail II, and Kendall Halliday]
"Klimaski and Vail acted as the spokesmen for the meeting. It was suggested that a parade be instituted in conjunction with the 16 May rally [as a "counter" to Armed Forces Day]. It was mentioned that a parade to the rally site, Rowan Street Park, Fayetteville, would have to develop on its own, but that a march on Fort Bragg would be more effective . . . ."

But in advance of this May rally, they also held free concerts. Military Intelligence again:

> On 30 April 1970, at approximately 2020 hours, seven male Caucasians and one female Caucasian departed the Quaker House, 324 Ray Avenue, Fayetteville, North Carolina, to distribute the May 1970 edition of <u>Bragg Briefs</u> . . . . Enclosed in each copy of the paper was a flyer . . . advertising a rally sponsored by the Fayetteville Liberation Arts Committee (FLAC) that will be held on 9 May 1970 at Rowan Street Park, Fayetteville. The flyer states that there will be live music, a theatre [event] put on by the Fayetteville Theatrical Association and art displays. The event is called 'Free Spring 3.'

These reports show conclusively that freedom of expression and association were being practiced regularly at Quaker House, along with making plans for peaceful petition for redress of grievances. All of which, it is worth underlining, was entirely legal.

For that matter, military investigators had other, more substantive crimes to worry about. On February 17, 1970, MPs were called to the home of Jeffrey MacDonald, a Special Forces captain and a doctor. There they found his wife and two young daughters murdered, clubbed and stabbed to death, MacDonald himself wounded, and the word "pig" written in blood on the headboard of the couple's bed.

MacDonald claimed that a gang of drug-crazed hippies had invaded the house, beaten him and killed his families. But within a few weeks he was charged with the crimes, later convicted, and at this writing is still serving a life sentence, while still proclaiming his innocence.

With such events in the background, when a local newspaper article that same spring called Quaker House, "the catalyst for dissent, the meeting place for young people bent upon challenging the social order in which they live," this was accurate, but it was not likely meant as a compliment. The article also noted that although the project is funded by Quakers, "religious services as such as rarely held" and that neither of the staff members are Quakers.

That was not the only complaint. Under another headline, "Fayetteville Angered by Protests," the paper spoke of "young activists" who had "congregated in [Rowan] Park spouting political beliefs and holding a series of free rock concerts – much to the chagrin of residents surrounding the park." The concerts, the article added, had attracted as many as 500 people, "who listened to music and watched performances by an organization called Fayetteville Liberation Arts Committee (FLAC) – a sort of 'street theater.'"

City Manager Gilbert Ray said that "many Fayetteville residents objected to the taste displayed by the movement in their literature." But some would soon find much more than that to object to, and would do more about it than call City Hall.

25

3. 1970: Jane Fonda and the Fire this Time

Ask anyone who lived in Fayetteville during the Vietnam era what happened here then and the first thing they'll say is, "Well, Jane Fonda came."

The May 16, 1970 rally was planned to coincide with, and challenge Fort Bragg's observance of Armed Forces Day, and was coordinated with similar protests around the country. The momentum of the plans increased after May 4, when four white college students were killed by National Guardsmen at Kent State University in Ohio, and two black students were killed a few days later at Jackson State University in Mississippi. A wave of outrage and mass protest welled up across the nation among the young and restless. And the stars came out to join them.

In Fayetteville, this meant actress Jane Fonda, who accepted an invitation to join the May 16 march and rally, along with Rennie Davis, a member of the Chicago Eight, a group of activists facing trial for notorious protests at the 1968 Chicago Democratic National Convention.

In the face of the looming protest, post commanders canceled their Armed Forces Day ceremonies and confined most of the troops to their barracks. Even so, hundreds of GIs somehow evaded the ban and gathered with several thousand others in Rowan Park. Fonda and others then took their protest right on to the un-gated turf of Fort Bragg, where they engaged soldiers in "rap sessions" about war and dissent. They were promptly evicted from the post, but then the soldiers, released from their confinement at nightfall, flooded into town, and according to one observer, Quaker House was completely swamped with visitors.

"When we came back we heard there had been the usual threats," Honeycutt remembers. Quaker House staff had become jaded about anonymous callers who threatened to "come over there and kill you" which usually followed high profile events. It had gotten to the point where Honeycutt would reply merely, "Yeah, yeah, we'll be lookin' for you" and hang up.

In the past the threats had always proven meaningless. This time would be different.

One such threatening phone call had come the previous week, in the days leading up to the big protest and action at Fort Bragg. The call was answered by Private John Vail, one of the lead organizers of *GIs United*, who happened to be at Quaker House at the time. The caller had asked Vail if the insurance on the house had been paid up and then said ominously, "It had better be" and hung up.

The next Tuesday night, GIs United had their regular weekly meeting at Quaker House, and reported the largest attendance ever. Afterward, soldiers hung around to talk until late, and one of them, Michael Ralston, who had been discharged from the Air Force that same day, decided to crash for the night on a couch in the entertainment room, while Gary Horvitz and J.C. Honeycutt slept upstairs as usual.

The serendipity of Ralston's presence may well have saved the staffers' lives. He could have gotten a lot closer to his hometown of Salinas, California if he had wanted to, but he ended up at Quaker House instead. Presumably because it was a place that felt safe to him. He was awakened at 2:30 am by fire and smoke so threatening and unbearable that instead of heading for the door of the room, he leaped through the first-floor window.

George Goodman, a neighbor who lived at 319 Mason St., looked out a window and saw the rear of Quaker House engulfed in flames. He saw Ralston running up and down the street and quickly headed outside and pulled a fire alarm.

"Gary [Horvitz] ran into my room and he screamed '*JC GET OUT!*' Honeycutt remembered. "I thought he had ... just gone psychotic, but I wasn't about to argue with him in that mood." She raced to the stairs and halfway down smelled the smoke.

"I got out the side door and when I got out I saw that the back of the house was on fire." According to Honeycutt, Horvitz ended up stranded on the sloping roof above the front door until the firemen came.

Standing on the lawn next to the still-burning house, Honeycutt and the rest of the neighborhood watched and listened as the electrical wires connected to the house sparked and popped. "My initial thought was 'Well I guess this time they meant it. But how stupid to think that they could make us stop doing this by burning our house down!'" she said.

Fire engines came quickly, and the fire was out before it spread very widely. Damage to the building was estimated at about $3000, and Horvitz at first hoped it could be repaired, for much less with volunteer labor.

In the available photo, the house does not look all that badly damaged. But that's because the fire was put out quickly. Honeycutt soon realized how close a call she and Horvitz had had: If Ralston had not been sleeping downstairs and been awakened by the fire, she and Horvitz would probably have burned to death."It really wasn't until a couple of days later that I realized you don't set somebody's house on fire at that time of night to send them a message—you do it to kill them. And when I realized that I felt pretty shaky."

Where, one wonders, were the police or Military Intelligence? Surely they had been around that night, with all the activity. But arsonists managed to set not one but two fires beneath the entertainment room at the rear of Quaker House. The crawl space provided excellent air circulation which fed the flames and they quickly ate up the dry wood at the bottom of the old house and reached toward the sleepers above.

27

An internal FBI Memo about the fire turned up in a sheaf of documents released to Quaker House years later. All of the text except for the heading identifying it as relating to the fire, is blacked out. What was being covered up here?

Is this just idle paranoia? No. Many of the GI organizing projects ran into serious trouble, including arson.

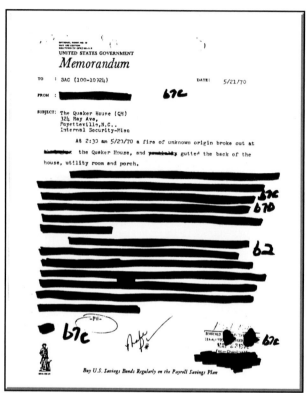

FBI Memo on the Firebombing of Quaker House

The list of possible suspects for the Quaker House firebombing is a long one. Several adjoining counties had been strongholds of the Ku Klux Klan, and in 1970 there were still billboards along highways not far from Fayetteville claiming the region as "Klan Country." Then there was the FBI's COINTELPRO program, which involved disruption and covert violence against "radicals." Closer at hand, there were numerous secretive units at Fort Bragg who were highly trained in such clandestine warfare. And for that matter, just across Ray Avenue stood a VFW post; and one can imagine some anti-antiwar veterans, their resentment given sufficient lubrication, slipping down along the creek, under cover of darkness, to give some payback to those they saw as disloyal subversives.

State and local fire officials made some show of digging into the charred remains of the rear part of the house, looking for signs that the fire was deliberately set, but this was already an established fact in the minds of many. Perhaps sensing that no matter what conclusion they came to it would be ignored, there was no investigation to speak of. "I don't remember really any contact with the police," recalled Honeycutt.

Except there was contact with city officials – who soon told the angry and now homeless staff that they could not return to the house, nor would they be allowed to repair it.

"It appears that the success of recent activities of the Quaker House and the unprecedented positive response of servicemen has been more than some citizens of Fayetteville could tolerate," Horvitz told the *Fayetteville Observer* the day after the fire.

Others in the antiwar network were ready to take them in, though. Army Specialist Bill Carothers, a stalwart of GIs United, had joined with some buddies to rent a house on Haymount Hill, not far away. They added Horvitz and Honeycutt to their motley crew.

Naturally there was fear among Quaker House staff and supporters of another attack. So it was much to their annoyance when the *Fayetteville Observer,* the day after the fire, printed the address of their temporary refuge: 223 Hillside Avenue, just off Hay Street. Horvitz took issue with the newspaper's decision, saying that the lives of the staff were thereby endangered.

A statement put out by Quaker House staff soon after the fire declared, "We feel that the fact of 1,000 GI's coming to the May 16 rally in Rowan Street Park and showing their collective strength frightened the right-wing element in Fayetteville. However, the right-wing may have burned us but they did it with the blessings of Fort Bragg Brass."

GIs United also issued a press release, stating that the group is "greatly concerned over the fire-bombing of the Quaker House." Police found no evidence to indicate a fire bomb was used, however. But there is also no evidence that they looked very hard.

"Almost all the damage was to the back room," Honeycutt said. Consumed in the flames were not only Honeycutt's record collection and sewing machine, but her beautiful German chess set. "[Losing] that was the worst because I paid a hundred dollars for that chess set!" she laughed.

But what about Quaker House? "I think there was a pretty general feeling that we shouldn't just pack up and leave," remembered Bob Gwyn. "I think it's a good clear testimony to faith—we did not have a plan. We were just going on faith that something would work out." Jeffries agreed, "There was certainly a determination to go on in one way or another."

The first thought was to maintain the organization at the same location. The Fayetteville *Observer* reported that the owner would permit the Quaker House staff to repair the damage. "We have tried to reopen our building," the Quaker House press release states, "but the city of Fayetteville claims that it was not being used as a residence and cannot be rebuilt. This is in spite of the fact that our staff lived there for a year." In fact, members of the Haymarket Square Coffeehouse organization had begun helping Quaker House staff tear the damaged room off the back of the house and make repairs to the wall. "Somebody from the building department of the city came over and told us if we didn't stop we'd be arrested," recalled

Honeycutt. After that, thoughts turned to renting or even buying a new home, but that had its own set of problems.

"When we went to investigate about buying or renting a house...it would suddenly not be for sale!" said Pulliam. "This was because of the feeling in the city towards Quaker House. And some people were afraid the house might be burned again if...we opened up." Quaker House was probably beginning to feel the same way about the city.

Flipping copies of *Bragg Briefs* out the window of the Moose Mobile was one of Honeycutt's fondest memories of this period of her life. But Holland's death and the attempt on her life were two of the worst. It had been a rough six months for J.C. Honeycutt.

In 2008, now past sixty and living in Charlotte, NC, Honeycutt works as an insurance fraud investigator, a field heavily populated with former police and retired military. "After having your house set on fire with you in it in the middle of the night, nothing is all that scary afterward," Honeycutt said. "Going to see somebody that I know has a criminal record is not that big a deal for me!" Whatever doesn't kill you only makes you stronger—the cliché is true for Honeycutt and it is true for Quaker House.

Quaker House passed its first anniversary in a state of disarray and frustration—with a touch of paranoia.

The Board and the staff felt that in spite of tragedies and vicious attacks, the project had clearly had an impact on Fayetteville and Fort Bragg. In a memo the Board drafted not long after the fire, they noted the substantial amount of counseling the staff had done and support for a formation of a women's rights group. The memo adds that "after the deaths of Dean Holland and Kaye Lindsey and after the recent fire, substantial numbers of soldiers and civilians expressed concern that Quaker House continue." Quakers are nothing if not deliberate and it was the Board of Overseers who very deliberately carried the organization forward in the aftermath of the fire.

Throughout the summer of 1970 while Quaker House was without a house, meeting for worship was held once a month during the Board meeting outside on the lot at 324 Ray Avenue. The small meeting included the Board of Overseers, the staff and typically one or two visitors. They all sat on folding chairs facing each other in the grass next to the scarred remains of the house they were prohibited from rebuilding. Throughout the silence of the worship service Cross Creek could be heard babbling, just as it had over 200 years ago when Newberry and other Quakers gathered for meeting.

With the slow speech and long pauses of an octogenarian but with the sharp memory of a life-long journalist and professor, Gwyn recalled those meetings: "It was particularly moving, sitting on the chairs outside the burned out building, watching the army intelligence across the street in unmarked cars taking notes. So you really felt like you were in the belly of the beast."

Another regular function that they tried to continue on the lot of the burned house was weekly movie night. It was a very popular event with GIs especially. During the summer of 1970 the folding chairs were set up in the grass facing the side of the house or a make-shift screen such as a bed sheet, and a heavy duty electrical cord was run out of a neighbor's house to power the projector.

Unfortunately, this didn't last long. According to Honeycutt, the supportive neighbor "came over and he told us that he had got a call from the Klu Klux Klan, and they told him that if he ever let us use his power again his house would be next."

The intimidation and threats did not stop there. The house at 223 Hillside Avenue, where Honeycutt and Horvitz were staying, was also home to the group organizing the new Haymarket Square GI Coffeehouse. More overtly "political" and "radical" than the church-sponsored Quaker House, the Coffeehouse too had its share of enemies in the city. Honeycutt said there was a very real fear in the Hillside Avenue house because "everybody in Fayetteville who could read knew that's where we were, and they might decide to come there and just take us all out at once." Following the publication of the house's address in the newspaper, the house near the end of a quiet dead-end street began to receive a lot of curious onlookers in cars, driving by and "rubbernecking," she said.

"At this point we were getting a little paranoid," Honeycutt explained. The members of the two organizations, with the help of a few GIs, began guarding the house in shifts. "They had a couple of guns," Honeycutt said, "I remember telling them that I would be willing to stay up and watch but I wasn't going to handle the gun because the farthest that I would be willing to go would be to tie somebody up and talk to them about Quakerism."

The amateur security guards predictably loused up their work but luckily no one was injured. "At one point, one guy who had had too much to drink got up in the middle of the night and was peeing off the back porch," Honeycutt recalled. "The guard thought somebody was trying to break in and ran around there with the pistol!"

The opening of the Haymarket Square coffeehouse in August of 1970–not to mention the unofficial but close association between it and Quaker House at the time–also made the Board uneasy.

Haymarket was one of dozens of GI coffeehouses and related projects that sprang up across the nation. The Pacific Counseling Center operated successfully out of Oakland, California, serving soldiers at Oakland Army base which, like Fort Bragg, was a primary embarkation point to Vietnam.

Harassment and even violence against these efforts was likewise hardly confined to North Carolina. Fort Knox, Kentucky may have set the record: a coffeehouse project there had been subjected to arrests of its staff, indictments by a grand jury, harassment from landlords, and not one but two firebombings. By late summer 1970, just as Haymarket Square opened in Fayetteville, their Fort Knox counterparts threw in the towel and closed for good. Coffeehouses and organizing projects in Idaho, Tennessee and near Ft. Dix in New Jersey were all firebombed as well; and a GI project in California was fired on twice.

But political and perhaps spiritual hazards were of more concern to the Quaker House Board. "They are not pacifist," a Board memo noted about the Haymarket staff. "They are anti-Vietnam War, but they are mostly concerned with radical change in the nation," with no claim to pacifism. In contrast, "A number of people still feel there is a role to be played by Quaker House...presumably it would continue to be a Quaker witness to non-violence and concern for the integrity of the individual personality. While we seek change in institutions that have become disfunctional [sic], we feel the only genuine change is through non-violence."

The difference between Quaker House and Haymarket Square was only one of many factors the Board weighed as it decided how to move forward. Board minutes during this period include sharp critiques of some of the workings of Quaker House. Among these criticisms, a weak "Quaker spirit" loomed large. As even the local newspaper reported–perhaps a bit to Friends' embarrassment–their Quaker peace witness project was staffed by non-Quakers. Non-Quaker literature predominated at the house and Board members were concerned that they had not been kept informed of the daily activities of the staffers.

Aside from guilt-by-association with Haymarket Square, Quaker House also faced skepticism and even opposition from some Quakers nearby. "When we started, Quaker House was not universally popular among North Carolina Friends. It was just too radical," Bob Gwyn explained. As with any other denomination, there were (and are) ideological rifts among Quakers. Friends who emphasize the Peace Testimony and other forms of progressive witness are greatly outnumbered, in North Carolina and the world, by Friends who more or less ignore these aspects of Quakerism. The latter group was more socially and politically conservative, inclined to be suspicious of "peace" activities, except for the very carefully-calibrated and respectable variety. For instance, in March 1970, before the firebombing, the minutes of Chapel Hill Meeting reported that the Peace Committee of North Carolina Yearly Meeting-FUM, which Bob Gwyn and others had been lobbying for support, "has indicated that it does not favor contributing to Quaker House."

Yet limited finances prevented importing Quakers from elsewhere with anything like the quality of the current staff. Clearly the overseers were torn–they appreciated the staff and thought that they basically were doing a good job, but wished to see more identifiable Quaker spirit, and some sensitivity to the broader denominational situation.

Other concerns included the lack of a strong Board (the responsibility had fallen on just a few), that the project had been a severe financial drain on the member meetings supporting it and the multitude of local concerns that could be occupying their energies without going to Fayetteville.

On the upside, they noted that there seemed to be interest on the part of some young people in Fayetteville in forming a Friends worship group that would meet weekly, not just when the Board came to Fayetteville once a month.

The "Quaker spirit" the Board was after was summed up, and rather sternly emphasized, in the articles of incorporation that were finalized on September 10, 1970:

"The purposes . . . are: to hold religious services, conduct religious and educational programs, lectures, meetings, and discussions, to form groups and associations and to develop, prepare and publish information, reports and other materials, all activities being of an educational and religious nature consonant with the beliefs of the Religious Society of Friends and in furtherance of the educational and religious functions of the Corporation."

The Board also worried about the public perception of their project. The highly visible actions and demonstrations that Quaker House had participated in during the fall and spring alienated many people in Fayetteville. But, the Board noted, local citizens "seemed to object less to the substance of radical activities than its style." Confrontation was inevitable, they concluded, so the desirability of the confrontation depended on its quality. For example, walking to Fort Bragg to speak to GIs about conscientious objection was confrontation, but of a non-violent, constructive kind. Overall, the Board members stressed that staff should consult with theBoardwhen faced with decisions about programs and major tactical decisions.

The situation soon developed another delicate aspect: Honeycutt and Carothers began dating (and eventually married), and this meant a Quaker project was being staffed by an unmarried couple living together. Such arrangements raised the specter of the "sex, drugs, and rock and roll" side of Sixties youth culture, which was sure to be a red flag with many traditional Quakers, even many who were otherwise peace-minded.

Gary Horvitz had drifted out of the Quaker House picture soon after the fire—he was identified as the manager of the soon-to-open Haymarket Square Coffeehouse just a month afterward when the newspaper reported on his arrest on a charge of disturbing the peace. In his absence, Bill Carothers had moved in. Already a stalwart of GIs United, as Military Intelligence reports duly noted, he packed parachutes with the 612th Quartermaster Company during the day and worked with *GIs United* on *Bragg Briefs* in off hours. The paper was paid for with money they made painting houses for Dave Moose, the original owner of the Moose Mobile.

The Board's agonizing about hiring Honeycutt and Carothers as staffers was further complicated when the pair openly expressed their solidarity with Castro's Cuba. They told the Board that they were planning to travel to the island early the next year with the Venceremos Brigade, an overtly Socialist group.

Virginia Driscoll, a Quaker House Board member from the New Garden Meeting in Greensboro, recalled that in regards to Honeycutt and

33

Carothers, "There was a lot of question by the authorities in Fayetteville about who they were and what their political sympathies were." Yet, "Bill was real solid at that time," Honeycutt said later. "If something needed to be done he didn't care if it was a job that was going to make him prominent or invisible, he was willing to do what needed to be done."

And what needed to be done more than anything else that summer was find Quaker House a new home. In October of 1970 Carothers, who had just been discharged from the army, made the crucial breakthrough: obtaining a Veteran's Administration mortgage with a 4per cent interest rate, he put about $200 down and bought the house at 223 Hillside Avenue. Then he turned around and offered to sign the deed over to the Board of Overseers of Quaker House, if they would assume the mortgage.

J.C. Honeycutt, 1970

The sincerity of Carothers' gesture left no doubt in the Board of Overseer's minds about whether the project would be safe in his and Honeycutt's hands, and his offer was accepted with relief. Some months later, after scraping together donations from several sources, the Board bought Carothers' $3200 equity in the house. The title was transferred to Quaker House from Carothers in November of 1971.

On Hillside Avenue, off Hay Street near the crest of Haymount Hill, fine old houses of various building styles sat on a quiet, dead-end street shaded with huge old oak trees. A number of long-time residents—one house served three generations of the same family—gave the street a feeling of permanence.

Prior to the Vietnam War, Hillside and Haymount was a bastion of the Old

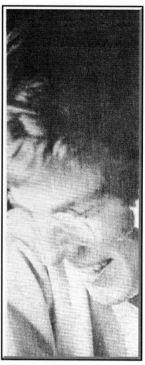

Bill Carothers, 1970

34

Fayetteville establishment. The prominent Rose family, one of whose younger members, Charles "Charlie" Rose, was the longtime Democratic US Congressman from the area, not only lived there but had built several of the houses on Hillside Avenue, including 223.

This house, one of the more modest on the street, was built in 1929, on a narrow lot that adjoins one edge of Rowan Park. In the craftsmen's bungalow style, all on one floor, it still had several unique features. Its roof, for instance, is very intricate, a double-cross gable with a third gable above the front room – a design clearly done by skilled craftsmen, rather than an architect. The maid-cook, presumably a person of color, also had a real toilet, which was quite an amenity at the time. Yet this facility was of its time, located under the back porch and flushed with a bucket. Heating was by three coal fireplaces, with cooking done on a woodstove.

Not long after the end of World War Two, the house was home to a young lawyer with political ambitions named Terry Sanford. His wife Margaret was part of the Rose family. Sanford went on to become Governor and US Senator from North Carolina, as well as President of Duke University (one can start arguments among native Tarheels as to which post was the most prestigious). They extensively remodeled the house, bringing modern appliances into the kitchen, and replaced the coal heating with an oil-based forced air system.

After the Sanfords' tenure, the house followed a path familiar in the neighborhood, and ended up as a rental. By the late 1960's and early 70's, this included some groups of young people with young ideas, commonly referred to as hippies. In some nearby parts of Haymount, the occasional house was repainted psychedelic purple and a heavy drug culture flourished. By the time Quaker House officially moved to Hillside Avenue in the fall of 1970, the Haymount district had lost some of its cachet.

"It was a very prestigious neighborhood," one long-time resident told the *Fayetteville Observer* many years later. "Then came the Vietnam War. The Quakers came in and Jane Fonda came to town. The hippies began coming to the park (Rowan) and began walking through the neighborhood."

It may not be easy for some contemporary readers to understand how unsettling such changes seemed to many older Americans then. But the Sixties culture had a definite dark side, as the Jeffrey MacDonald "drug-crazed hippies" murder case illustrated.

Thus by the time Quaker House officially moved to Hillside Avenue in the fall of 1970, the Haymount district had come downscale a bit, and would later prove a prime candidate for a round of gentrification. And in mid-1970, what went on at the new establishment in 223 raised more than a few eyebrows. "We did counseling, we would advise people who wanted to get out of the military or wanted to file for conscientious objector status or wanted to desert," Honeycutt remembered.

During the months after the fire at the old house, Honeycutt received training in military counseling, nonviolence and the basics of military law. Through the AFSC Peace Education Committee chaired by Bill Jeffries,

Chip Cole came to work at Quaker House alongside Honeycutt and Carothers.

"We were taught that we couldn't encourage people to desert and so we would say something like 'Well I can't encourage you to desert but if you should make up your mind to do so, this is a list of the Friends meetings closest to the border in Canada and they would probably be sympathetic to your situation,'" Honeycutt recalled.

According to the daily activities reports the staff was directed to submit to the Board, sometimes two or three folks and sometimes 30 or 40 would show up. In other words, "no day is typical." The staffers counseled GIs, convened meeting for worship every Sunday at 1 pm, arranged speaking engagements for visiting activists and hosted meetings of local groups. One of those local groups was the women's liberation collective, of which Honeycutt was a member, that would eventually publish a newspaper called *New Carolina Woman.* They found acceptance and welcome at Quaker House that they found no where else. Some 60per cent of the group's members were GI wives.

Some of the activity report entries were more than a little tongue-in-cheek. For instance, the cryptic entry on January 18th reads, "Chip returned with a hitch-hiker and an English setter." The most outrageous entry appears on April 1st 1971:

> The Legions of Rome and the Sabine women led by Rev Bean, a local God-fearing fundamentalist missionary, attacked Quaker House. A howling mob they were, trying to torch the house by lighting copies of the Sermon on the Mount while thinking they were putting on the whole armor of God. Really they were just putting on. But through nonviolence Mrs. Garcia and I defeated them with love. Later that morning I convince the 82nd Airborne to desert. Gurynedd, our dog, decided her bite should be worse than her bark (pretty serious considering her bark) and ate both of the sweet ladies who live next door. And I got reclassified 1-A by Brother Nixon, a small q Quaker. Visitors: Legions of Rome, Sabine Women, Rev. Bean, two sweet old ladies, Brother Nixon, Spirit of God (thankfully)

"The most difficult things were the day-to-day organization and running of the house," Honeycutt remembers. "We had to go out and check the yard everyday because people would throw drugs in the yard, you know there was always the idea that we would be framed for something." The harassment didn't end there. "We knew the phone was tapped because if you didn't hang up right after your call you would hear your call being played back to you," she explained. "That was always kind of a joke."

According to Bill Jeffries, the early Quaker House staffers knew they were in the midst of a hotbed of opposition. "They were very brave and gutsy to spend a night there," he said. Chapel Hill Meeting shared Jeffries' sentiment, noting in their minutes that "living [at Quaker House] takes considerable courage, as some harassment is expected and the house is easily entered"

No doubt about it, Fayetteville was (and still is) hardship duty for peace movement people. A woman's position was particularly difficult – Honeycutt recalled verbal and physical harassment while passing out *Bragg Briefs* on Hay Street. "It's important to be where you're needed," Honeycutt said, and overall that's what kept her there, a sense of being needed.

Change was a constant, however.

4. 1970-71: This One Is Completely out Of Control . . .

After more than two months of volunteer work refurbising a large empty building at the corner of Bragg Boulevard and Hay Street, the Haymarket Square coffee house opened on August 1, 1970. Located at the edge of the Strip, Haymarket aimed to provide a haven and an alternative for dissident soldiers who wanted something other than to throw their money and their minds away further down the street.

GIs United soon moved its weekly meetings and production of *Bragg Briefs* to Haymarket Square. In November, an antiwar conference was held there, which was monitored by Military Intelligence. A few excerpts from their report may be suggestive of the controlled chaos of the movement in those days of turmoil. The chairman, a soldier named Phil Frederick, argued that GIs United

> should attempt to improve the over-all quality of Bragg Briefs (BB) In order to accomplish the improvement, the editorial staff would have to discontinue the use of profane and vulgar language directed at law enforcement officers and "Brass," and begin the use of more constructive articles. . . .In the past, meetings of GIUAVW had not followed any semblance of order but future meetings would follow a more orderly manner.

Despite organizational disarray, constant money troubles and fears about drug busts, Haymarket kept busy. Bluegrass and rock music was also featured, along with many rap sessions. And the kind of social change the Haymarket staff envisioned was also evolving rapidly. In November, GIs United morphed from an antiwar protest group into the GI Union.

The idea for a serviceman's union had been spreading for some time, spearheaded by Andrew Stapp, a soldier-turned labor organizer who was closely associated with the Socialist Workers Party. It issued a list of demands, which was published in *Bragg Briefs,* and dealing with issues of working conditions and soldiers' rights, in addition to ending the war.

For that matter, the war was changing too. President Richard Nixon had announced a policy of "Vietnamization," in which US troops were to be replaced by anti-communist Vietnamese forces. While troops had begun to return home, and draft calls were reduced, opposition to the war was still widespread.

The first half of 1971 was in many ways the zenith of the GI movement around Fayetteville, and perhaps in the nation. At the end of January, the unofficial "Winter Soldier" hearings were held in Detroit, at which over a hundred former GIs testified vividly about the wrongs and horrors of the war. In February, Jane Fonda and Donald Sutherland organized a troupe of antiwar actors and performers for the "FTA Tour." FTA was taken from a recruiting slogan of the time, "Fun Travel, Adventure," which was revised to mean either "Free The Army" or "Fuck The Army," depending on the speaker's judgment of the listeners' tolerance for profanity.

In this venture, Fonda tried to balance her fame as a film star with a commitment to the group. "The press has a tendency to concentrate on Donald [Sutherland], Peter [Boyle] and me," she complained to a *New York Times* reporter insistent on an interview. "One of the things we're doing in supporting the GI movement is developing an alternate lifestyle, another way to look at things, at entertainment as well as at the war. We're a collective. Everyone is of equal importance. And so we decided that no one of us would speak individually to the press." (Though she did, reluctantly.) One rising young cast member, singer Holly Near, was to return to Fayetteville for an encore solo engagement more than 35 years later.

Fayetteville was one of the troupe's first destinations. Barred from Fort Bragg after the May 1970 "incursion," Fonda and company turned to Haymarket Square. The *New York Times* covered the show as if it were a new Broadway hit.

In one skit, Fonda played Pat Nixon, rushing in to see her husband (played by actor Gary Goodrow) in the White House:

> Fonda (agitated): Mr. President . . .
> Goodrow: What is it, Pat?
> Fonda: Mr. President, there is a massive demonstration going on outside.
> Goodrow: There's a massive demonstration *every* day, Pat.
> Fonda: But this one is completely out of control.
> Goodrow: What are they asking for today?
> Fonda: Free Angela Davis and all political prisoners, out of Vietnam now, and draft all federal employees.
> Goodrow: All right. We have people to take care of that, Pat. Let them do their job, you do yours, and I'll do mine.
> Fonda (hysterical): Richard, I don't think you *understand.* They're about to storm the White House.
> Goodrow: I'd better call the Army.
> Fonda: You can't, Richard.
> Goodrow: Why not?
> Fonda: It *is* the Army."

All three of the FTA Fayetteville shows over the weekend of March 13 and 14, 1971 were triumphant, noisy, standing-room only affairs. The

FTA troupe went on to perform for tens of thousands of cheering soldiers and sailors at shows from Fayetteville to the Philipines; they would have gone on to Vietnam if military authorities hadn't stopped them.

Poster for the suppressed 1972 film *FTA*, drawn from the tour.

A superb documentary film was made of the tour, entitled *FTA*; true to the collective ethos, it vividly evoked the variety and creative intensity of the cast members, and the wildly enthusiastic response of their audiences. It appeared in theaters in the summer of 1972 and ran for a week, then was suddenly and mysteriously withdrawn; the director, Francine Parker, was convinced that pressure from the White House led to its suppression. Almost no one outside the studio ever saw it.

Meantime, more than ten thousand protesters were arrested in Washington DC during the MayDay actions, followed in Fayetteville by a second successful protest rally aimed at the Armed Forces Day observances on Fort Bragg.

On the same weekend as the Armed Forces Day protest, a new bombshell burst over Fayetteville: on May 15, 1971, the *Fayetteville Observer* published an ad headed, "We the undersigned concerned officers . . ." in which twenty-nine officers at Fort Bragg and Pope Air Force base publicly denounced "the immoral and wasteful war in which our country is embroiled," and demanded the withdrawal of all US forces and advisers from Vietnam by the end of the year.

The group called itself the Concerned Officers Movement (COM), and it was the brainchild of two West Point graduates, David Vaught and

Cornelius Cooper, who had been holding quiet meetings since the autumn of 1970. Cooper was a black officer, who had found the combat training for Vietnam sobering. As he told *Village Voice* writer Lucian Truscott in late 1970:

"I was made project officer for the Laotians in my Ranger school class late 1970. The Ranger school people were calling them 'gooks' and 'slopes' behind their backs. I threatened to quit, and then decided not to because of my Ranger buddy. He was a Laotian. I

Concerned Officers Movement ad in the *Fayetteville Observer,* May 1971.

guess I identify more with the 'gooks' we're supposed to hate than with any officer. West Point? You're not given much time to think there, but I've had plenty since I got out. And that's what has mattered. A little thinking about these things, and you begin to get straightened out."

The Fayetteville COM ad was soon followed by similar declarations from COM cells at bases as far away as Minot North Dakota and Alaska. Several months later, the same ad was published in the *Washington Post,* this time including well over one hundred officers' names.

These ads, and related COM actions, caught the attention of the higher-ups. As the appalled Marine Col. Robert Heinl wrote, in his piece, "The Collapse of the Armed Forces":

At least 14 GI dissent organizations (including two made up exclusively of officers) now operate more or less openly. . . .Only a short time ago, for example, a dissident group of active-duty officers, members of the concerned Officers' Movement (COM), filed a sweeping lawsuit against Defense Secretary Laird himself, a well as all three service secretaries, demanding official recognition of their "right" to oppose the Vietnam war, accusing the secretaries of "harassing" them, and calling for court injunction to ban disciplinary "retaliation" against COM members. . . .

As for the officers, said a four-star admiral, "We have lost our voice."

The foregoing may be true as far as admirals are concerned, but hasn't hampered short-term junior officers (including several West Pointers) from banding together into highly vocal antiwar and antimilitary organizations, such as the Concerned Officers' Movement (COM). At Norfolk, the local COM chapter has a peace billboard outside gate 2, Norfolk Naval Station, where every sailor can profit by the example of his officers.

Yet despite Heinl's trumpeting of the military's impending doom, COM didn't last long. Most of those publicly identified with it were pushed out of the military, pressured into resigning their commissions. In fact, neither Cooper's nor Vaught's name appeared on the May ad, because both were out of the army by then. Yet it seems clear that COM's audacious public statements shook the pillars of the Pentagon.

Despite this fever of activity, by mid-1971 many forces were at work to undermine the GI movement. Besides the relentless harassment, there was the steadily rising tide of drug use among the thousands of soldiers returning from Vietnam. This was one symptom of what would, a few wars later, be called PTSD (Post Traumatic Stress Disorder), but which had no accepted diagnosis then.

In addition, the ideologically shapeless fervor of earlier years began to settle into more familiar patterns, reflecting the influence and rhetoric of older Marxist groups. The formation of the GI union was one example. But along with the old Left influence, came its tradition of sectarian rhetoric and infighting, which combined to drive away the mass base they were always lusting after.

More broadly, amid the increased brutality of the war itself, the Nixon administration was steadily decreasing the number of US troops in Vietnam, and moving steadily toward an end to the military draft. Soldier organizing was also undercut by a Pentagon decision in December 1971 to permit tens of thousands of overseas returnees and troops with less than six months service to receive immediate honorable discharges merely by asking. This was less an act of compassion or leniency as much as a desperate attempt to rid the military of potential resisters and to stave off further resistance from within. The president was also known to believe that an end to the draft would sap both the student-based and GI protest movements of much of their energy, and in this he proved to be right.

Thus despite the triumphs of the spring and summer, by the end of 1971, the Haymarket Square staff were running out of money and enthusiasm. In February of 1972, the coffeehouse closed, blaming not only greedy landlords who wanted higher rents, but also the strain of constantly having to watch for dope pushers and undercover cops, both of which were increasingly plentiful in and around the downtown Strip. Between the lines, though, could be read the beginnings of the epitaph of the GI and Sixties antiwar movement: fatigue, frustration, and fragmentation.

At Quaker House, things were not much better. J.C. Honeycutt and Bill Carothers left for Cuba in early 1971. Without GIs United and *Bragg Briefs* as an operational focus, the project faltered. Further, by the fall of 1971 the project was without staff, a hiatus which lasted into the following year. It was all the more painful and dispiriting because of the way in which it happened.

Following the departure of Honeycutt and Carothers for Cuba, the Board interviewed a interested couple, Harry "Scotty" and Sara Scott. On paper they looked ideal: married, for one thing; and Quaker too, members of the Adelphi Meeting outside Washington DC, with a record of being active and active in the youth Friends movement. Scotty's father served on the Executive Committee of the Friends World Committee and his mother worked with American Friends Service Committee office in Baltimore.

At a meeting in April of 1971 the Board enthusiastically received a long letter the Scotts had written explaining their interest in working at Quaker House and the couple's ideas on the operations and goals of the project. The Board noted that Sarah Scott would be a considerable asset to the growing women's rights group which met regularly at the house on Hillside Avenue. "It was the consensus of the Meeting to send Scotty and Sarah an invitation to take over duties at Quaker House in mid June," the Board concluded.

"They came highly recommended and we were just thrilled that they were coming," remembered Pulliam.

Enthusiasm for the Scotts was short-lived, however. They moved in in late June, but by August they were missing in action. Pulliam called and visited the house frequently but found no one there.

In one sense they had not gone far; in another they had: Pulliam reported that, "They decided that Quaker House was not politically orientated [sic] enough and so they just left and without telling the Board, and we did not know about it until about two weeks later." The Scotts had chosen instead to work with Haymarket Square Coffeehouse.

The Scotts discovered, upon arriving, that they would have to build up the programs from scratch at Quaker House whereas "right down the street [at the Haymarket Square Coffeehouse] there were projects up and running." "[The Coffeehouse] was more exciting and there were more people," Scott said.

During their brief stay at Quaker House the Scotts focused on involving the wives of GIs more than in the past. "The women's group did end up building a lot more community ties with the wives of service men," Scott remembered. "They had quite a little group going there."

Scott also attempted to continue the efforts, begun by AFSC staffer Chip Cole, to expand Quaker House's services to Marines at Camp Lejuene, a hundred miles east in Jacksonville, NC. In addition to these fairly new functions, they hosted meetings of *GIs United*, the women's rights group and the editors of *Bragg* Briefs. Notes also indicate they were helping out at the Coffeehouse, which was short staffed at the time.

But overall, the Scotts felt very isolated at Quaker House. "With all the stuff that had happened with the firebombing, that made people worried about the Quaker House," Scott remembers. "We didn't have a huge community base with the Fayetteville community other than the GIs we were working with."

In 2008 Scott taught first and second grade in Huntingdon, Vermont. "We came to Fayetteville to work at the Quaker House, and very quickly found that the work the folks at the coffeehouse were doing was what we wanted to be doing," Scotty Scott recalled. His decision to leave Quaker House "in the lurch" was definitely an unfortunate one, Scott admitted.

The Scotts' letter of resignation (delivered to the Board after they had moved out of Quaker House) gave a very critical account of the organization from within. Scotty Scott accused the Board of using their identity as a married Quaker couple from a family with long involvement in Quaker issues to get legitimacy and financial support from the more conservative elements of North Carolina Yearly Meeting. The Scotts also objected to having been grilled by the Board on their political beliefs, they said, with a tape recorder running. Yet evidently one of their central misgivings about Quaker House was that it was not "political" enough.

Between the Quaker Peace testimony and the radicalism of the Haymarket Square Coffeehouse, they chose the latter. Scotty wrote, "Because we are oriented toward political programs the counseling has to be done in line with a political philosophy. Therefore, we have many questions about the form counseling should take. Right now we aren't prepared to do the necessary work to straighten that out."

About regular meeting for worship he wrote, "Although we would enjoy participating in it, we don't have the time and energy to organize it and take responsibility for it."

Bob Gwyn noted that he understood some of the young couple's reasons for leaving, but felt some of them were the result of misinterpretation of the Board's words or actions by the Scotts, and some were their own identity issues.

Four decades later, Scott acknowledged that "The Quaker House is the thing that has been enduring. I think that's a real admirable thing. I'm sure they were feeling quite isolated, I'm sure people have felt at different times that they were pretty lonely."

"Quaker House is now closed, except for an occasional meeting,"

Bob Gwyn wrote dejectedly in late 1971. Would it now reach the same dead end that was looming for the coffeehouse?

The Board of Overseers considered its options. It had become clear that interpreting the Board's idea of the Friends Peace Testimony to politically-minded young people, even Quakers, could be difficult. Some Board members predicted that the project would continue to lose staff to the "more glamorous, better financed Haymarket Square Coffeehouse." The challenge, as they saw it, was for young people at Quaker House to maintain their own integrity and the Quaker character of the project, alone in Fayetteville, while avoiding being diverted to the secular political path embodied by Haymarket Square.

The Board also weighed the alternative: laying the project down and contributing any remaining funds to a similar organization.

Just as after the firebombing pushed them out of the original house on Ray Avenue, Board members went back to their respective meetings for input. Should we continue to support the Quaker House in Fayetteville? They also searched their own feelings. The process definitely took its toll on the organization.

Among those who thought it was time to lay the project down was Gwyn, one of the co-founders and the clerk of the Board of Overseers. "It seems to me that the committee is beginning to see Quaker House as a permanent institution with the attendant cautiousness and structure," Gwyn said. "Given the present situation in Fayetteville I think it will be very difficult to design any kind of unique program."

For instance, Gwyn said, Haymarket Square reportedly had a lawyer available, and thus could do a much better job of military counseling than Quaker House could. In addition,"Finding and keeping staff who can work in a vacuum is going to be equally difficult." Furthermore, Gwyn said, "It is going to be increasingly difficult to encourage Chapel Hill Meeting to put money into Quaker House because there is a feeling that if the folks in Fayetteville want a permanent project, they should pay for it."

"The Chapel Hill Meeting would leave it in the hands of the Overseers, but there is some feeling that it is time to lay Quaker House down," reported Gwyn. "It is hard to work with Haymarket and retain identity, and it is hard to keep proper staff." As for himself, he said "I think you need someone who can give this job more enthusiasm than I can," and he resigned from his position as the Board Clerk .

John Gamble reported a similar sense at the Durham Meeting.

On the other side were those like Lloyd Tyler, from Raleigh Meeting, who strongly supported keeping Quaker House going. "I do not feel we have given the House a real chance to be established and gain all of the local support it is capable of getting," Tyler wrote. "Quaker House in Fayetteville should not become a permanent institution as far as support from outside Meetings is concerned, but I think many of us think of its being more than a 'flash in the pan.'"

"If Fayetteville were other than the type of city it is, I would feel somewhat differently about it," Tyler continued, "but I don't think we should be unrealistic about the situation there. In fact, I would have been surprised if a self-supporting house could have been established in two years."

Another Raleigh representative, Isabella Cannon, said that "the young people from Raleigh have really been committed to the idea of Quaker House. The two years of work that has gone into it already and the growing financial base are reasons for hope."

Bob Driscoll, from the Peace and Social Justice Concerns Committee of New Garden Meeting in Greensboro, said his committee was much in favor of keeping Quaker House open. He felt that the sense of the entire Monthly Meeting was similarly positive. Virginia Driscoll, Bob's wife and another Board member from New Garden Meeting added, "We have really been tested over the last several months but if we come out of this we will be stronger and have purposes better defined." Bill Jeffries reported on the sense of the AFSC Peace Education Committee which he worked for: as far as his group was concerned, there was a need to keep the project open as an antiwar witness in Fayetteville even after the Vietnam war was over.

Community members from Fayetteville chimed in also. Frank Berardi, a member of GIs United, said "If it weren't for Quaker House the antiwar movement would have had a hard time getting along." Bruce Pulliam added that "Many feel locally that Fayetteville will never be the same as it was before Quaker House."

David Moose echoed both sentiments, "The Quaker witness here has been wonderful...We would have it as a permanent contribution to anti-militarism and anti-imperialism." Moose noted presciently that Haymarket's effectiveness was waning and said that Quaker House would be needed when the coffeehouse inevitably disappeared.

Honeycutt, back from Cuba and headed for Charlotte with Bill Carothers, said that she had become discouraged with the antiwar movement, but was encouraged by the concerned support expressed for seeing Quaker House continue.

In September 1971 members of the Board of Overseers told the *Fayetteville Observer* that although some members believed Quaker House had served its purpose and should be closed, the majority opinion was to keep the house open as a permanent contribution to anti-militarism. The newspaper reported on the Board's plans to emphasize the project's religious nature, its dedication to nonviolence and to play down "political" activities. Quaker House, the article stated, will "maintain a cooperative relationship with the antiwar movement without being merely another part of it."

The announcement of the "re-orientation" of the project in the *Fayetteville Observer* marked the end of the newspaper's harsh treatment of Quaker House and ushered in a new era of more empathetic portrayals of the project as a family place. The *Observer* still had very little understanding of who Quakers are or why they came to Fayetteville. But in a county with more than three hundred churches, what the readership could easily understand that less "politics" and more religion must be a good thing. With a few small exceptions, the paper would not have to report on any more large street protests associated with Quaker House for the next three and a half decades.

Across the nation, military counseling centers and GI coffeehouses that sprang up, like Quaker House, in the late sixties, were closing down, due to a combination of harassment, internal quarrels, lack of funds, and just plain fatigue. A major factor in this decay was rising drug use, a plague that was very much an aspect of the war coming home to the US. Again, Col. Heinl, with his purple prose, came very close to the mark:

> At Fort Bragg, the Army's third largest post, adjacent to Fayetteville, N.C. (a garrison town whose conditions one official likened to New York's "East Village" and San Francisco's "Haight-Ashbury") a recent survey disclosed that 4per cent (or over 1,400) of the 36,000 soldiers there are hard-drug (mainly heroin and LSD) addicts. In the 82nd Airborne Division, the strategic-reserve unit that boasts its title of "America's Honor Guard", approximately 450 soldier drug abusers were being treated when this reporter visited the post in April. About a hundred were under intensive treatment in special drug wards.
>
> Yet Bragg is the scene of one of the most imaginative and hopeful drug programs in the Armed forces. The post commander, LGen John J. Tolson, and the 82nd Airborne's commander, MGen George S. Blanchard, are pushing "Operation Awareness," a broad post-wide program focused on hard drugs, prevention, and enforcement.

However effective "Operation Awareness" might have been, *Bragg Briefs* reported in the same month that Heinl's article appeared that the program was so under-staffed as to be barely functioning. The pattern of the military starting highly-trumpeted new programs for social problems, and then failing to put sufficient resources into them is one that will surface again.

In any event, the surge of early 1971 was spent. Within six months after the September report on the future of Quaker House, Haymarket Square Coffeehouse was gone too.

Before long, and without seeking the distinction, Quaker House in Fayetteville would remain as the only survivor of the wave of dozens of Vietnam-era organizing projects around US military bases. There were still a few military counseling groups, like the Central Committee for Conscientious Objectors, but they were based in large cities. US involvement in the Vietnam War was winding down, the draft was nearing its end, and GI dissent was losing momentum.

"We never thought the war would go on that long," Jeffries remembered. "But it was obvious that [Quaker House] was having a purpose, that there was a continuing need. There were still [conscientious objectors] and if it hadn't been for that, it might have gone by the wayside. It wasn't just

47

inertia that kept it going."

Quaker House was different in that it was basically religious, directed toward finding and speaking to that mysterious "Inner light" or "that of God" which Quakers postulate is part of every person and therefore every soldier. From a spiritual perspective, war and violence damages and dims that light, so the aftermath of conflict is a crucial time to be listening and counseling.

While steadfastly opposed to the Vietnam War and the militarism underlying it, the Quaker Peace Testimony was based outside "politics." It aimed to see into the condition of each individual spirit, not simply on the material or political conditions of groups of people. But could this different basis help Quaker House survive the looming end of the Vietnam War and the antiwar movement? Could it adapt and continue as the conditions on which it initially thrived had all but disappeared?

At the end of 1971, with Honeycutt and Carothers gone to Cuba, and the Scotts moved to Haymarket Square, which itself was on the way out, the fate of Quaker House was likewise very much in doubt.

5. 1972-74: Recipe For Survival Pie: Pacifism & Broccoli

On a Thursday night in 1972, a soldier walked into Quaker House. He was a tall, good-looking young PFC stationed at Fort Bragg and in the crook of his arm was a warm casserole dish filled with beans and rice. A piece of tape on the lid had his name on it–Philip Dixon–so that at the end of the night he could find it again amidst the jumble of other pots and lids.

Dixon had joined the reserves while still living with his family in suburban Detroit. It was a seven-year hitch but "it kept me out of Vietnam, and me and the family and everybody thought that was great," he said. After basic training at Fort Polk in Louisiana there were several months more of medical training in San Antonio, Texas. Dixon did his reserve duties while in college in Michigan but, "it kinda overwhelmed me mentally," Dixon said. In 1970 he was sent to Fort Bragg as a medic with the First Corps of Medical Support Command for the 82nd Airborne Division.

When he arrived, Fayettenam was in full swing. Tens of thousand of soldiers came through there, some just back from the horrors of Vietnam and the rest waiting to ship out. Many of the returnees flocked to the Strip, to lay waste to their bodies and obliterate their nightmares; in similar ways, the rest tried desperately to avoid thinking about the inevitable. One writer called the town a "carnival before death" (Lutz). With his free time, Dixon could have been amongst thousands of other GI s in downtown, getting drunk, fighting and ogling prostitutes.

On the other hand, "if I stayed on the post I had a heroin addict in my face," Dixon said. "That was my reason to get off the base."

His girlfriend, a teacher in Fayetteville, had heard about Quaker House first. "Even though I was just a PFC nobody talked about that," Dixon said of the peace movement and the protests that were going on all around them. "I don't think I went to any protests." Yet no matter what he thought about the war in Vietnam, he knew he needed to escape the environment on post. His world in the military was warped–bogus rules, hypocrisy, violence, drugs and lies. He and his girlfriend, Linda Jones, longed for something that felt comfortable, relaxed, familiar, familial, supportive, normal.

Now, to the rest of Fayetteville, everything "the boys" were doing downtown and on post was, if often troublesome, still made out to be utterly, completely, patriotically and religiously *normal*. Yet whatever was going on at the house at 223 Hillside Avenue was alien and suspicious. Granted, things had calmed down a bit since the old place on Ray Avenue had burned down two years earlier–no more marches in the street, no more disruptions on post and, best of all, no more Jane Fonda.

By this time, it's worth noting, Fonda was in the throes of being turned from a activist ally into an object of undying hatred for many Vietnam vets who felt let down by their countrymen after the war. In a triumph of right-wing mythmaking, her tireless pro-GI crusading in the FTA tour was skilfully being buried under the ever-rising mountain of self-destructive bitterness that saw so many Vietnam era vets homeless, suicidal and otherwise damaged. Decades later, her name could still spark automatic reflexes of rage.

Kenn and Ellen Arning at the "new" Quaker House on Hillside Avenue, 1972.

After months of the house standing mostly empty, a young married couple had come down from New Jersey and settled into it in January, 1972. The Board of Overseers "unanimously and with great joy approved the appointment of Kenn and Ellen Arning as new directors." Within six weeks they had turned the Quaker House into a home with soft sofas, spring flowers and the smell of freshly brewed coffee. "The new image of Quaker House has come in its improved neighborhood relations on Haymount Hill," the newspaper reported. "The house was the center of the antiwar movement two years ago and was regarded with suspicion and animosity by some in the Fayetteville community." The Arnings changed that attitude.

Like the Scotts, the Arnings were Quakers, members of Moorestown

Monthly Meeting in Moorestown, New Jersey and graduates of Rutgers University. Before coming to Fayetteville they had travelled in Europe, visiting Friends in Norway, Denmark and Germany. By all accounts, the couple were striking to look at. Both were tall, lean and handsome. Kenn wore his thick black hair a little bit shaggy, but not unkempt. His black beard had a rough sort of pious look about it. A photo in the newspaper, taken during a counseling session with a GI shows Kenn's dark eyes fixed in an intense gaze as he leans forward, putting his weight on his palms that rest on his knees. In contrast to the "tall dark and handsome" thing that Kenn had going on, Ellen was like a sunflower. She had long blonde hair, a bright smile and a strong jaw.

"They were young, attractive, and they made quite an impression in Fayetteville among the non-Quaker community here, among young couples particularly," remembered Pulliam.

When the Arnings moved in they invited their neighbors for coffee and dessert and a chance to talk about the purpose of the project. "We try to keep good relations with the community because they are important," Ellen told the Fayetteville *Observer*. At the original Quaker House on Ray Avenue some of the closest neighbors were the USO and the American Legion. Bridge building of the sort the Arnings undertook would have been impossible back then. The neighbors on Hillside Avenue reacted positively to this outreach.

The newspaper reported approvingly that while previous Quaker House staff persons were "activists," the Arnings showed "dedication to Quaker principles of peace and humanism" and that this is the basis of the "more peaceful relationship with the community." This phrasing skated carefully past the inconvenient facts that the only violence associated with the project was a firebombing directed against it, which aimed to kill the staff. There had not been a single incident perpetrated by the staffers themselves.

So what had changed? Was it that the Arnings were married and therefore more socially acceptable? Clearly they were appealing and irenic in their style. But probably just as important was a change in atmosphere in the city. The GI resistance movement had died down to a great extent. After the Haymarket Square Coffeehouse closed down, the remaining "radicals" opened a storefront GI Center in Spring Lake, still close to Fort Bragg but ten miles from Fayetteville. The GI Center offered films, meetings, and tried to do GI counseling. But like the coffeehouse, it struggled, ran short of money and eventually closed.

With the draft soon to end, and most US troops out of Vietnam, the social temperature was lower – like a once boiling pot with the fire turned down. In 1973 the newspaper ran a story about the Arnings with the headline, "They Came to Help G.I.'s." That, of course, had been the headline of the Quaker House story for the past four years.

And one of those GI's was Philip Dixon. He entered Quaker House on that Thursday night for the weekly potluck, greeted the dozen or so other guests and breathed deep. He took in the aroma of Ellen's fresh baked oatmeal bread, a broccoli and cheese casserole, and perhaps a blackberry pie. But the food was just a side-light to the real attraction—the atmosphere.

"These are like normal people!" Dixon recalled thinking at the time. "They've got kids and things other than drill sergeants!" Dixon sat among the other guests, plates of food on their laps, on comfortable couches and chairs in the big living room and chatted. No one needed to watch what he or she said because, unlike up on post, there was no hierarchy and no rules to break here—other than the "No alcohol, drugs or other de-humanizers" policy on a sign by the door. "It was my breath of normalcy," Dixon said.

This was also true for some locals. Walter Vick, a native, remembered that "In the Seventies there were only two places to go in Fayetteville. One was a jazz club on Bragg Boulevard. The other was the Wednesday night potluck at Quaker House."

The weekly potlucks were open to anyone who wished to learn first-hand about Quaker House and its programs. The event was intended to induce people to visit. The Arnings especially welcomed people with views different than their own. "We have a person who comes here who is just exactly the opposite of everything I believe in...he's very firmly committed to the Army; a West Pointer, and you can't get much more opposite from us than that," Ellen told the Fayetteville *Observer*. "But that doesn't make him a bad person; he's a very lovable person, in fact. Quaker House exists to get people to think through their opinions, she said, and the potlucks are just one way to do that.

"I've heard the objection (expressed by various activists) that we are somehow 'selling out' by welcoming people who aren't pacifists, aren't determined to change this society," Ellen said to the newspaper in 1972. "I see no reason to think that my views are 'watered down' because I present them with a smile and with a liking for the other person."

Dixon was honorably discharged from the Army as a conscientious objector in 1972, just three months shy of the end of his hitch. " I didn't save any time, but I made a point," he said. He explained that the process of applying for conscientious objector status is like a series of essays. By the time he asked Kenn to help him get the right forms, "I had all the questions answered in my mind" Dixon said. For him, the process had begun in his conversations during potluck suppers at Quaker House.

While attending New Garden Meeting in Greensboro and teaching at the Friends School there, Judy Hamrick (later Judy Dixon) met Bob and Anne Welsh who recommended that she represent the Meeting on Quaker House's Board of Overseers. She served on the Board for eight years.

"One of the things that really struck me about all these Quakers," she said, "is that they are very good listeners as a group, and they're very upbeat people. I was young then and it was very interesting for me to see. I learned a lot from them."

"We always had a program and we had officers and everybody sort of did their job but when it really got down to it, when you were dealing with the GIs, people sort of shut down and let them do the talking," Dixon remembered.

The opportunity for the Board members to listen to the GIs and their wives came after the conclusion of the Monthly Meeting for Business which took place at Quaker House. The military folks joined the Quakers for a meal and, following the meal, there would be an informal "rap session." Dixon remembers in particular the presence of wives of the GIs.

"When their husbands are overseas and if the wives are at home, a lot of them would come to Quaker House with their children because they were lonely and they wanted to talk to people who understood what was going on," Dixon said. "There's always been a need [for Quaker House] for the wives as much as for the husbands."

"There was a lot of laughing that went on," Judy Dixon remembered. "Folks would just have these funny little stories of things that happened, but there was also a lot of crying too. There were always boxes of Kleenex. They didn't overdo it, but you know there was always crying there."

Buddies killed in action, the pain of separation and divorce–these were common themes in the stories Dixon and the other Board members heard. Some of these things she could relate to directly, all of them she empathized with. "We weren't counselors," she said of herself and the other Board members, "we were just people who were doing our best to help out Quaker House."

Luckily for the GIs and their family members, trained counselors were on staff every day of the week. "Guys would come in and just be basket cases and they just had a way of speaking to those young men to sort of help them get back on their feet," Dixon said admiringly about the Arnings. "They were very hard-working."

Not that everything was always smooth sailing. In the spring of 2008, an email came to Quaker House from Norway, with the subject line, "Quaker House Alumni Checking In." In it, Barbara Bach Berntsen, describing herself as "Quaker House Class of 1971-73," described a different kind of visit to Quaker House in this period:

> Subject: Quaker House alumni checking in
> I was only 18 years old when I married a young GI stationed at Fort Bragg and we spent a lot of time at Quaker House back in the day! Quaker House changed the course of both of our lives. My then husband . . . has been an active Quaker for over thirty years and lives in [a western state].
> I have a Quaker House story of my own to tell. In about May of 1972 we were living at Quaker House. I think Kenn and Ellen [Arning], a young Quaker couple from New Jersey, were running the place then. I was about as sick as I ever have been in my life with genuine influensa, in bed in the back bedroom.
> In the middle of the night, there were literally rifle butts thumping at the front door. My husband answered the door and there were

armed, masked men there, asking questions about me. I had heard about the bodies being stuffed with heroin from a GI, and had said so right in the middle of my on-base Psychology Class at Bragg only days before. The masked men told my husband to get control over his wife's mouth .

(Although disputed and unproven, the heroin-smuggled-in-dead-solders'-bodies story has had a long life around Fayetteville, and even figured in the plot of the 2007 feature film, *American Gangster,* starring Denzel Washington. What is beyond doubt is that the illicit drug trade thrived in those years, and has not disappeared since.)

Berntsen added,

I am now 55 years old, with streaks of white in my hair and my three kids are all grown ups. I have lived in Norway for more than 30 years. I am a historian at The National Archives of Norway and have taught archival science at the University of Oslo .
I was in Palestine during the 2006 war, and returned from Cairo 10 days ago, where people are being murdered in bread lines and most of the candidates and their lawyers were in jail for the recent elections.
No doubt about it, Quaker House alumni most definitely had the course of their lives changed! If the garage is still there, you will find my PX ID tucked under one of the shingles. My name back then was Barbara Black. Bet I look a LOT younger on the picture!
(Note: alas, no such ID has turned up as of late 2008.)

And despite the generally more "peaceable" atmosphere portrayed in the newspaper articles, public controversy had not been completely banished from Quaker House. At two AM on September 12th 1972, a 22-year-old PFC named Keith Dallman knocked on the door of Quaker House and requested religious sanctuary there.
Once they found out that Dallman was absent without leave from the 82nd MP Company at Fort Bragg the Arnings immediately called Bruce Pulliam. They were unsure of the legal ramifications of providing religious sanctuary for a man in Dallman's position.
"Is it OK for him to stay here?" the Arnings asked. Pulliam made calls to other members of the Board and eventually got word back to Quaker House. "Of course," Pulliam told them. "We're not going to turn anyone down."
Dallman, a native of Green River, Wyoming, had wrestled with moral convictions against combat service before entering the Army in 1971, but decided to join a support unit rather than go to jail, and became a military policeman. During the summer of 1972 he applied for a conscientious objector discharge. But this was denied because he qualified his objection to

war, saying that he could have served as a soldier against Hitler. Dallman was fully aware of the distinction he was making. Conscientious objector status was reserved only for those who object to all wars on moral or religious grounds.

Dallman claimed the right to be a "selective" conscientious objector, a stance which has still not been recognized legally.

"I think it should be the individual citizen's right to question a war that was never made legal by Congress, which is the only body that has the right to declare war," Dallman told the *Charlotte Observer* at the time.

Following Board instructions, the Arnings called both Fort Bragg and the local newspapers with the message that they were providing religious sanctuary to a GI who had left his company. When reporters arrived Dallman told them, "I plan to stay here indefinitely until the Army removes me or a petition on my case is heard by the federal court." According to Pulliam, pictures of the handsome young blond in the newspaper created a fervor among teenage girls in town who rushed over to Quaker House to get a glimpse of him.

On September 15th, 1972 three days after Dallman arrived, military authorities and sheriff's deputies in civilian clothes walked, unannounced, through the unlatched front door and apprehended Dallman as he sat in the living room where meeting for worship was held every Sunday afternoon.

The following week it was reported that Dallman was receiving an Article 15 non-judicial punishment rather than face desertion charges and a possible court martial. "I'm very surprised that he hasn't been charged with desertion," Arning told the newspaper. "They had grounds for it. I think this humane, this tolerant treatment could mean something important."

Although much was made in the press about the leniency with which Dallman was dealt, it was a different aspect of the situation that concerned Pulliam. He sent a letter to the commander at Fort Bragg protesting the invasion of a Meeting House and a private residence when Dallman was taken into custody. The *Fayetteville Observer* received letters to the editor on the question of whether churches should offer religious sanctuary to AWOL soldiers. According to Pulliam, many of the church-goers who wrote expressed the same, disgusted "No!" coupled with, "Send 'em to Quaker House."

It wasn't just servicemen and their family members that the Arnings had a knack of speaking to. Fortunately for the organization, the Arnings were also gifted fund-raisers. "They were a married couple so they were considered more middle class," recalled Virginia Driscoll who served on the Board of Overseers with Dixon. "They could talk to Friends meetings and Quakers much more comfortably and were much more accepted in terms of doing fund-raising than their predecessors had been." (This comment might seem to confirm the suspicions of the Scotts about their marital status being "used" for the project's financial benefit. But the Arnings did not seem offended to find that their wholesome appearance was an advantage in this area; after all, funds did have to be raised if the project was to continue.)

55

It's important to note here that there are actually two Quaker groups called "North Carolina Yearly Meeting" in the state. (This can be confusing, so bear with us.)

Both claim the same ancestry in the 1600s, but they parted ways in 1903. The smaller group, called North Carolina Yearly Meeting-Conservative (NCYM-C), sought to "conserve" traditional forms of silence-based Quaker worship and a church structure which did not include paid pastors. By the 1970s, despite the "Conservative" in their name, many of these Friends were somewhat politically progressive-minded, and often disposed to support the pacifist expression of the Quaker Peace Testimony which Quaker House represented. Their "Conservative" label was also a reaction against the "innovations" which had been gradually adopted by the other, larger body. These "innovations" centered around replacing silence-based worship with "programmed" meetings in a revivalist style, and hiring paid pastors.

This larger Yearly Meeting was affiliated with an umbrella group called Friends United Meeting (FUM), so it will be abbreviated here as NCYM-FUM. Along with its adoption of more conventional Protestant church forms, much of the NCYM-FUM constituency had absorbed Southern attitudes about social issues, including war, gender, and race. The FUM-affiliated group had more than eighty member congregations, whereas the Conservatives could claim no more than eight, several of which were quite small.

Wood Bouldin had been the first Quaker House representative to make a presentation to the North Carolina Yearly Meeting-Conservative. Bouldin met with the group in 1969, not long after Quaker House opened. It received no official support, but minutes indicate that the Yearly Meeting on Social Concerns felt positively about the project and urged smaller meetings "to get under the weight of this project and make financial contributions as way opens" and many did.

The next reference to Quaker House in that Yearly Meeting's minutes is in 1973 when the Arnings, along with Keith Dallman, presented to the group again. The budget committee reported that "after hearing Ken and Ellen Arning's remarks about Quaker House the Yearly Meeting encourages Monthly Meetings and individuals who wish to contribute to that effect to forward their contributions to the Yearly Meeting Treasurer who will forward them to Quaker House."

Financial and spiritual support from the small North Carolina Yearly Meeting (Conservative) was undoubtedly crucial for Quaker House. But an endorsement from the other, much larger FUM Yearly Meeting could produce more financial support.

At its beginning, Quaker House was turned away by the Peace Committee of the larger body, NCYM-FUM. But later, in August 1972 a representative from NCYM-FUM visited Quaker House and recommended "that FUM support this effort at Fayetteville, NC." Support for the project, however, hit a stumbling block with the members of NCYM-FUM's Joint Social Concerns Committee, who believed that further interpretation among

North Carolina Friends would be advisable before they approved a proposal to sponsor Quaker House.

One of the committee members spoke to a group of fifty members of the Yearly Meeting, all of whom had negative feelings towards Quaker House, dating from before the Arnings. "Our impression from these discussions," he reported, "is that the Arnings' ministry will receive widespread approval among North Carolina Friends as soon as it is generally known."

So they put off concrete sponsorship but reported that "the concern to keep Quaker House open was so strongly felt that delegates to the umbrella Friends United Meeting from three other Yearly Meetings (Baltimore, New England and New York) pledged to raise the $200 a month needed until direct FUM sponsorship could be considered."

That consideration came at the gathering of the NCYM (FUM) in 1973, when the Arnings spoke to the group. A representative from FUM later wrote to the Quaker House staffers that "from all reports I can only observe that you scored a 'hit.' Your presentations were very well and laudably received. You succeeded in inspiring a great deal of confidence in your program in Fayetteville."

In the Quaker House Newsletter Arnings sent out in the spring of 1973 they wrote: "NCYM-FUM has become a co-sponsor of the ministry to the military carried on at Quaker House. This is an important step and many persons have worked in co-operation to make it a reality... Friends from North Carolina to Indiana to Maine have contributed to this fine effort."

By the summer of 1973 Phillip Dixon and Linda Jones had been attending Fayetteville Friends Meeting for over a year. The Meeting for Worship at Quaker House had grown under the Arnings such that weekly attendance varied between 10 and 15 people and it was formed officially as a Preparative Meeting (*preparing* for full monthly meeting status) under the care of Raleigh Monthly Meeting.

"This step further stabilizes the Quaker presence in Fayetteville and aids in gaining recognition for the non-violent Peace Center at Quaker House," the Arnings wrote in the Newsletter. One of the first things the fledgling Meeting did was perform a traditional Quaker wedding.

When Dixon and Jones decided to get married, Pulliam, the Arnings and others formed a Quaker "clearness committee," which "acted sort of like counselors," according to Dixon. Some years later, after Judy Dixon's death, he married Judy Hamrick, also under the care of a Quaker meeting. The committee helped the young couple achieve clearness on the importance of what they were doing. They also helped the couple celebrate.

"The church we were married in was decorated with flowers by our new friends through Quaker House, the ones we'd met at potluck suppers," Dixon remembered. The ceremony took place in a Methodist chapel downtown. But no minister conducted the ceremony or sanctioned the union—the couple exchanged vows and married each other before God and the gathered witnesses, "after the manner of Friends." There was a period of silent worship and at the rise of the meeting, all present, including the youngest children, signed the wedding certificate as witnesses.

Everyone then gathered at Bruce Pulliam's house and planted two trees—an apple and a pear—to bless the union. Dixon and Jones, surrounded by the Arnings and Pulliams stood around one of the seedlings a bit apart from the others, who were dressed in casual summer clothes and seated on a straw bale and on the grass.

The wedding seemed to cement Quaker House's new relationship to the community. It marked quite a turnaround: in early 1972, the Arnings were handed a project that seemed doomed. It suffered from internal weakness and the public perception wasn't much better. Under their stewardship the organization navigated the turbulence of the end of conscription and the beginning of the volunteer army. In the long tradition of Quakers they acted on the needs of a new generation of soldiers willing to resist war. Through the attention given to Dallman's case they showed the community and other Quakers that there was still Quaker support for soldiers who refused to fight for reasons of conscience.

Potluck suppers brought different elements of Fayetteville's community together in a new way. The formation of Fayetteville Friends Meeting (Preparative), and the new support the couple put into the project showed in the way it was flourishing by the end of the summer of 1973.

But no summer lasts indefinitely. In late 1973, the Arnings separated, and Ellen left Fayetteville; Kenn departed in June of 1974. After they left, a volunteer from Durham Friends Meeting kept Quaker House open until new fulltime staff arrived in early August.

6. 1975-77: Intermezzo – A Pause Between The Wars

The Vietnam War may have been almost over by late 1974, but its bloody trail still led back to Fayetteville, among other places inside the United States. One incident that year stands out. On December 3, a woman's nude body was found in the woods on Fort Bragg. She had been choked, beaten, and repeatedly stabbed.

Not Happily Ever After: Richard & Beryl Mitchell. In 1975 Richard Mitchell was convicted of her murder on Fort Bragg.

Her name was Beryl Mitchell, and she was an Australian immigrant. Two days later, her husband, Richard Mitchell, was arrested and charged with murder. Richard Mitchell was a Special Forces Captain and a Vietnam veteran. He was later convicted of the crime and spent twelve years in prison. Mitchell's children, a daughter Christine, age nine, and a one-year old son, were placed in the custody of their paternal grandmother. Christine's long struggle to come to terms with her mother's death would eventually bring her full circle, back to Fayetteville and Fort Bragg, and to a place she had never heard of there, Quaker House.

The new residents at Quaker House were Stan and Diane Rodabaugh, and their young son Benjamin. They arrived from Richmond, Indiana where Stan had recently completed his Master of Ministries studies at the Earlham School of Religion. Stan, a trained military counselor, took on primary duties. He was a native of Chicago, but had spent his early years traveling through the Midwest and the Southwest with his father, a minister in the Church of the Brethren.

"The Church of the Brethren and Quakerism are very similar," Stan explained to the *Durham Morning Herald*, which ran a piece on Quaker House. "Both stress leading a simple life and living out one's beliefs."

Diane grew up in Philadelphia and was studying abroad as a student at Temple when she met and married Stan in Germany. The couple served together at a boys home and a half-way house for allied prisoners of World War Two in Germany.

The economic distress that was widespread in America by 1975 was a boon for the Armed Services. Any worries that there would not be enough enlistees for an all-volunteer Army vanished as recruiting and re-enlistment goals were exceeded across the country. "All in all we're very, very pleased," Colonel William A. Greynolds, chief of the Army's Recruiting and Re-enlistment Division told the Associated Press in April of 1975. "The quality we saw increasing before the recession now is dramatic."

The military had a tough time making the argument that it was not an employer of last resort and in an effort to downplay the fact that the dreary economy was a prime enlistment motivator, they used language about the quality of recruits since more and more high-school and college graduates were joining up. The fact that in Vietnam the North Vietnamese forces conquered the entire country, bringing the Vietnam War to a definitive end, no doubt aided in the recruiters' success. To many, perhaps most potential recruits, a military career looks more attractive between wars.

The military also took advantage of this relative personnel surplus to weed out dissatisfied soldiers by granting lots of discharges, including for conscientious objection. As a result, Stan and Diane felt "grossly under-engaged" in the primary mission of the project, which they saw as working with military personnel whose conviction of faith and conscience had led them to believe that military service was wrong.

"There has been a drastic decline in inquires about conscientious objector discharges," Stan told Quaker House supporters in the Newsletter in 1975, "We attribute this to the increase in discharges being given by the military for the convenience of the same."

"Nevertheless, just the presence of an open, nurturing, peaceful sanctuary in this military community served a real need," Diane explained.

At Quaker House Diane organized a natural and whole foods cooperative which operated out of the back porch at the rear of Quaker House. There was a door into the kitchen from the outside and it was always open. Inside, great glass jars and bags of dried beans, grains and nuts filled the shelves. Prices were just above cost.

The Friendly Food Co-op was popular with the small number of vegetarians in Fayetteville like Ann Ashford. "You couldn't find things in Fayetteville for a vegetarian diet," Ashford said. It operated successfully even after the Rodabaugh's departure.

"While our immediate neighbors were very open about their opposition to the work of Quaker House, they were very cordial with us personally, and really enjoyed our children," Diane explained. Their second son, Aaron, was born while they were living on Hillside Avenue.

One of the changes during the Rodabaugh's time at Quaker House was that, for the first time in the project's history, it hosted both silent, unprogrammed meetings for worship and the more modern, more widely-recognizable form of worship, known within Quakerism as "programmed" meetings.

The latter were pastored by Clyde Lane of the Bethesda Friends Meeting in Dunn, a small town not far north of Fayetteville. Since the mainly pastoral Friends United Meeting was providing financial and spiritual support for the project at the time, it made sense to incorporate the programmed meeting. This was also the style more familiar to the Rodabaughs from the Brethren background.

The Thursday evening potlucks at Quaker House, begun by the Arnings, continued with the Rodabaughs there. Despite the decrease in inquiries about conscientious objector discharges, there was a steady stream of soldiers coming to Quaker House for help.

And while the counseling load started small, at a skimpy eight people in the first three months at the end of 1974, it grew to 25-30 people per month by the end of 1975. To advertise Quaker House's services the Rodabaughs placed simply-worded public service announcements on the radio. The ad said merely:

> If you are in the military and would like information about your rights, conscientious objection, AWOL, discharges or upgrading a discharge contact Quaker House in Fayetteville, North Carolina from 7 pm to 9 pm Tuesday through Sunday.
> Phone number 919 485 3213.

It was clear from the response to the ad that an increasing numbers of the enlistees felt they were not being treated well.

"We don't foresee a decline in the need for a place like Quaker House," Diane explained. Besides conscientious objection, "there are other questions to be answered, too, concerning other kinds of discharges and information on servicepeople's rights." As a sign of the Board's intentions to stay, a new roof was put on in 1973 by a work party. The original roof was of fine cedar shakes, but these were covered over by a layer of much cheaper tin. Some years later the tin was replaced with asphalt shingles.

Due partly to the decline in conscientious objector counseling and partly to the disappearance of an active peace movement among GIs and civilians, there was a sense that the project was in a time of transition. Despite the solid foundation the Arnings had built for the program after the tumultuous early years, Quaker House was still seeking its identity in the community and trying to relate this to dollars and cents.

In this period, attendance at Meeting for worship and at Board Meetings was sparse. There was also a lack of interest in planned, organized peace education events even among participants in Quaker House programs and supporters. A discussion group on Quakerism failed after two meetings.

Former Board member Virginia Driscoll said, "I think we hit a low point around 1975-76, it was very hard to get people to understand why we needed a Quaker House, why we needed to do that work at all." Yet, "After the treaty ending the Vietnam war, we wanted Quakers to understand that just because the Vietnam was over there were still issues for GIs that needed to be addressed."

A Chaplain at Fort Bragg who was interviewed for a story about Quaker House in 1975 told the newspaper, "We don't have many people any more trying to get out because they are conscientious objectors or anti-military so this type of operation is almost out of business."

At least in the early days of Quaker House, resistance from within the military establishment proved to the Friends that they were indeed confronting an institution of violence. But times had changed. "Since we have been here the most hostility has been from chaplains at the ministerial meetings," Stan told a newspaper in Durham. "As soon as I say Quaker House they would walk away from me in mid-sentence."

Stan wanted to go into area churches and teach about war and peace in the Biblical tradition. But, as one of the local pastors explained to him, none of the ministers in town would risk their position or reputation to invite Stan to speak.

Friends were no doubt asking themselves, 'What does a pacifist need to do to get an outpouring of hostility around here?' The idea they hit upon was challenge military recruiting in high schools.

Among Quaker House supporters, "there

Stan & Diane Rodabaugh, with their son, Benjamin.

was an interest in talking about the peace movement and choosing peace over war, and talking about that in high schools," according to Driscoll. "We were looking for ways that we could counter the [military's] rhetoric in high schools."

"I am asking the high school counselors to let me come into the schools so the students can hear our side of the Army, the alternatives," Rodabaugh told a Durham newspaper reporter. "Even if they don't agree with me I want them to know I'm a halfway decent guy that can be trusted."

But the attempts by Rodabaugh and Driscoll to get into high schools in Fayetteville and Greensboro were met with a lot of resistance. "That helped people understand that that effort needed to continue after the end of the Vietnam war. We had to continue that whole discussion around peace education and the idea of militarism as a system," Driscoll explained. Quaker House's first peace education efforts like this were ultimately frustrated, but they laid the groundwork for future successes.

After one and a half years in Fayetteville, the Rodabaughs moved on. One of the difficulties the young family faced was living in a public house and they recommended the Board seek staff persons without children. They returned to Indiana and did organic market farming before Stan was called to pastoral ministry in his home denomination, the Church of the Brethren. He served as an ordained minister in two different congregations over thirty years, until retirement.

In the final Overseers meeting Stan attended he was told gratefully that the Quaker House program "is in better shape than we have ever been when staff left before."

After the Rodabaughs left, the search committee of the Board of Overseers publicized the opening at Quaker House far and wide. Announcements went out to Quaker colleges like Earlham and Swarthmore, Quaker publications such as *Quaker Life* and *Friends Journal*, and Quaker Organizations like the Central Committee for Conscientious Objectors and the American Friends Service Committee.

But they also crossed the traditional boundaries and placed ads in Catholic Worker, Unitarian, Brethren and Mennonite publications. Though they cast their net wide, the next director of Quaker House came from Durham, just a hundred miles up the road from Fayetteville. Three months after the Rodabaughs left, John and Ruth Wenberg and their young son Jack moved into the house at 223 Hillside.

Sunday mornings must have been hectic for Wenberg. He was a United Methodist minister who preached at two churches outside Fayetteville at staggered hours each Sunday morning, then hurried home to tend to Friends meeting at Quaker House at 1 pm. Wenberg told the *Fayetteville Observer* that although the Methodist Services "demand a whole lot more of my energy," he received more spiritual nourishment from the Quaker Meeting. He had found out about the opening at Quaker House because he had been attending Durham Friends Meeting at the time.

Wenberg told the *Fayetteville Observer* that the Methodist Church had adopted a strong statement against the militarization of society, but because it was such a large and diverse denomination, it could not speak with the united voice that Quakers did. [Though, as we have seen, the Quaker "voice" was considerably less united than it seemed to some outsiders.] Generally, he said, other churches tried to help conscientious objectors and several denominations supported the National Interreligious Service Board for Conscientious Objectors in doing this. Nonetheless he felt that his duties at Quaker House were compatible with his own views on the subject of the military.

Wenberg, a native of Wilmington, North Carolina, attended Campbell College and received a Master's degree in Divinity from Emory University in Atlanta. He served parishes in North and South Carolina and completed clinical chaplain training at a hospital in Chapel Hill.

His wife Ruth was an elementary teacher from Smithfield, North Carolina. She continued the Friendly Food Co-op and taught yoga and meditation classes Quaker House.

"At one point I took a yoga class at Quaker House," remembered Ann Ashford, a Fayetteville resident. "The teacher was Ruth Wenberg... and after the yoga practice, Ruth held a meditation." Ashford had been interested in yoga and meditation, but it was her first experience at Quaker House. Thirty years later, Ashford is one of the mainstays of Fayetteville Friends Meeting.

During Wenberg's time at Quaker House, Fayetteville Friends Meeting was released from its preparative status under the care of Raleigh Meeting, and became an independent Monthly Meeting within North Carolina Yearly Meeting (Conservative). Charlotte Kleiss was the Clerk of the small Meeting and Francie and Earl Myers were the Recording Clerk and Treasurer respectively.

High numbers of servicemembers continued seeking out Quaker House for help. On one occasion, Wenberg prepared to drive a soldier to the bus station. But as he backed out of the driveway, the street suddenly collapsed under his car, opening an eight foot deep hole from a collapsed sewer or storm line.

After extricating himself and his passenger from the vehicle, Wenberg called city hall, which sent workers out who with some effort managed to haul the car up from its watery crypt. Wenberg insisted that the city should pay for repairs on the automobile, but officials at first denied responsibility.

The *Fayetteville Observer* stepped into the breach, carefully covering both sides of the dispute. "This was an act of God," said the city. "I work for God," Wenberg retorted, "and He had nothing to do with it!" In the end the city yielded and fixed the car in its own shop.

Wenberg estimated that he counseled Marines to soldiers at a four to one ratio. The explanation for this lay in the treatment of unauthorized absence (UA) in the Marines as opposed to being absent without official leave (AWOL), its equivalent, in the Army. These infractions comprised the bulk of the problems servicemembers came to Quaker House for help with during this time.

As Rodabaugh had also noted, the Army was granting discharges fairly easily. A soldier returning from being AWOL was likely to receive an expeditious discharge. In contrast, a Marine returning from UA was more likely to serve time in the brig and face a court martial. The unequal and harsh treatment caused many Marines to seek help outside a system that was apparently deaf to their problems. A few years later, Quaker House would establish a Camp Lejeune Outreach Program with a dedicated staff member and counselor to deal with this issue.

Wenberg's credentials as a Methodist minister with Chaplain training meant that he was also allowed in to visit military prisoners in the brig at Camp Lejeune. He told the Board, "Prison visitation probably is one of the most meaningful things I do. Several men have broken into tears during my visits. The impact of having someone not wearing a uniform visit and express concern cannot be underestimated."

"Many of the people who seek counsel from us lately," Wenberg explained to the *Fayetteville Observer*, "are youngsters of no more than 17 or 18 years old. They are often totally unaware of what they are doing. Many have received a bill of goods from recruiters which never materialize." It might take practice shooting at a human form target for some to realize that they're in the wrong place. But while it would be simple for a civilian to leave a job they don't feel comfortable with, leaving a job in the Armed Services can be a crime."

On top of his counseling cases, Wenberg continued the community outreach and peace education components of the Quaker House program. "The Thursday night potluck has been having a large attendance," Wenberg wrote in a report to the Board of Overseers in 1978. Speakers and programs provided, "our version of Daniel in the lion's den."

"Sometimes the lions win, sometimes Daniel can hold his own, but the discussion is usually heated and intense," Wenberg reported.

But there was more to the sessions than political talk. Ruth Wenberg, in particular, had the instincts of a matchmaker. And for one young single mom named Peggy Cruse, Ruth had just the man in mind. It was Walter Vick, who worked for a local architect. Vick's trademark contribution to the potlucks was one or another variety of Breyer's ice cream, and Ruth was soon suggesting he should ask Peggy for a date, telling him that Peggy was interested. (She was, at the same time, telling Peggy that Walter was interested too, but shy.) Finally Walter took the bait; and one thing led to another.

In September of 1977, a year and two months after his arrival, Wenberg announced his resignation from Quaker House. Like Rodabaugh, he and his family found the pressures of living in Quaker House bearable for only a short time. Wenberg also had differences with Pulliam and other Board members, some of whom, he said, criticized his programming for being "not spiritual enough" and others for it not being political enough. He recommended changes in the oversight of staff members and emphasized the need to grow Fayetteville Friends Meeting to give staff at Quaker House more support. In 2008 John Wenberg was Senior Pastor at the Englewood United Methodist Church of Rocky Mount, NC. Ruth, now Hamilton, was a member of Chapel Hill Friends Meeting.

Minutes from Board meetings show that Friends in Fayetteville strongly supported the continuation of the project after Wenberg left. Others within the committee weren't so sure. Was there, one might ask, an urgent need for Quakers from Chapel Hill to sustain a food coop and yoga classes in Fayetteville? No one doubted that there was still a need for military counseling and peace education. The evidence was the number of soldiers and community members getting involved with the project. But, others argued, despite the continuing need, present operating conditions at the house seem inevitably to lead to burnout. Staffers suffered from a lack of emotional support in Fayetteville. Slim resources for wages didn't help–Wenberg was paid about $400 a month.

To add to the dilemma, financial support from one of Quaker House's largest backers was made contingent upon who succeeded Wenberg as director. FUM sources told Board members that it could justify putting Quaker House in its budget only so long as the Board sought strong Quakers for staff who could increase the ties with FUM-affiliated meetings in North Carolina.

The Quaker process of decision-making is a unique one. When Friends can't agree, they will frequently call for a moment of silence and begin discussion after that with the hope that during the silence, Friends were able to get more clarity on how they were being led. If everyone is listening to God's Spirit, the theory is that the way forward will become clear. Quakers try to make collective decisions based not on finding solutions that everyone is willing to live with (as in consensus models) but in determining God's will, or "a sense of the meeting."

Decision-making in this manner can seem time-consuming and impractical, but many Friends believe it works well, allowing a group to ultimately find "unity" (which, they add, is not the same as unanimity) for decisions on the most contentious matters. By the time a decision is recognized, they point out, the important issues have been worked out so taking action is easy.

In this manner, after more consideration, the Board of Overseers of Quaker House felt led to continue the project.

Another phrase from Quaker terminology describes how the Board moved forward. "Proceed as way opens" means to undertake a service or course of action without prior clarity about all the details but with confidence that divine guidance will make these apparent and assure an appropriate outcome.

When they welcomed the next director of Quaker House (along with continued financial support from FUM), surely there was happiness, but not surprise, since they had acted simply on how they felt led to move forward.

7. 1978-80: Seeking Out The Secrets

After eight years in the military, Bill Sholar of Chapel Hill, North Carolina discovered that the maneuvers he had been teaching pilots to avoid being shot down by enemy planes were ineffective. Yet as a records custodian with access to classified documents, he told the *Fayetteville Observer,* he learned that he was not allowed to instruct pilots in effective evasive action, because a military regulation excluded those pilots from the personnel classifications which would have given them a right to know .

"I said, 'If that's the case we need to change the information we're teaching,'" he said. Sholar was rebuffed: "I was told to teach the old information." Sholar protested, but according to him the response was, "'We'll make the decision on what is right and what is wrong and even though this information is incorrect you can change it later. If a war starts we'll then let you tell the pilots.'"

"For the first time in eight years in the Army I was being told to do something that I really considered wrong," Sholar said. "They just as easily could have given [the pilots] the evasive information that could have saved their lives."

When Sholar found himself in the position of teaching American pilots how to keep from being shot down by missiles and knowing that what he was teaching them was not true,"That was my rebellion point," he said.

"To me, the responsibility is mine. I couldn't shift it to somebody else, so I said, 'Who's in charge of my life?' I eventually decided I have to decide for myself. I can't let somebody else make the decision on whether what I'm doing is right or wrong," said Sholar.

During this time Sholar was living with his family in Germany where he was stationed and working for the Army Security Agency. A Chapel Hill native, he had attended the University of North Carolina before entering the military and doing two tours in Korea and a couple years in the inactive reserves. The same spirit that guided him to act according to his own conscience within the military guided him to begin attending Quaker meeting in Germany.

To deal with the situation at work, Sholar first requested duties requiring no access to any classified information. "I didn't want to become another Daniel Ellsberg," he said. "I basically told the Army, 'You get me out of that situation and I'll keep secret what I've learned, but I'm not going to guarantee what I'm going to keep secret tomorrow. They were very willing to cooperate." Within a few months, however he realized that the implications of this new consciousness of his went beyond just handling classified information.

"If I was in a situation in which I was taking orders of any kind from someone else I had to rely on that person to know right from wrong and I had to subject my own conscience to that person's conscience," he said. Having to subcontract out his conscience was where the connection he felt to the military began to break down. Upon returning to Chapel Hill he received a conscientious objector discharge from the Army. While attending Chapel Hill Friends Meeting he learned about Quaker House and moved to Fayetteville in January of 1978 to direct the project, which had been without a staff person for three months. Joining him there were his wife Sue, who worked as a secretary, and their 5 year old son Billy.

Sholar's realizations during his service in Germany formed the basis of his ministry at Quaker House. There had been a change in the program, he announced. "Today, the Quaker House emphasis is on the individual," he told the *Fayetteville Observer* a month after his arrival. "Although Quaker house remains as a statement for peace and social justice, the antiwar marches and demonstrations of past years have given way to a renewed concern for individual rights and dignity."

Bill Sholar, on the front porch at Quaker House.

Sholar even went as far as to say, "We're not anti-military, we're just pro-individual."

"At first, Quaker House seemed to serve angry men and women opposed to the war in Vietnam," Sholar wrote in a Newsletter in 1979. "The men and women we serve today are not so outspokenly angry but are still troubled and in need of honest straight forward professional military counseling."

Was this change truth or perception? Mostly the latter–anyone who thought that the project was not dedicated to serving individual soldiers right from the start wasn't paying attention. What had changed more than the disposition of the troubled men and women in the Army over the first decade of the project's existence was the political climate and Quaker House's post-Sixties efforts to be more respectable.

That's not to say the message hadn't changed at all. For instance,

Sholar told the *Fayetteville Observer* in 1979 that "Most of what I do, when you get right down to it, is tell people what their first sergeant should have told them in the first place." Ten years earlier Holland had explained to the *Greensboro Daily News* that talking to GIs is the most important thing they do at Quaker House:

> "We tell them about some of the forces in our society that are responsible for things like the Vietnam War–the military industrial complex and the general influence the corporate structure has over our society. Vietnam is not an isolated problem. It is a coherent result of the way the United States is. Things like Vietnam are not going to be prevented by changing government officials. It will be prevented only when our society as a whole is changed."

You're not going to get that from a first sergeant.

Sholar's experience in the service and his journey to Quakerism is instructive. You either know that you're opposed to military service from birth or you're a war supporter, right? Wrong.

A more typical pattern, as Sholar put it, was that a recruit joined the service without having really thought out the implications of what he or she was doing. Then, at some point, the soldier was exposed to something that was too much for them. "For somebody it might be bayonet training in basic training when they're given a bayonet and told to stab a human dummy and yell 'Kill!'" said Sholar. Or, in his case, to learn that what he was teaching pilots is ineffective and dangerous to them, but being prevented from correcting the error.

"Frequently the person who reached the decision that he or she is a conscientious objector after joining the military does not come from a pacifist family, obviously, or he wouldn't join the service," said Sholar. "Therefore, the decision they've reached is their own decision and their families aren't going to be very supportive." There is very seldom any support from friends because they are in the service too. This, he said, describes most of the people Quaker House serves.

"These people are ordinary young men and women who happened to be susceptible to smooth sales talk of recruiters. Others like them bought used cars at inflated prices and were stuck with 36 months of payments," he explained. "These people are stuck with 36 months out of their lives."

Smooth talk is one thing, but outright lying by recruiters is another. Sholar helped one young soldier named James Walker find an attorney after his request for an administrative discharge from the Army was denied. A recruiting sergeant in Iowa allegedly told Walker that he would not go overseas during his first tour of enlistment and assured him that there was a job waiting for him with the 26th Combat Support Battalion at Fort Bragg.

When Walker arrived at Fort Bragg, he discovered that the 26th Combat Support Battalion didn't exist at Fort Bragg or anywhere else. When he was given orders to deploy to Germany, he took his case to court. His breach-of-contract suit against the Secretary of Defense and the commander at Fort Bragg was heard before a U.S District Court during November of 1978.

When told that the unit with which he promised Walker employment did not exist, the man who recruited Walker testified, "I know that now but I didn't know that then. How was I to know? I've never been to Fort Bragg." Attorneys for the Army pointed to the clause in Walker's enlistment agreement [often erroneously referred to as a "contract"] that states that any promise not written in the contract will not be honored. Although the non-existent unit was printed in the contract, the attorneys then argued that the valid portion of the contract concerning location was only "Fort Bragg" and not the unit.

Walker lost his case; the court was unwilling to make untruth a criterion for invalidating military enlistment forms. Before Walker shipped out to Germany, he spoke to the *Fayetteville Observer* and gave young people thinking of joining the Army some advice, "Whatever you do, don't trust what a recruiter says. All a recruiter wants to do it meet his quota for enlistments. He may promise you anything and I learned in court that neither the Army or the government consider a recruiter's promises binding."

The fat year of 1975, with its surplus of recruits, was long past. In a refrain that was to echo down the following decades, Sholar said that recruiting abuses were largely the result of pressure on recruiters to fill high quotas. These were in turn the result of manpower shortages in the Armed Services, which, according to Sholar, were the result of poor treatment.

Official Pentagon statistics from January of 1978 showed that at the time over 2300 soldiers, sailors and airmen were going AWOL each week and over 20 per cent of enlisted Marines were missing at any given time. The AWOL rate for the Navy was at an all time high–triple that of Vietnam war days. Over 40 per cent of first termer enlistees were being discharged before their enlistment was completed, because they were 'inept, incompetent and usually have bad attitudes' according to the Army.

"To meet that manpower gap," Sholar explained, "recruiters get super high quotas which they can't meet any other way."

"It is a problem because of the way the military treats people," Sholar told the *Fayetteville Observer* in late 1979. "Very few of them would come here if they were treated the way they were supposed to be treated...people are still being treated as draftees."

In March 1978 the Army asked Congress to allow women in combat roles, citing "manpower shortages due to the baby boom." Sholar attacked the spin in a well-worded letter to the editor in the Fayetteville *Times*. "Far more serious than any shortage of manpower caused by a declining birthrate is the manpower shortage caused by AWOL and desertion rates within the services," he wrote. "It's no wonder the Pentagon wants to fill up the ranks with women–they can't keep men around!...When the women go AWOL who is the Pentagon going to recruit next?"

The Board of Overseers were overjoyed with Sholar's work. "Bill is doing an outstanding job as our staff person," noted Judy Hamrick Dixon, then Clerk of the Board. "He has spent the summer visiting various Meetings and Yearly Meetings in the state to familiarize Friends with our work. He is producing excellent newsletters, doing research and reading...I really cannot praise Bill high enough." It seems that Sholar was a complete package–military experience, conscientious objector experience, a married Quaker with a family and a good communicator.

Thirty years later, Dixon remembered Sholar as "Sort of quiet, he was always the kind of person that paid very close attention to what everybody else was saying and suggesting and then he would just come up with these wonderful ideas of how this person could be helped and what the counselor could do and all."

Another thing that made the Board happy is that on November 11th 1978 they burned the mortgage on the house, thanks to a $4000 donation from Raleigh Meeting.

Probably Sholar's most notable contribution to the Quaker House program was the Discharge Upgrade Project he initiated in early 1979.

Military discharges are something like the rungs on a ladder. At the top is "Honorable," which requires a clean record and completion of the full term of enlistment. The next rungs down are General Discharges, which could be "Under Honorable Conditions," which is less positive than it sounds, involving some level of unsatisfactory performance. A General Discharge "Under Other Than Honorable Conditions," hinted at more serious disciplinary problems. Then comes a "Bad Conduct Discharge," which is meted out by a military court for serious but not the most grave military offenses. For these is reserved the worst, "Dishonorable Discharge." To qualify for full veteran benefits, a GI needs an Honorable Discharge; on the lower rungs, eligibility for benefits is sharply or completely eliminated.

A lower level discharge can sometimes be upgraded, and there are many myths about automatic upgrades that circulate among ex-GIs. For a brief time, however, there was some substance to the myth: in 1978, court decisions and a bill passed by Congress allowed many veterans an opportunity to receive a discharge upgrade in many cases, even if they have been denied by discharge review panels in the past. A stipulation in the court required that agencies such as Quaker House be provided with the reference material to assist veterans.

The Armed Forces were required to notify each of 45,000 veterans who had been recently denied an discharge upgrade about the new standards. The fifteen-year statute of limitations for upgrading a discharge was suspended until the end of 1979. According to Sholar, more than 70 per cent of the discharges that would have expired under the statute of limitations were being shown to be unfair and in some cases, illegal.

"An upgraded discharge means a new chance for a job, education and life," Sholar wrote in a Quaker House Newsletter, as well as access to veteran benefits. This was an issue that only a veteran could appreciate. Many

71

antiwar activists without military experience would never have noticed an issue like upgrading discharges, but Quaker House has never been the average antiwar project.

On each of those 45,000 notices, Quaker House was listed as one of only five agencies offering help and the only one in the South. After the notices went out, Sholar reported receiving ten calls a day. Although half the callers needed nothing more than clarification of what the government letter meant, the discharge upgrade cases took up so much time and so much paper work that a printer was purchased for the first time and typing services were contracted for one day a week.

These activities were a departure from Quaker House tradition, Sholar said in that they were in cooperation with the Department of Defense. "We don't generally see eye-to-eye with the Pentagon," Sholar told the local newspaper, "but in this case we are cooperating with a Defense Department request that we help them reach several hundred thousand 'bad paper' veterans before their eligibility to apply for an upgraded discharge expires at the end of this year." In that it was nonviolent assistance to victims of war, Sholar said he viewed it as within the scope of the Quaker House project.

One result of all this work was a *Discharge Upgrading Handbook* which Sholar produced himself. Hundred of copies were mailed to college veterans advisors and Veterans Service Officers across North Carolina.

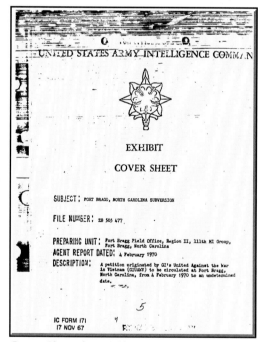

In contrast to the seemingly cozy relationship between Quaker House's Discharge Upgrading Project and the federal authorities, it was Sholar who requested FBI and CIA files regarding the Quaker House's activities during the tumultuous early years through the Freedom of Information Act (FOIA). It was obvious to Holland, Honeycutt, Gwyn and many others who helped found the project that federal and local authorities spied on and harassed Quaker House despite its peaceful approach. But the chance to see the documents about that era was irresistible.

In response, Sholar

Cover Sheet for a Military Intelligence surveillance report, dated February 4, 1970, released to Bill Sholar.

received a sheaf of documents, from Military Intelligence and the FBI, some of which have been quoted earlier. There were indications that more existed which were being held back.

Sholar sent FOIA requests to both the FBI and the CIA at the same time. "Now we really didn't figure that Quaker House would have a file in the CIA, but we just wanted to check all possibilities," Sholar reported in the Newsletter.

To his surprise, he also received a response from the CIA, stating that not only was there a file on Quaker House at the CIA but that it was so secret it could not be revealed. The letter quoted two provisions of the FOIA as authority for not releasing the file–exemptions dealing with undercover agents and information vital to the national security.

"It seems we had more agents of the intelligence agencies visiting Quaker House than soldiers needing help!" wrote Sholar.

Thus, ten years after the raucous founding of Quaker House, amidst the cultural revolution of 1969 and all the attendant messiness, the project was being run by a veteran with eight years of Army service who was focusing energy on upgrading discharges from dishonorable or general to honorable. This was a far cry from the high-visibility contentiousness of the first years. But what does it reveal about the Quaker spirit of the project? Quite a bit. All of Bob Gwyn's (and the rest of the Board's) vocalizations about not being too "narrowly political" come true in the Tenth Anniversary moment.

On June 1st, 1980, two and a half years after he arrived, Sholar and his family left Fayetteville. In his final Newsletter as Director, Sholar writes, "In many ways it seems more than an employee, the staff person at Quaker House is an individual freed by the support of concerned friends, so that the staff person could seek to answer his own concerns, which are shared with those Friends who support us."

73

8. 1980-87: Growing Up Quaker In Fayetteville

Gwen Gosney, nicknamed Gwendy as a child, hated hot weather. She vividly remembered when she and her parents moved into the house at 223 Hillside in mid-June of 1980. It was typical summer weather in Fayetteville and the 1929 house was hot and stuffy. There was no central air conditioning. The heat made the relocation from Richmond, Indiana even more difficult on the fair-skinned seven year old.

The soil of the Carolina Sandhills releases moisture much more readily than the nearby Piedmont's clay-loam or the soils of the Coastal Plain. This allows more energy to be used for heating the surface. The result is high humidity that makes the heat stick and keeps the breezes down. In addition, given the same amount of energy, sandy soil gets hotter than others.

Then, within a week after Gwendy arrived in Fayetteville, the sirens began. The civil defense sirens that rang out were unlike anything she'd ever heard, a sound chilling and surreal. Soon after that, artillery practice began on Fort Bragg. Even though it was ten miles away, the blasts shook their walls and rattled the windows. Clearly, Fayetteville meant big changes for Gwendy Gosney.

In Fayetteville she was enrolled in public school for the first time, at Pauline Jones, a poor and predominantly African American elementary school located a block from the Grove Street Terrace public housing project. Previously, she had attended a liberal Quaker school in Indiana. To a girl accustomed to circle time, learning to sit behind a desk was a lesson in and of itself.

Despite a number of white children of similar ages that lived on her block, she was the only caucasian in her third grade class. "They [other whites] either went to private school or had gotten some kind of out-of-district dispensation voucher," Gosney said of her neighbors. Vouchers like that presumably weren't hard to come by for likes of Congressman Charlie Rose's relatives and friends whom Gosney played with on the weekends on Hillside Avenue. Because of her father's low salary as director of Quaker House, Gosney qualified for free lunch throughout her public school years in Fayetteville.

"My weekend friends weren't my school friends," Gosney said. "It was an interesting transition."

After three years at Pauline Jones, where she had on occasion received threats and harassment, she began middle school at Hillcrest Middle, which required another total cultural shift. "It was like those John Hughes movies," Gosney laughed, referring to the director of many popular slapstick comedies of cultural juxtaposition. Whereas at Pauline Jones she shared the classroom with the children of the infantrymen of the 82nd Airborne, Hillcrest Middle was for the officers' kids. Pauline Jones had had an inner city feel to it, but up on Haymount Hill, two miles west, it was all suburban, white, cliquish and, according to her, "horrible."

Luckily, "school was never primary," she said. "I'd get much more out of going to the library with my Dad." In fact, she decided to go into library work when she grew up, which she did.

Bob Gosney, Gwen's father, accepted the position as Director of Quaker House soon after Sholar's departure in June of 1980 and, together with his wife, Barbara, raised their family on Hillside Avenue

Gwen Gosney Erickson, right, and her sister Mary Enid, in Fayetteville. Gwen is now archivist at Guilford College, in charge, among others, of the Quaker house archives.

for the next seven years, the longest stay of any of the project's directors in its first thirty years.

When Gwen and her younger sister Mary Enid weren't playing with Nicole Ray in Rowan Park or Congressman Rose's kids at their basketball court, they could be found keeping Eileen "Granny" Moffit company. Moffit's house shared a driveway with Quaker House and on hot afternoons the young girls sought refuge in her kitchen where they were treated to cold soda and stories of old Fayetteville. Moffit, then 80-years old, had been a newspaper reporter before she retired.

There was a Christmas tradition in which the neighbors went caroling together, down one side of the street and back up the other. Afterwards they all met at the Ray's House for a party.

"It was a really great neighborhood," Gwen Gosney remembered. "I think it helped that my family was from the south so you could fit in on the street culturally in some ways."

"I knew there were things they were wary about," she said about her neighbors' attitudes towards Quaker House, "But it didn't come up in our personal interactions. They had the attitude that it could be a lot worse."

From the neighbors' point of view, even if they didn't agree with Quaker House's stand on important political issues such as nuclear weapons or the possibility of a draft, at least they kept the house up. On the end of the street that Quaker House occupies there were a number of elderly widows and Bob Gosney–being the fit young man that he was–frequently helped one or another of them out.

Although occasional events spilled out of the house, most of what

Bob and Barbara Gosney.

went on at Quaker House went on indoors and unobtrusively. "We were just a house that entertained more than other houses," Gwen Gosney said.

.

During the summer of 1968 Bob Gosney got a draft notice. He wrote back to the draft board explaining that he was opposed to participation in war and why he had not filled out the proper forms to get status as a conscientious objector.

When he was ordered to report to his draft board and failed to do so, he was charged with a felony and received a visit from US Marshalls. Through the ACLU he got a lawyer and eventually the government dropped the case. Instead, they sent him back to his draft board, where he was classified as a conscientious objector and ordered to complete alternative service.

Along the way, one of his wife Barbara's co-workers helped Gosney get draft counseling through the Charlottesville, Virginia Friends Meeting. It had been his first experience with Quakers and it convinced both him and Barbara to begin attending Charlottesville Meeting.

"I was teaching after my work in alternative service and I had decided to stop teaching and at that point was thinking about making some changes," Gosney said. He was earning a living making ice cream while he and Barbara deliberated about the next steps.

Their first impression of Quaker House was intimidating. Another young couple attending Charlottesville Meeting had recently moved there from Fayetteville. "We became aware that Quaker House in Fayetteville had an opening for staff," Gosney recalled, "and they said 'You don't want to move to Fayetteville. You have a young daughter and it's a military community.'" The Gosneys took their advice and moved to Richmond, Indiana where Bob enrolled in a Masters program in Ministry at Earlham School of Religion. But the next time the Quaker House post came open, Bob was ready to chance it.

"We felt we were older, more experienced," Gosney said. "I felt like having had that couple of years to reflect I was better able to consider getting into something like Quaker House." Gosney's family would define and personify the project throughout most of the decade after they arrived.

Camp Lejeune is a major Marine base, roughly 100 miles east of Fayetteville and Fort Bragg, adjoining the coastal town of Jacksonville NC. It is a 246 square-mile training facility, in operation since 1941. Along with its satellite facilities and nearby Marine Corps Air Base Cherry Point in Havelock, NC, it is home to the largest concentration of Marines and US Navy sailors in the world. Its 14 miles of beaches make it a major area for amphibious assault training, which attracts military forces from around the world for bilateral and NATO-sponsored exercises. Its proximity to two deep water ports–Wilmington and Morehead City–facilitate rapid deployment. Its brig, can house 280 inmates. Military prisoners from Fort Bragg are often sent here to serve their time, since Fort Bragg in recent decades has not had a brig of its own.

Camp Lejeune has also had its share of government scandals. Apparently, the water which Marines and their families drank and bathed in on and around the base was laced with toxics and carcinogens from 1957 to 1987, when the base's wells were shut off. Authorities knew about the contamination, but hid the information for decades. As of late 2008, investigations were proceeding.

In 1980 Gosney found himself unable to cope with the high volume of calls coming from Marines and sailors at Camp Lejeune. The distance, coupled with a corporate culture that was different from the Army, made adequate counseling those service members difficult without extra help.

At the time, a young minister, Mac Legerton, a recent graduate of Union Seminary in New York City, was attending Meeting for worship on Sundays at Quaker House. "I first went to Quaker House because of the faith community there," Legerton said. At the time he was still discerning his own relationship to the institutional church. "As a contemplative, I felt totally at home with Quaker spiritual practice and culture and its perspective on peace," Legerton recalled.

"I always felt pulled toward community ministry rather than pastoral parish ministry," Legerton explained. In 1982 he was ordained to Community Ministry through Eutaw United Church of Christ in Fayetteville.

Gosney and Legerton discussed the need for counseling at Camp Lejeune and proposed a solution to the Board. In August of 1980 the Mary Reynolds Babcock Foundation awarded Quaker House a $7,580 grant to pay for a car and a salary for Legerton to visit Camp Lejeune 5-10 days a month.

"I felt my role was to be a loving and healing presence to those who were victimized," Legerton said. "It went beyond issues of conscientious

objection to war." Over the period of the Camp Lejeune Outreach Project, Legerton's dedication to being that presence would be obvious to everyone. "I became so well known at the hotel I would stay at in Jacksonville that the marquee would say 'Welcome Reverend Legerton!" he laughed.

Camp Lejeune was different in many ways from Fort Bragg, with which Quaker House had always been so closely associated. First of all, to be relevant at Camp Lejeune, Legerton needed access to prisoners in the brig. To get it, he joined a group called Prisoner Visitation and Support (PVS), which was founded in 1968 (as Prisoner Visitation Service) to serve the increasing numbers of GIs who were resisting the Vietnam War and were being sent to brigs and stockades for their acts of conscience.

Any Marine returning to the base from an unauthorized absence, or UA, the Marine equivalent of AWOL, was thrown into the brig. "That was the safest place for them. If they went back to their units they'd get beat up," Legerton explained. "You didn't want to send them back to their commanding officers – they'd take it personally if a Marine went UA."

Marines who were UA often called Quaker House and Legerton would be put in touch with them. "I would encourage them to return to the base and resolve this issue so they could get on with their life," Legerton explained. Once back in custody, Legerton would package their case by interpreting to the legal teams charged with prosecuting the young men why this particular person had decided to go UA.

"I became like a mitigation specialist for the legal team," Legerton said. He would continue visiting his counselees throughout their incarceration in the brig.

"I found the personnel on the base and their legal teams very supportive of my presence," said Legerton. "I think it helped that I had the status as a Protestant Minister...I know I would have been treated differently if I hadn't had that institutional form of authority."

Another difference between Fort Bragg and Camp Lejeune was the particular culture of the Marines at the time. According to Legerton, many Marine officers felt that all family members, particularly spouses, were almost a problem because anything that took the focus of the Marine from their military duty was a problem. When ever there was a family need that required their husbands to request time to deal with family issues "many spouses felt alienated and felt that they were treated less than honorably," said Legerton.

By that time in the early 80's, the Army had loosened some of its authoritarian grip (its recruiting slogan as the draft ended was "Today's Army Wants To Join You!" followed for the balance of the 1970s by, "Join The People Who've Joined the Army") and had made an effort to be more "family-friendly" as well.

"But the Marines were really proud to remain in that authoritarian, autocratic culture," recalled Legerton. (Counterpart Marines recruiting slogans: "We'd promise you sleep deprivation, mental torment, and muscles so sore you'll puke, but we don't like to sugar-coat things." And: "Nobody likes to fight. But somebody has to know how.") The treatment of military personnel as isolated and totally dedicated to the military mission caused a whole set of problems for Marines beyond what those serving in the Army had.

In this kind of atmosphere there is little tolerance for deviation. Fear, intimidation and harassment was much stronger in general in the Marines than in the Army, and in particular to a person with conscientious scruples. "That sense of spiritual strength as moral weakness was much stronger in the Marine Corps than in the Army," remembered Legerton. "It was a much different experience than what the majority of the Army personnel were experiencing at the time."

Sailors were another story altogether. Many had joined the Navy because it was considered the least restrictive of the services, but they didn't realize that many Navy personnel were assigned to Marine bases. This too led to major conflicts with the tightly wrapped Marine culture, particularly for those who joined the Navy because of their service in the field of health.

Legerton carried an average of 15 cases per month, providing counseling, prison visitation, advocacy, and family support. Each case involved about three to four months of direct counsel and constant communication and a majority of them involved a high level of emotional and financial trauma. Nintey-five percent of the Marines he counseled were between 17 and 21 years old and almost as high a percentage came from low income background and said they joined the Marines with a lack of direction in their lives.

Of particular note to Legerton's credit is that he reported that ninety per cent of the discharges given his counselees were "Good of Service" discharges instead of bad conduct ones. In a report to their funders, Gosney reported that "Over and over again we are told that without this program many more Marines would now be UA." This was the goal–to stop the further victimization of young men who are already victims of war.

The project was laid down in August 1984, but not before producing "It's Our Right," a guide to GI rights that is specifically targeted for active duty service men and women. Both "It's Our Right" and "Should You Enlist?" a booklet aimed at pre-enlistment education, were produced by Gosney and Legerton and mailed out to meetings and churches in the vicinity of Army posts and Marine camps across the country.

"Its such an important practice and witness," Legerton said about Quaker House. "I'm just so grateful that the supporters and leaders and staff…have sustained it and created an institution that now has a respected presence in the Fort Bragg and Fayetteville community."

Legerton was still in Pembroke, NC about 35 miles south of Fayetteville in late 2008, where he was Co-Director of the Center for Community Action.

Bob Gosney came from a family of builders, so he knew something about fixing up houses. This came in very handy, in that the Board's approach to such matters was strictly "do it yourself," with the help of occasional volunteer work parties. He saw several aspects of Quaker House that needed renovation. Someone had partially enclosed the former screened back porch, and he turned it into a functioning room with large windows. Below it, in what was originally storage space, he dug out part of the sandy floor so an adult could stand up in it, then laid a concrete floor and put in a window and air conditioning, to make a pleasant space that could be used for First Day School for children at Fayetteville Meeting.

Such rebuilding work had to be sandwiched in between an increased counseling load and the press of other peace issues.

While the military draft ended in 1973, draft *registration* for all males reaching age eighteen was reinstated under President Jimmy Carter in June of 1980, in response to the Soviet invasion of Afghanistan. Government and military officials, however, had not forgotten the massive draft resistance of the Vietnam years. As former general and Secretary of State Alexander Haig told a French interviewer, "There is a Jane Fonda on every doorstep."

But Haig's evocation of the much-vilified Fonda had its intended effect. Thus administrations since then have (as of 2008) hesitated to take that next fateful step. Ever since, however, questions about the return of actual conscription, and how young men can prepare for possible CO claims, have been a constant for Quaker House staff.

Yet despite scattered protests, the return to registration did not spark significant resistance. (And Jane Fonda, for that matter, turned away from protest and spent much of the 1980s making hugely successful exercise videos.)

Besides, in the early 1980s, the deep recession and high unemployment of the first Reagan years again meant that military recruiters were reaching their enlistment goals. As a result, Bob Gosney's load of counseling cases was relatively light. While at times he had five or six counselees, usually it was more like two or three active cases.

That left Quaker House available to respond when community members in Fayetteville began agitating for more local action around a wide range of peace issues. One main result of this was the Fayetteville Peace Center, which came together in 1984, centered at 223 Hillside. A series of Friday Forums on issues of the day were one of its major efforts.

One forum in 1986 was especially memorable: there could not have been any more people inside Quaker House that night. "I thought I would never get in the front door and they just kept squeezing in!" Ann Ashford remembered.

Motlalepula Chabaku, a South African refugee, feminist, humanist minister, and anti-apartheid activist, speaking at Quaker House, in 1986.

"I was scared the floor joists were going to give in and that the fire marshal was going to show up," laughed Gosney, who estimated the size of the crowd at 200. "There were probably people in my bedroom!"

This size crowd was totally unprecedented for a Forum session. After all, a previous forum on ecological issues attracted only five or six participants. The topic of this event—the situation in South Africa—apparently had more appeal in Fayetteville. Announcements in predominantly African American churches in the area brought people out too. Even more impressive was that this

particular forum deviated from the schedule, and was held mid-week–
Wednesday March 19th 1986.

At the center of attention was Motlalepula Chabaku, a South African
refugee, feminist, humanist minister, and anti-apartheid activist. She was then
on a US speaking tour. "You couldn't see her," remembered Gosney, "only
hear her booming voice."

From other presentations on her tour, here are a few of her themes:

> I was born and brought up on the outskirts of
> Johannesburg. In Johannesburg, the indigenous people to
> whom I belong, the Africans, are forbidden by law to live in
> the city. We are forcibly housed outside the city. I am one
> of seven children from a very poor family. My parents were
> able to educate us only up to the sixth grade. As I was the
> second eldest daughter there were more difficulties for me;
> there was preference for educating a boy over a girl. I now
> also realize the pressures my mother faced. There was
> pressure on her to give birth to a boy to retain the lineage,
> as daughters cannot carry on the family name. Even before
> that, there was hostility toward her marriage because it was
> a marriage of choice instead of one arranged by their
> parents. And, too, they did not have a dowry as expected,
> and they were poor– so when my mother gave birth to
> another girl, that was an added problem.

What Gosney recalled most about the night is Chabaku's story about
the rubber ball that her father had in their house in South Africa.

> My parents always used to tell us how we were loved, how
> special we were, how we were meant to be greater than
> what we were. My father used to take a tennis ball and say,
> "You are like a tennis ball. People can squeeze you, but
> always bounce back as who you are. They will even try to
> bounce you down, but the harder they hit, the higher up
> you should go. Be like this ball, the harder they throw you
> down, the further you come back up."

In 2008, Chabaku was a provincial legislator in the now
post-apartheid south Africa. But in 1986, as she explained,

> I am still a South African, although I am now without
> citizenship by decree of the white South African
> government. I still love Southern Africa. We are going
> through a very painful but exciting moment. We are people
> at the bottom of the mountain struggling to go up, and
> saying to those in power who are on top, "Come down,

meet us halfway so that we can live and share and be together." And the longer they delay coming down...well, we are coming up, and the harder they will fall when they finally tumble down.

The Fayetteville Peace Center was really an expansion of the Fayetteville Area Nuclear Freeze Campaign, which was initiated by people meeting at Quaker House out of concern for nuclear arms issues.

The Nuclear Freeze campaign burst on the scene in 1981, sparked by Dr. Randall Forsberg, a peace researcher and activist in Cambridge, Massachusetts. It called on both the Soviet Union and the US to freeze and then reverse the nuclear arms race. The movement spread rapidly, and became the focus of intense public interest and much enthusiasm. In June 1982, the Freeze brought out the largest peace rally in US history, close to a million people in New York City's Central Park.

On June 12, 1982, the largest political demonstration in the history of the country took place in Central Park, New York City. Close to a million people gathered to express their determination to bring an end to the arms race.

An example of the energy the Freeze expressed was the statement of Harvard chemistry professor George Kistiakowsky, who had worked on the first atom bomb. At eighty-two, dying of cancer, his last published article, in the *Bulletin of Atomic Scientists* in December 1982, was dramatic for a lifelong scientist: "I tell you as my parting words," he wrote: "Forget the channels. There simply is not enough time left before the world explodes. Concentrate instead on organizing, with so many others of like mind, a mass movement for peace such as there has not been before."

This enthusiasm soon spread even to Fayetteville. "We had people in the community come to us and say 'We need to organize in this community around this issue, this is something that concerns people,'" Bob Gosney explained. "As is true of most of the people involved in the nuclear freeze movement," Gosney wrote in a Newsletter at the time, "the folks who started this group have not had any previous participation in 'peace movement' activities."

One of those people in particular was a Jewish woman named Helga Baer. Baer was a concerned citizen who told Gosney at the time, "'Something needs to be done. You're the people do things!'" Gosney repeated this with a great laugh. "After that, we sent out some notices and we had a little meeting about the issues at one of the branch libraries and people really flocked to that." Before long, there were 40 or so members of the group including people from both civilian and military communities and various faith backgrounds.

Ann Ashford and her husband John had been attending St. Paul's in the Pines Episcopal Church in Fayetteville when they got involved in the group. "I think what really brought me to [Quaker] worship was when we started the Nuclear Freeze Campaign," Ann Ashford said. At Freeze meetings she met Sister Dorothy Ann, a Catholic nun, and Denny Burnett, a liberal Presbyterian minister, both of Fayetteville.

When the Nuclear Freeze Campaign joined with other local groups such as the Shalom Group and the Fayetteville-Obninsk Friendship Sociey, they called the new group the Fayetteville Peace Center.

"The Fayetteville Peace Center itself is not focused on any one issue. We're working on different issues," Gosney told the *Fayetteville Observer*. "We're not saying 'This is the way to have peace...we don't have a ready answer."

"The main idea of the Peace Center is people," he continued. "We think there needs to be a group of people that has a vision of peace and who has informed themselves about the different kinds of information available." The group sponsored a peace vigil, lobbied local leaders, organized conferences and support for local and national legislation.

Perhaps the culmination of all this community organizing was "We Are the World: A Retreat for High School Peacemakers." This was a weekend-long camp for high-schoolers that took place in October of 1986 at Camp Rockfish, outside of Fayetteville. It was directed towards high school juniors and seniors "who want to begin learning how to live in a world that is not of their making, and how to begin to shape this world into a more peaceful and just society" according to the brochure.

"Although many would not expect it to happen in a military town like Fayetteville," Gosney wrote in the Quaker House Newsletter at the time, "the population of doves seems to be increasing around Quaker House." Gosney and Ashford, remembering it 25 years later, were both still impressed at how it all came together–so active, so diverse and so ambitious. The peace education component of Quaker House's mission which had up to this point proven elusive, began to come into its own with the establishment of the Fayetteville Peace Center.

The 1980s were also the years of US involvement in wars, overt and covert, in Central America. One of the bloodiest battlegrounds was El Salvador. There the assassination of Catholic Bishop Oscar Romero in March 1980 helped set off extended fighting between a left-wing rebel coalition and a right-wing US-backed government. Many tens of thousands, mainly farmers and civilians, were killed in the struggle.

During the first two months of 1982, events there brought antiwar protests back to Fort Bragg's doorstep. When word got out that about 1,000 soldiers from El Salvador had arrived on post for training, organizers with the Coalition in Solidarity with the People of El Salvador rallied with over 200 people at the gates of the Army post. They were met by a colonel who accepted a letter from the protesters. The colonel said he had decided to meet with them because, "they have been very orderly. They haven't disrupted anything on Post."

Although Gosney and Quaker House stayed behind the scenes of the antiwar protests at Fort Bragg in 1982, two years later, as involvement in

Central America escalated and expanded into Nicaragua, they stepped forward. After leftist Sandinista rebels in Nicaragua overthrew the longtime Somoza dictatorship in 1979, the US response went from tepid acceptance in the last years of Jimmy Carter's presidency to active opposition under Ronald Reagan. US funds and military resources went into backing the "Contra" rebel attacks on the Sandinistas and many apolitical ordinary citizens. Many US activists mounted protests of this involvement.

Along with the Carolina Interfaith Task Force on Central America and the New York-based Fellowship of Reconciliation, Quaker House co-sponsored "An Open Letter to Soldiers at Fort Bragg" which ran a whole page in the *Fayetteville Observer* on December 11th 1984.

Signed by close to 150 people in North Carolina, Georgia, South Carolina, Tennessee and Virginia, and sponsored by national groups, the letter presented facts about the popular support enjoyed by the Nicaraguan government, how the Contras were formed and supplied by the US to topple a non-aggressive government and how the conflict had little to do with the defense of the United States.

The real strength of the letter is its appeal to soldiers as individuals:

> We understand that just because you are wearing the same uniform at the same base does not mean that you all think alike and it is to each of you as individuals that this letter is addressed...We understand that you volunteered to become part of the US Armed Forces out of a dedication to the defense of this country and ideals of freedom. We respect your sincerity and your willingness to endure hardship for what you believe...In this situation we realize you may feel in a bind. Your loyalty to our country is without question. At the same time, each of you is a person who cares about what is right and what is wrong...Should the orders to move against the people of Nicaragua come you do have other options. Although they too could bring personal difficulties, conscience and conviction have the capacity to override whatever hardships might come.

This approach was in part an effort to apply a lesson from the Vietnam years. Much opposition to Quaker House then was based on the perception that by being against war the protesters were also against the rank-and-file soldiers. In this ad, the antiwar stance passed no judgment on the soldiers as fellow humans.

During a press conference following publication of the letter Gosney said, "We are not advocating any particular response. What we are advocating is that [soldiers] take a position before anything happens."

But some on the post were not swayed. "It's saying if you don't want to fight, you can desert and we'll give you legal aid," Cpl. Troy Bowman of Alpha Company, 325th Regiment at Fort Bragg told the newspaper. "It's promoting people to go AWOL." Bowman claimed that every soldier he had discussed the letter with was enraged.

Every member of Bowman's company signed a rebuttal letter to the paper. "We are the instruments of our country's foreign policy—wherever and whatever our elected representatives might decide that may be," the letter stated. "We believe and are ready to die for your freedom of speech and right to opinion but our opinion is that your opinion is wrong."

"The response was immediate and mostly negative," Gosney wrote in the Quaker House Newsletter after the Open Letter appeared. "[The letter] and responding to it have emotionally, spiritually and physically drained us at Quaker House." Response to the letter among Friends was mixed: a few raised questions as to whether or not it fitted in with the purposes of Quaker House. Many more indicated that the letter was one of the most significant projects for Quaker house in some time.

Fayetteville's largest annual cultural event is the International Folk Festival, which takes place every September. It draws many thousands of people for a weekend of food and music representing cultures from around the world, showcasing the city's ethnic diversity. The Fayetteville Peace Center showed up there with a table full of information on the nuclear freeze campaign and other hot button issues.

Aside from pamphlets and petitions, Ann Ashford, the whole Gosney family and Peace Center volunteers had with them huge boxes of frisbees printed with the Peace Center's logo. "We were convinced we were going to sell them and get rich!" joked Ashford. After all, who doesn't like to play frisbee, right?

Unfortunately for them, the Fayetteville Peace Center's frisbees were competing for the festival goers' dollars with homemade kim-chee from Korean, sweet gulub jamun from India, and Turkish kebobs hot off the grill, among any other appealing delicacies.

No one was buying the frisbees, so they lowered the price. Still no takers. "We lowered the price again, and no one bought them," said Ashford. "Before long, we gave them away!"

The free toys did attract the attention of a little girl who approached the group for a Frisbee. What Ashford recalls most vividly about that afternoon was what happened next. "Before she got too close her Momma yanked her away by the arm and reprimanded her, 'Don't talk to them, they're not nice people.'"

"I couldn't imagine nicer people than those Gosney girls," Ashford said sadly. "That hurt me."

"I have a lot of good memories of the Gosneys," Ashford said. "I was really glad to find them." Over the seven years they were there, hundreds of counselees were glad to find them too. Quaker House under the Gosneys was valued, not just because it was the sole full-time military counseling center in the southeastern US, but because it was a family household.

Visiting GIs yearned for a respite from the military atmosphere. "I remember one [counselee] in particular going back in the kitchen and cooking with Barbara," Gosney said. "It was just a way to have somebody to relate to who didn't have something to do with the military." A GI seeking to become a conscientious objector faced a particularly driving taskmaster in Gosney when they sat down to write the statements that would become the crucial parts of their application.

"[The counselees] would take a break from working...and would spend time with Barbara, also sometimes with the girls," Gosney explained. "They really appreciated the family environment."

"The bad part," Gosney said, "was on occasion we had people come in and it probably wasn't best that we had a family there. There was an intensity there that wasn't really congenial to living as a family."

"I don't think that's a kind of work you can do for an extended period of time and bring the kind of energy to it [that] it needs to have," Gosney said. After Legerton left, Gosney remained as the sole counselor. "It was difficult because even though it wasn't a huge case load, you were always on call and there were some very intense cases," he said.

This intensity took its toll on the family, and in the summer of 1987, after almost seven years, they moved to rural Halifax County, in the northeastern part of North Carolina where Gosney began counseling abused and neglected children. A few months later, he wrote to the Quaker House Board. "I want to say thank you ...for your concern for us over the past seven years," the letter said. "I have delayed writing to you to see if I could express my appreciation in a better way. I find I cannot. There is no way I can express what your support and encouragement has meant and means to us."

"For the rest of us this was a cause apart from our regular lives," Ann Ashford said about Gosney's approach to the Peace Testimony. "For him it was so peaceful. He was so clear and able to act. I thought, 'I want to be like that,'" Ashford said.

Anne Matthysse, a Board Member at the time, said Gosney "had a lot of the qualities that a good minister would have" and as a result was very well respected in the religious communities both in Fayetteville and also on the base.

9. 1987-1994: War & Rumors of War

There were obvious advantages to having a Director stay for several years at Quaker House. It gave time for building wider contacts in the community. It made possible an orderly response to new issues and movements. It burnished the project's sheen of respectable dissent. This had been true with the Arnings. It was particularly so with the Gosneys.

Such continuity also eased the workload for the Board. But perhaps their work became too easy. When the Gosneys left, the Board was evidently not ready for the transition, because the house was without staff for almost a year.

It's not as if events stood still while the Board got its act together. In 1988, the Soviet Union began its descent into disintegration; Congress cut off funds for the ongoing Contra war in Nicaragua (and the Reagan administration continued to fund it, illegally and, for a time, secretly); Russian troops withdrew from Afghanistan, after years of fighting US-backed militant Islamic groups, some of which were later to coalesce into what was called Al Queda, and others into the Taliban Militia; Chilean dictator Augusto Pinochet was forced from power after seventeen brutal years; and US military recruiting was surging toward its post-World War Two peak.

Many of these faraway events reverberated at Fort Bragg. There was still plenty for Quaker House to do. But who could be found to do it?

When Greg Sommers registered with Selective Service in 1980 he noted on the form that he was a Mennonite and a conscientious objector. Many Mennonites, along with Quakers and the Church of the Brethren, have had similar beliefs about war, that Jesus advocated nonviolence and that fighting for nations or governments is contrary to Christian morality.

Sommers was born in 1962 in the Mennonite stronghold of Goshen, Indiana and raised in California and Pennsylvania, but returned to Indiana to study the Bible and Religion at Goshen College. Later he spent several years working for the Midwest Committee for Military Counseling (MCMC) in Chicago, where he became Program Director. Much of his work there involved knowing the Army regulations, listening to the soldier's needs and matching those up, whether it be a compassionate reassignment or a hardship discharge. This was about as good a fit with the Quaker House tradition that the Board could hope to find.

Indeed, his introduction to Quaker House came while he was working at MCMC. "I had referred somebody to Quaker House in early March of 1988 and found out that they were not functioning at the time,"

Sommers exlained. This was during the long months the project was without staff after the Gosneys left. "Bruce Pulliam called me back and he talked to me and I said 'Ok I might be interested in moving down there'," Sommers said.

Greg Sommers takes a call; the counseling load skyrocketed with the buildup to the Gulf War of 1990-91.

Within the month they flew him down and offered him the position. He liked the idea of working at Quaker House and besides, the deferment on his student loans was coming to an end and the $65 a month he was paid in Chicago wasn't going to cut it. He arrived in Fayetteville during the summer of 1988. He looked so serious with his round spectacles, sport coat and close-cropped hair and beard, but the scholarly exterior belied a jocular manner.

"We've been real busy since August," Quaker House director Greg Sommers told the *Fayetteville Observer* in late December of 1990. During the first seven months of the year, Sommers had seen only about one new counseling case each month. But in the month prior to the newspaper interview, twenty-eight new counselees had contacted him – almost one per day – seeking medical discharges, hardship discharges or compassionate reassignment. Half of them were seeking discharge on grounds of conscientious objection.

"I'm not out there telling people to do this," Sommers said to the newspaper. "But what we're facing now is a lot of people saying they don't think this particular conflict is right."

By "this particular conflict," Sommers meant the buildup for war in the weeks after August 2nd 1990, when Saddam Hussein's Iraqi Republican

Guard had invaded adjoining, oil-rich Kuwait and declared most of it to be the new 19th province of Iraq. In response, President George H.W. Bush declared that "this will not stand," and began what his administration insisted was a "wholly defensive" mission, ostensibly intended to prevent Iraq from moving on to attack Saudi Arabia. (Something, it turned out, Hussein had had no intention of doing.)

A massive military buildup, dubbed Operation Desert Shield, began days after Hussein's invasion. It would eventually reach 543,000 troops, more than three times the number used in the second US invasion of Iraq in 2003. Polls showed upwards of eighty per cent of Americans in support of the troop deployment.

"Within three days 120,000 Iraq troops with 850 tanks poured into Kuwait and moved south to threaten Saudi Arabia. It was then that I decided to act to check that aggression," President George H. W. Bush explained in a speech on September 11, 1990. The Pentagon claimed that satellite photos showing a buildup of Iraqi forces along the Saudi border were the source of this information. This claim was later shown to be false when a reporter for the *Saint Petersburg Times* acquired commercial satellite images made at the time in question, which showed nothing but empty desert.

Despite the seemingly broad public support for the buildup to war, there was plenty of protest against it, in hastily-organized rallies large and small, most ignored by a seemingly war-hungry media. In addition, there were plenty of soldiers and sailors who had doubts about it, doubts strong enough to send them visiting Quaker House, and jamming the phone lines at other similar agencies, such as the Central Committee for Conscientious Objectors in Philadelphia, and the National Interreligious Service Board for Conscientious Objectors in Washington DC.

As early as August of 1990, Marine Corporal Jeff Patterson, sat down on the runway of a Hawaii airfield, refusing to board a plane for Saudi Arabia. Instead, he requested a discharge. He wrote that,

> "I have come to believe that there are no justified wars.... I began to question exactly what I was doing in the Marine Corps about the time I began to read about history. I began to read up on America's support for the murderous regimes of Guatemala, Iran under the Shah, and El Salvador.... I object to the military use of force against any people, anywhere, any time."

Patterson, who was later discharged without a court martial, was one of the lucky ones. The military acted swiftly to prevent the re-appearance of any organized GI resistance. Army regulations were changed so that CO applicants scheduled to deploy to the Gulf would be shipped out anyway, before their claims were processed. This would put them thousands of miles away from counselors or lawyers, not to mention uncensored media.

Many dissident marines were shipped to Camp Lejeune, which is also in an isolated location. More than a dozen Marine reservists there filed CO applications. One of them, Erik Larsen, stated,

> "I declare myself a conscientious objector. Here is my sea bag full of personal gear. Here is my gas mask. I no longer need them. I am no longer a Marine. ... It, to me, is embarrassing to fight for a way of life in which basic human needs, like a place to sleep, one hot meal a day and some medical attention, cannot even be met in our nation's capital."

There were many other soldiers, marines and sailors who resisted the call to what is referred to as the Gulf War. Yet few of them gained much public attention. One that did was an Army reservist from Murphysboro, Illinois named Stephanie Atkinson. She was very close to the end of her six-year reserve hitch when the call to active duty came. She felt, however, that the American buildup in the Gulf had more to do with oil than any ideals, and declined to report.

"My conscience is my guide," she told an interviewer, "and it tells me not to take part in what President Bush is planning in the Gulf." When a reporter challenged her about breaking the oath she had taken when she joined, Atkinson replied, "What do you want? That every eighteen year-old who joins up stay at exactly that same level of political and moral understanding for the rest of his or her life?"

Atkinson was ordered to report to Fort Benjamin Harrison, Indiana later that same month, for training and deployment to Saudi Arabia. When she did not show up, she was picked up and placed under house arrest. The next month, Atkinson was given an administrative discharge "under other than honorable conditions." An Army historian says this was to avoid a long and highly-publicized legal fight.

Several weeks of bombing began in mid-January 1991, after Congress authorized the use of force to drive Hussein's forces from Kuwait in the slimmest margin authorizing force since the War of 1812. An actual invasion began on February 24, and Saddam Hussein's forces retreated in disorder. The ground campaign lasted only one hundred hours before a ceasefire/victory was declared.

Despite the quick end to the fighting, the surge in activity at Quaker House continued – Sommers handled 59 cases within the first five weeks of 1991. In contrast, he had handled 102 in total for all of 1990. Service-members from all branches of the military called seeking help on a wide range of issues, including five soldiers at Fort Bragg who were seeking conscientious objector status.

"Our evidence is that the Gulf War was not universally supported, particularly by those who had to fight it," Sommers said in October of 1991, months after active hostilities had ended. Part of the problem was the way the Army had been advertising for the years prior to the conflict. The recruiting slogans (primarily, "Be All That You Can Be,") had emphasized self-realization and benefits, such as money for college.

"It wasn't 'Army of One' yet so people were joining for all the wrong reasons," Sommers said referring to a US military recruiting slogan that came later. "The 'Money for College' advertising was an effective campaign for the military to get people in, but the downside was they got people in who were not interested at all in being in the military."

Also problematic for military morale was the 'total force concept' which military authorities had put into place prior to Operation Desert Storm. This plan depended on keeping the number of troops in the standing Army at a lower level, then mobilize National Guard and Reservists for international conflicts. "Previously they [the reserves and Guard] were mostly homebodies," Sommers said. "When the rules changed, these folks who signed up for two weekends a month realize suddenly they're going to be leaving their families."

The reality was that most of the soldiers who Sommers counseled were not conscientious objectors, even if they called saying they were. "I screen my clients carefully and make sure they are really conscientious objectors," he said. "It's not something to take lightly...If somebody's trying to misuse the [conscientious objector status] I have a real problem with that."

"I was there to help military personnel with various things," Sommers explained. "[Conscientious objectors] primarily, but if they were troubled in a way that wasn't that, I wasn't going to put a square peg in a round hole."

One of the hardest things for Greg Sommers to get used to in Fayetteville was the Quaker practice of working by the "sense of the Meeting" when doing business. This process draws in part from biblical sources, such as Jesus' charge to the disciples, in Matthew 20:25-26: "You know that the rulers of the Gentiles lord it over them, and those in high positions use their authority over them. It must not be this way among you! Instead whoever wants to be great among you must be your servant . . . ." Also the account in Acts 15 of the first, ad hoc church council among the new Christians, in which there was wide debate and discussion, summed up by the Apostle James and then reportedly agreed to by the entire assembly.

The Quaker application of these examples has produced a model of voteless decision-making, in which discussion continues, coordinated by a presiding Clerk, who attempts to sum up a discussion when it reaches a point where a decision represents the "sense of the meeting," which then is drafted into a decision minute.

This method explicitly rejects both simple majority rule and unanimous consent. Thus when there are differences, discussion can be quite protracted, until a broadly acceptable resolution is reached.

One way of maintaining (or regaining) calm during ardent discussions is for a Friend to ask for the group to have a period of silence. This happened at Quaker House Board Meetings, and the practice tried Sommers' patience. "I was like a young child, I always wanted to finish what I was saying!" he laughed. "But God works through all that," he added, acknowledging its usefulness. In 2008 Sommers, an administrator at the Warwick River Christian School in Norfolk, Virginia, joked, "I wish my current board would do that!"

In 1989, Sommers explained his stance against war to the Greensboro *News & Record* thus: "The Beatitudes are more than just nice words. I feel they are a social mandate. Basically, God exists in everybody. To harm that is wrong." Throughout his stay in Fayetteville he attended a Mennonite church in Raleigh and as a result was not as involved as his predecessor in the life of Fayetteville Friends Meeting, but in all other regards he fit right in at the project.

Sommers said he felt that the conflict in the Persian Gulf dominated his time at Quaker House. By the end of 1991 he had counseled over 146 new clients that year alone, mostly as a result of Operation Desert Storm. This is up from 102 during the previous year. Of the new clients 57 were in the Army, 19 were Marines, 2 were Air Force, 9 were in the Navy 1 was Coast Guard, 22 were reserves. "As a result of our experience during the first quarter of [1991] we are more eager than ever to get information of the realities of the military service to students in high school before they enlist," Sommers reported in the Newsletter.

The struggle by non-military groups to gain a modicum of access to high school students comparable to that military recruiters are allowed is a very long and uphill battle, one that continues to this day. Sommers was invited more than once to speak to students at high schools around Chapel Hill, but just up the road from Quaker House at a school named for a former resident of 223 Hillside, Terry Sanford High School, he had been rebuffed. Unlike in the Research Triangle, which draws students from the liberal communities that surround the universities, Terry Sanford's student body is comprised largely of military dependents. Military recruiters were in its facilities constantly.

The brushoff was no surprise. Fayetteville and surrounding Cumberland County ranked 13th in the nation in number of Army recruits in 2006. Chapel Hill and its Orange County, didn't make even the top 100.

Luckily for Quaker House, one of its Board members had more than a little pull at Terry Sanford. She was not on the School Board, nor a teacher, nor was she a member of the PTA–she was a senior.

Sarah Hennessey had begun attending Meeting with Gwen Gosney when the two were just ten years old. She had appreciated the respect that the adult Friends gave her there. "I'd been going to lots of different churches, but [Quaker Meeting] was the first time any adults had looked me in the eye," Hennessey said. "I felt like I was being recognized as a spiritual seeker even though I was ten years old." Before long, she became Recording Clerk of Fayetteville Friends Meeting.

Thanks to Hennessey's activism, Sommers met with the principal of Terry Sanford and Quaker House was given access to present three pamphlets on alternatives to military enlistment every few months. Hennessey reported back to the Overseers. "The Board felt very optimistic and a sense of breakthrough regarding this opening at the Fayetteville, NC high school," they wrote. "Congratulations to Sara and Greg!" The access was short-lived. Hennessey graduated, and after further seeking joined the Roman Catholic church. In 2008 Hennessey was living in St. Paul, Minnesota where she was a Franciscan Sister and was earning a Masters degree in Theology at the University of St. Thomas. Her parents still lived in Fayetteville.

Sommers kept a busy schedule but made time to volunteer in the community. One project was to mix up six gallons of soapy water and cart it down to the International Folk Festival. There he showed kids how to blow bubbles with their hands and using the plastic rings from six-packs. Service to the community was a way of breaking down the barriers between people who don't agree, he explained. It was a way of becoming accepted as a peace activist in an Army town.

Greg Sommers displaying another of his skills – with bubbles.

After two decades, Quaker House itself had gained a certain measure of acceptance as well. On the day Quaker House celebrated its 20th anniversary in 1989, The *Fayetteville Observer* ran an editorial praising its "practicable approaches like counseling young soldiers about their rights as possible conscientious objectors or as military people who have decided that the profession of arms is not for them." It recognized the project's courage "to brave the opprobrium of the majority" and commitment to peace and non-violence. "In the midst of one of the world's largest military communities, the Quaker House carries on its program in a matter-of-fact

94

way, demonstrating its commitment to peace by being peaceable itself." It added, "The Cumberland County community can thank heaven for the practicable, peaceable work of the Quaker House and wish it well for at least another twenty years of service."

Sommers was measured in his comments on the occasion:

> "Some people just aren't meant for the military," he told the paper. "Some aren't conformists. Some aren't team players. And they are causing the military a lot of problems.
>
> "There is what I call a poverty draft," he said. "A lot of clients don't have an alternative - they are poor and they need money to go to college. They're told, 'We'll pay you to learn a skill.'
>
> "But kids don't see the other stuff," Mr. Sommers added. "The military's main purpose is not to make you a better person; it's not to give you money for college; it's not to give you job training. It is for defending our country or foreign intervention or whatever you want to call it."

Like many people around the world, Harry and Rebecca Rogers of Columbia, South Carolina, watched as two laser-guided bombs from U.S war planes destroyed the Amiriyah blockhouse, killing hundreds of Iraqi civilians.

The bombing happened on February 13, 1991, but the couple saw it happen hundreds of times after that. Scenes of burned and mutilated bodies were broadcast and controversy raged over the status of the bunker, with some stating that it was a civilian shelter while U.S officials contended that it was a center of Iraqi military operations and the civilians had been deliberately moved there to act as human shields.

There was no disputing the outcome of the attack. Estimates of Iraqi civilian deaths due to the "wholly defensive" Operation Desert Storm range between 20,000 and 200,000.

"Both of us watched the news and were horrified at the coverage," said Harry, a Vietnam veteran.

Rebecca was stunned by the footage and remembers watching with tears in her eyes. "The world felt cold and negative," she said. Months earlier the couple had begun researching different faiths in hopes of finding a community that felt right. In their hearts they resisted the county's move to war and had become increasingly isolated from those around them.

But soon they found what they were looking for. A letter to the editor, signed by a member of a Quaker meeting in Columbia, appeared in the local newspaper decrying the war and defending peace and nonviolence.

"Seeing the letter that [the Quakers] put in the paper, there was this epiphany," Rebecca recalled. The Rogers' quickly tracked down the phone number for the letter's author and inquired about the local Meeting. The couple soon became active members of Columbia Friends Meeting.

They first became involved with Quaker House when Sommers came down to visit. Hearing about the project sparked their interest and both

Rebecca and Harry would eventually serve as representatives on the project's Board of Overseers. But making contact with the Columbia Friends Meeting would prove fateful for Sommers as well. Through the Rogers he met Susan Leatherman, a Mennonite from Berkeley, California who was attending Friends Meeting in Columbia.

"We got married because of those busy body Quakers," Sommers joked.

Friends in Columbia, like those in Fayetteville, found themselves in the midst of a military culture. Fort Jackson, located in Columbia, is the Army's largest training base in terms of sheer numbers of soldiers who undergo training there. Most of it is for basic training, or boot camp. Inspired by Quaker House's ministry, the Rogers were trained as military counselors, and Columbia Friends Meeting took out an ad in the Fort Jackson *Leader* advertising free counseling for GIs with concerns.

"When I talk to people about [Quaker House] I say that it is as powerful a witness against war as there is," Harry said. As a veteran himself he feels a particular responsibility to do counseling with active duty soldiers. It produces a ripple effect as each counselee then influences those around him or her.

"For a small organization in Fayetteville, we've had far reaching effects," Rogers said. It would not be the last time Friends in another area took strength from the witness in Fayetteville and started their own similar project in their own community.

"While we read of the closing of military bases and reductions in the Pentagon's budget, we see Ft Bragg, Pope AFB and Camp Lejeune adding to their ranks," Sommers wrote in one of the last Quaker House Newsletters he would author. "It is evident that Quaker House—the only military counseling facility in this militarized region—is still needed."

But after the intensity of his time in Fayetteville, Sommers needed a change. "The lack of motivation has been a problem in working for Quaker House. I talked to Bob Gosney and discovered that this is not a problem unique to me," Sommers told the Board. The expectation that staff would stay only a brief period was an issue too. "That's OK as far as planning to look for replacements," he reported, "but I think it may lead to attitudes in both the Board and the staff that are counter-productive." He also cites "burn out," not surprising given his hectic travel schedule of public meetings, workshops, interviews and Friends' gatherings.

"He has been an outstanding director, worked exceedingly well with people [and] represented Quaker House in an outstanding manner," Board members wrote upon his departure.

"After spending six years in the Army Reserves feeling powerless over myself and the world at large I now feel I am in a position to contribute to positive change," Stephanie Atkinson wrote in the March 1992 Quaker House Newsletter. "After declaring myself a [conscientious objector], being arrested, jailed, discharged and swept up in a whirlwind of media attention, I found it hard to return to normal life." Atkinson's "normal life" prior to these incidents had been full of frustration and apathy.

At the time of Saddam's invasion of Kuwait, Atkinson was studying English at Southern Illinois University. She had joined the Reserves to help pay for her college education, but when her unit was mobilized to ship out to Saudi Arabia, she stayed behind. She felt duped by recruiters and realized that the Army was not the place for her. Atkinson addressed hundreds at an antiwar rally in Cambridge, Massachusetts and her case was debated in the opinion pages from the Boston *Globe* to the Chicago *Tribune*.

A writer in the Chicago *Tribune* summed up a widely held view-point: "Ms. Atkinson broke the terms of her military contract, so the Army's decision to discharge her serves as a deserving action against a soldier who owes her country and American tax payers for her college education."

Afterward, working as an intern for the American Friends Service Committee's National Youth and Militarism Project in Philadelphia helped her regain some of the confidence that she had lost during her time in the military. "Now there is nothing more exciting for me than helping another young person like myself apply for a discharge or speaking to high school and encouraging them not to enlist," Atkinson wrote.

Atkinson, 25, was energetic, motivated and clearly committed to doing peace work. She was not a Friend herself, but having worked with the American Friends Service Committee, she had experience working with Quakers and it appeared that her dedication to peace was spiritually based. When she applied to succeed Greg Sommers as Director of Quaker House, Board members thought she would bring a noticeable intensity to the job.

One reservation the Board did express about her was her age. Her youth would be a boon to connecting with high-school students for her recruiting work, but as far as daily life in Fayetteville, they knew the town would be difficult for a creative, energetic young woman with no local friends or connections. Since the departure of the Arnings in 1973, most staff had been slightly older and had arrived with their families to support them. A notable exception was Sommers, a young single man who had stayed more than three years. He worked part-time to help train Atkinson when she arrived in March of 1992.

Sarah Hennessey was friends with Atkinson and remembers her well. "I think her story was so striking because she had such conviction and had been in the middle of it all," Hennessey said.

During her stay as Director of Quaker House, Atkinson dealt with a range of issues. She continued what she had begun at AFSC, developing materials for Quaker House to distribute to high school students. "With a new focus on outreach to young people who are so eagerly sought after by the military, Quaker House hopes to help others develop skills to counter the information students receive from the military," she wrote in the Newsletter.

She also helped bring attention to an emerging issue, sexual harassment of women in the military. In late July of 1992 *USA Today* ran a piece about sexual harassment within the military which featured a picture of Atkinson and her Quaker House counselee, Heidi Balla. Atkinson's experience with the military and the media clearly had an impact on Balla.

Not So Funny: an unofficial patch made in response to the Tailhook controversy.

"[Balla] was quite scared when I initially talked to her, but is now quite willing to go public," Atkinson wrote. A former Navy petty officer, Balla said the men teaching her about submarine repair on a work ship in Charleston, South Carolina asked about her sex life and urge her to "try one of us" according to the newspaper's report. The harassment reached the point where Balla went AWOL.

"It [military service] ain't *China Beach* where you have all these beautiful women who have these affairs," Atkinson told *USA Today*. ["China Beach" was an ABC TV series from 1988-1991 about a group of nurses working in Vietnam military hospitals] Atkinson's advice to female would-be soldiers was clear: "Expect sexual harassment in the military."

Balla's case gained media attention as one of a series that came out of the Gulf War and its aftermath. The number of women in the military had risen since the Vietnam years, from about three per cent to eleven, and more than 30,000 women GIs served in the Gulf war. In particular, the weekly *Army Times* had recently reported that twenty-four women soldiers had reported being raped while serving in Iraq.

The Navy had likewise been rocked in September 1991 by news of rampant sexual harassment and assault at the annual Tailhook convention, a semi-official gathering of supporters of naval aviation, in Las Vegas. The 'Tailhook Scandal," as it became known, sparked investigations that went on for years and involved many high naval officers and Pentagon personnel.

Thus, in the *USA Today* article which quoted Atkinson, military spokespeople were quick to play down the report. "Women are safer in the military than they are on the streets of most of our major cities," said Jeanne Holm, a former Army officer and author of *Women in the Military: An Unfinished Revolution*.

"The Gulf attacks are 'not indicative of an army out of control,' says Brig. Gen. Thomas Jones, the Army's human resources chief. He says 24 cases are relatively few in a force of 334,000 soldiers, 26,000 of them women."

Significantly, however, the article also acknowledged that, "The Pentagon doesn't keep tabs on complaints, so it's hard to assess the problem in all services. But in 1990, the Army had 0.47 reported rapes per 1,000 service members, compared with 0.41 among civilians."

Note the key term, "reported." This issue of the lack of reliable record-keeping was to surface again, in even more serious contexts.

Heidi Balla was given a general discharge under honorable conditions, which meant that she could not access funds she matched with the Navy's education program for college. "The Navy's discharge is an attempt to close the case," Atkinson wrote.

Atkinson also mobilized support for fellow Persian Gulf war resister Tahan Jones, who was the last conscientious objector from that conflict to face charges. Of the dozens of Marines CO applicants known to have filed claims at Camp Lejeune, not one was approved. And virtually all the war resisters there were court martialed and served jail sentences. At a court martial hearing at Camp Lejeune on June 15, 1992 Jones was sentenced to eight months in jail, a dishonorable discharge, total forfeiture of pay and a reduction in rank.

"Whenever military regimentation and uniformity seem to reduce the individual to a cog in a machine, we are there to recognize each person as a human being with inherent rights and dignity," Atkinson wrote.

Despite the sense of high energy that the Quaker House Board perceived in Atkinson, this was a role she found more than she could handle. In October 1992, only eight months after arriving, Atkinson resigned. "Moving directly from one side of the military fence to the other and working within a new set of values and consciousness has been an incredible experience," she told Quaker House supporters. "I am discovering however, that being a 'super-activist' is not a role I am ready for."

"It was an intense period in her life and I think that it was overwhelming for her," Hennessey said of Atkinson's time in Fayetteville.

Her departure gave the Board an opportunity to focus on one aspect of the Quaker House mission that had been neglected by staff for the past four years: growing the tiny Fayetteville Friends Meeting. Meeting for worship was an emphasis of the program from the start, but the strength of the connection between it and the program carried out by staff persons has always varied.

"The Fayetteville Meeting is very small and in need of nurture," Bob Gwyn wrote in the Newsletter. He had returned to the Board and was its Acting Clerk. He emphasized that future staff members should carry out a regular program of advertising about the Meeting and connect with isolated Friends around the region in an effort to increase the size of the Meeting. This effort to hold the Meeting in the light was to have impressive results.

10. 1993-1998: Race, Murder & The Politics of Faith In Fayetteville

Seventy-five miles south of San Francisco, on the northern tip of picturesque Monterey Bay, Santa Cruz, California boasts a mild climate year-round, idyllic beaches, and unique coastal redwood trees. The town's history of social activism and liberal politics has made it a bastion of alternative lifestyles and counter cultures. At the University of California Santa Cruz campus, there is no ROTC program, and students voted in 1986 to select as the school's official mascot the Banana Slug. The City Council was the first in the country to denounce the Iraq War (in 2003), and later issued a statement opposing the USA PATRIOT Act. In 2005, the city government opened an office to aid residents who wanted to obtain medical marijuana.

"It's hard to imagine two places more different than Santa Cruz and Fayetteville," said Sandra Jean Sweitzer. When she moved from Santa Cruz to Fayetteville in 1993 to be the Director at Quaker House, "it felt like jumping off a cliff."

In Santa Cruz she was the director of the Conflict Resolution Center, which promoted mediation and diversity trainings as alternatives to solving

Culture Clash: Banana Slug Meets The Troops, Fayetteville 1993

problems and avoiding violence. She lived in an intentional community. Before that, she had grown up near the campus of Earlham College, a Quaker school in eastern Indiana, which also has no ROTC program.

Sweitzer wanted to be closer to her family in Indiana, so when she

Sandy Sweitzer, in a quiet moment during a not-so-quiet era at Quaker House.

saw the Quaker House ad in Friends Journal, she called and talked to Bruce Pulliam. To induce her to come, Heidi Hannibal, a Quaker who attended Fayetteville Friends Meeting and lived on Fort Bragg with her husband, a military doctor, sent Sweitzer a long letter detailing the good things about Fayetteville. "Mostly they involved the public library!" Sweitzer laughed. Sweitzer and her husband, Rob Lamme, a freelance journalist, sold a lot of belongings, packed up their one year-old son, John William, and headed across the country.

What they found when they arrived took them aback. For one thing, the condition of the house needed attention. Their crawling son got splinters from the old wood floors. The paint on the outside had darkened from deep green to almost black. Floors had to be sanded and the house was painted a gray blue before they could settle into it. Installation of central air conditioning in 1993 also helped.

Then the couple, who were used to living in a community of like-minded liberals, found that their new neighbors were Christian conservatives and commandos.

And that wasn't all. If she wanted to take John William to the public library, for instance, Sweitzer had to roll her son's stroller off leafy, quiet Hillside Avenue, down Haymount Hill and then through the Hay Street Strip downtown, which was just blocks from the house. She passed the strippers hanging out on the sidewalk in front of the bars and walked under the marquee of Rick's Lounge, advertising "Donna 40 Triple F–This Weekend." That's when she vowed to move away before her son learned to read. Back at home at Quaker House, she could often feel the ground shake and the windows rattle during artillery practice on Fort Bragg. She felt under siege.

"It was really hard. I think we were both pretty shell-shocked for a long time," Sweitzer admitted. Under siege and shell-shocked in a military town–Sweitzer wasn't the first or the last Quaker in Fayetteville to feel that way.

Then things began to change. The neighbors across the street, the ones who were involved with the Christian Coalition, had a little boy the same age as John William. One day the woman offered to introduce Sweitzer to some friends of hers. "'They're Democrats,'" the neighbor said cheerily, 'I think you'll really like them!'" Sweitzer consented, met the couple, and they became fast friends.

"And through them we met the other ten progressives in Fayetteville!" Sweitzer laughed.

The diversity trainer realized there might be a lesson for her in all this. Sweitzer is what is known to Quakers as a birthright Friend, one who was born into a Quaker meeting. Her father was a conscientious objector during World War Two who worked at Earlham School of Religion. Sweitzer received "the full Quaker indoctrination" she said, attending Westtown School, a Quaker boarding school not far from Philadelphia, Pennsylvania. Then she was back at ROTC-free Earlham for college. After training with the Brethren Volunteer Corps–a service-oriented witness sponsored by the Church of the Brethren–she moved out to California and worked at the Center for Nonviolence and various political campaigns.

In short, Fayetteville had a dynamic that she had no experience with. "I thought people in the military were stupid and mean-spirited," Sweitzer admitted. "I'm embarrassed to say it, but [my opinion] was really negative."

Sweitzer thought that kids who joined the military got what they deserved because "everybody knew that this whole thing about job training ormoney for college was a lie," she said. "Surely they knew what they were getting into. But clearly they didn't."

Living in Fayetteville and working at Quaker House began working a change in Sweitzer's whole perspective. She realized her stereotypes were completely wrong. Despite the fact that she disagreed fundamentally with the Armed Forces, how as a Quaker could she think "that of God in everyone," which is one of Quakerism's most cherished beliefs, didn't apply to soldiers?

In October 1994, for Quaker House's 25th Anniversary, she asked two soldiers to lead Quakers who had come from all over on tours of Fort Bragg. The Quakers' reaction to their charismatic and likeable tour leaders proved memorable. For many it was the first time a soldier had appeared so human.

At the 25th anniversary celebration, in October 1994, all seemed sweetness and light. Fayetteville Mayor J.L. Dawkins gave an honorific proclamation to Bob Gwyn, the once and again Board Clerk. An ice cream social was held, and Dean Holland's parents Richard and mmary were the honored guests. An officer from Fort Bragg came and told the gathering that Quaker House was a boon to the Army, because it helped commanders identify recruits who were not suited to military service, and could be separated, to mutual advantage.

It's important to put this event in context: at that time, the US was "between" major wars. The administration was downsizing the active forces, so it was no exaggeration for Quaker House to be told it was helping the military reach its own goals. Add to this the fact that Quaker House was led by an appealing, outgoing staff couple, and it's no wonder an atmosphere of good feeling prevailed.

Ultimately, Sweitzer wondered, "How do you oppose the military without opposing the people in it?" In 1994, the answers seemed clear.

Dean Holland's parents, Richard and Mary Holland, with the memorial plaque that hangs in the Quaker house office, at the 25th Anniversary celebration, October 1994.

Fayetteville had more surprises in store. Soon after Sweitzer and her family arrived on Hillside Avenue, two gay soldiers renovated an old house nearby and moved into it together. They became good friends with the Quaker family and introduced them to other gay soldiers. In Santa Cruz, the gay and lesbian community had been very active and visible, and Sweitzer said she and her husband didn't expect to find anything like that in Fayetteville. But in fact there was a gay and lesbian population here too, if much quieter in public.

There was no Gay Pride Day in Cumberland County, no parades or festivals; the few bars that catered to such a clientele kept a very low profile. Although the new President Clinton had attempted to repeal restrictions on gays serving in the military when he took office in January 1993, this effort had been defeated, and replaced with the "Don't Ask Don't Tell" policy, under which being openly gay in uniform was still illegal.

Sweetness & Light: Fayetteville Mayor J.L. Dawkins, right, presents a plaque to Bob Gwyn at the Quaker House 25th Anniversary celebration, October, 1994.

And there were risks beyond regulations. On August 6, 1993, not long after Sweitzer arrived, a soldier named Kenneth Junior French walked into Luigi's, a popular Fayetteville restaurant. Pulling out a shotgun and pistol, he shouted, "I'll show you, Clinton, about letting gays into the army," and started shooting. Before he was finally subdued, French had killed four, including the couple who owned the restaurant, and wounded seven. (As of 2008, French was serving a life sentence.)

In October 1995, another case brought national media attention. Early on October 27, 1995, Sgt. William Kreutzer, hiding in bushes near a field crowded with hundreds of his fellow paratroopers preparing for morning exercises, opened fire with a high-powered military rifle. His barrage killed an officer and wounded eighteen other GIs, before he was tackled by several Green Beret troops who had been on a run nearby and saw him.

Following lengthy proceedings and a plea of insanity, Kreutzer was convicted of murder and sentenced to death. After nine years on the Army's death row at Ft. Leavenworth, Kansas, Kreutzer's conviction was set aside, on grounds that his counsel had been incompetent, and a retrial was ordered.

Although Kreutzer admitted to the shootings, he maintains that he was mentally ill at the time. His second trial proceedings began in mid-2008, but were then delayed until 2009.

Although these cases did not impact Quaker House directly, they reinforced the "Fayettenam" image of the city. And violent crime would later have a more direct effect on Sandy Sweitzer's work.

Among other things, the broad, almost undefinable nature of the Quaker peace testimony means that the job description of Director of Quaker House can be tough to pin down precisely. The Board of Overseers has always encouraged the staffperson to create the program as they see fit, and when Sweitzer arrived it was no different. "The job was described as anything I wanted to make of it," Sweitzer said. Counseling GIs was central but not dominant. The program's fluidity also made it possible to respond to whatever situations might arise, as Sweitzer ended up doing to a great extent.

"When I got [to Quaker House] not only did I not know much about military counseling, I frankly wasn't all that interested," Sweitzer remembered. "I'm embarrassed to admit it now!" Ironically, within two years of her arrival, Sweitzer was to play a key role in the development of the GI Rights Network, which greatly expanded the Quaker House counseling program and integrated it into a new, nationwide scheme of support for military personnel.

"My interest was really with diversity training and working with the community on different issues," she said. In Santa Cruz, Sweitzer had founded a local chapter of the National Coalition Building Institute (NCBI), a nonprofit leadership training organization dedicated to eliminating prejudice and solving conflicts peacefully. NCBI works by training local leaders with a series of "prejudice reduction" and conflict resolution workshops and then supporting the local team to be a resource in their own communities. Sweitzer was interested in continuing this work in Fayetteville and "the Board was very supportive of me doing that."

Friends and other community members who helped write a grant to the Z. Smith Reynolds Foundation saw a need for this work in Fayetteville. Although there are large African-American and Native American communities as well as smaller communities of Vietnamese, German, Korean, Latin American, Greek and Asian Indians in the city, Fayetteville remained a segregated town where issues of race were rarely mentioned in the community's single daily newspaper. Radio stations generally targeted exclusively black or white or, more recently, Hispanic audiences. The two ministerial associations in the county were segregated by race.

In her book *Homefront* which is a study of Fayetteville and Fort Bragg published in 2001, anthropologist Catherine Lutz described the city as "a place of stark racial tension and inequality."

Quaker House got the grant and, by the summer of 1995 had conducted three day-long prejudice reduction workshops in Fayetteville for over 40 participants. One of them, a staff person at the Army's Equal

Opportunity Office at Fort Bragg named Keith Choate, would become the national representative for Cumberland County's NCBI Chapter.

Harry Rogers, the Vietnam veteran Friend from South Carolina, attended one of the sessions. "It was a diverse workshop in terms of age and race and ethnic background. I learned a lot," he said. "You think you don't have stereotypes and that you're not at all prejudiced or you're not at all racist, but it made me look inside myself and make great changes."

The Board of Overseers applauded Sweitzer's work in forming the NCBI chapter and her work with the Cumberland County Dispute Resolution Center as important examples of how Quaker House could offer the community positive, practical models for non-violent conflict resolution.

Sweitzer's months of work on racial reconciliation issues in the community left Quaker House almost ideally positioned to respond to a shocking crime, involving a homicidal quest for a spiderweb tattoo.

December 7th, 1995. Midnight on Hall Street, less than two miles from Quaker House. Hall Street was an unpaved stretch, in a poor neighborhood, where street lights were rare, houses dilapidated and often boarded up, their residents mostly black.

Michael James was walking down Hall Street with Jackie Burden. James was 36, recently out of prison after serving time on a drug charge. His family said he was getting his life together and going straight, though still unemployed. He had expressed hopes of being able to reunite with an estranged wife and children, who were living in New Jersey. Jackie Burden was 27, and reporters later had few details to offer about her.

A car pulled up behind them, and two men got out. Taking a few steps toward them, one of the men raised a 9 mm Ruger pistol and fired twice. One bullet grazed James's skull. The other drilled into the side of his head, killing him instantly.

Burden started to run, reaching into her pocket for a small knife. The man fired again. The bullet struck her in the back, and she skidded to the street. The shooter walked up, and coolly put three more bullets in her head. The knife, and a few coins, were scattered in the dust near her body.

The two men turned and ran down side streets until they found a taxi to take them out of the neighborhood.

Their driver, parked in the darkness, heard the shots and wondered where they had gone. He walked down Hall Street in the direction where they had gone, and found the bodies of James and Burden at about the same time police cars arrived. He surrendered without resistance.

The driver, Randy Meadows, was a soldier from Fort Bragg's 82nd Airborne. He told police that his passengers were James Burmeister and Malcolm Wright, also paratroopers. The pair rented rooms in a trailer, he said, in Spring Lake, just across the line into Harnett County.

Police arrested the two in the trailer the next morning, finding both sound asleep. A swastika flag was on the wall in their room, along with white supremacist literature.

According to Meadows's statement, Burmeister and Wright were racist skinheads, and Burmeister had been talking about earning a particular status symbol of his circle, a spiderweb tattoo on his elbow. To qualify, though, he had to kill a black person or a homosexual. (Other

Flowers left on Hall Street in memory of the 1995 murder victims. Photo by elin o'Hara slavick, used by permission.

reports said that Jews might qualify as well, and that Burmeister had talked about attacking Fayetteville's synagogue.)

A spokesman for the 82nd Airborne Division told the *Fayetteville Observer* that it was an isolated incident. "You've got to consider that the 82nd is simply a reflection of society. We do some great things. Sometimes we have a small number of people who do some bad things."

"I was saddened though not surprised by the incident," Sweitzer explained to Quaker House supporters in the Newsletter following the event. "Racism is alive and well in all of our communities–civilian and military." As a result of her membership in the largely African American Fayetteville Cumberland County Ministerial Council and her position on the city's Human Relations Commission (where she succeeded Bruce Pulliam) Sweitzer was asked to be one of four community speakers at a "Reconciliation Rally" which took place after the murders.

The rally drew eight hundred people, mostly African-Americans. They packed into the Friendship Baptist Church, a block from the site of the murders, in the Campbell Terrace housing project. The atmosphere was expectant and there was a lot of anger. "The program was held not to defuse the situation or speak to it," Ann Ashford said. "Not so much to calm people down as to let people know that this was noticed and abhorred by most people, black and white."

Sweitzer took the podium, very pregnant with her second child. "Make friends with and get closer to someone who seems very different than you," she told the gathering. "Whether they're from a different race, a different religion, a different economic background."

Response from the community and the local media focused mainly on healing and reconciliation. There was little mention of the city's culture of militarism. Burmeister and Wright were later convicted of murder and given life sentences. Meadows testified against them and served seventeen months.

Following the killings, interest in the newly formed NCBI chapter grew. In February, 1996 Sweitzer led a day-long "Building Bridges" workshop for over sixty African American and white ministers sponsored by the ministerial council. It was a reflection of Quaker House's growing credibility in the black community that the Council trusted Sweitzer to take them through the process. The three-day "Training for Trainers," which had been planned before the murders, took place in March 1996 with over fifty people in attendance.

"It was particularly powerful to see people who have lived in Fayetteville for many years be inspired and moved by each other," Sweitzer wrote in the Newsletter.

For much of 1995, Trey Rogers kept a secret from his parents, Harry and Rebecca. He had signed up to join the Marines through the Delayed Entry Program and was being wined and dined by the recruiter who had signed him up. They played ball and lifted weights out at Fort Jackson, near Columbia, South Carolina where Trey lived with his parents.

How could he tell them? They were Quakers, pacifists and peace activists. They were outspoken in their opposition to war and the military. They participated in antiwar vigils downtown. Their home phone number was listed in the local newspaper as a way for soldiers and Marines to get help if they needed to get out of the Armed Services, not into them. What would they say?

After she found out about it, Rebecca Rogers was less concerned about her son's decision to join the Marines than she was about the constant telephone calls from the recruiter that bordered on harassment. When Trey finally did come clean, his parents told him "Whatever you decide we'll be behind you." But they didn't let the matter rest before Harry and Trey visited Quaker House together. If Trey had spent so much time listening to the recruiter talk, he could certainly listen to what Sandy Sweitzer had to say.

At the time, Sweitzer was involved in the formation of a new, nationwide network of civilian support groups for military personnel. The idea came out of the Central Committee for Conscientious Objectors (CCCO) in Philadelphia, and was proposed there by CCCO staffers Alex Doty and Sam Diener. Its genesis was in the rush of calls that had had the phones ringing almost nonstop in all the military counseling groups during the Gulf War of

1990-91. This was followed by later bumps in calls when US troops were sent to Bosnia and to Haiti. Diener and Doty thought there ought to be a better way to spread and manage this growing workload.

"We also wanted a way to prepare for new surges," Doty recalled. "We thought that future wars would be like the 1991 Gulf War – a big buildup, with a rush of calls from all over the country, then an invasion or battle, and then it would be over." Such a feast-or-famine rhythm was hard on a group like CCCO. During the buildup, Doty said, they were all going crazy, trying to answer calls, and prepare new counseling materials at the same time. Their fundraising also suffered: People were ready to donate during the rush, but they weren't able to take time to plan our fundraising. Then when the rush was over, many donors lost interest.

Doty and Diener at CCCO consulted their counterparts at several other groups about the idea – including the Military Law Task Force in California, the AFSC office in Dayton, the Midwest Committee for Military Counseling – and Quaker House.

Quaker House was ready. Already, telephone counseling was becoming an expensive undertaking. At one point in 1995, Quaker House was counseling three people applying for CO status: one at Fort Bragg, one at Guantanamo Bay, Cuba and one in Spain. "The phone bills are especially high due to the overseas call," Sweitzer told the Board in June 1995. All three were discharged with conscientious objector status. Sharing this growing burden with other groups was clearly attractive.

Doty and Diener suggested forming a network of military counseling groups, which would operate a nationwide toll-free phone number. When GIs dialed it, their calls would be automatically routed to the nearest network group's phone, so counseling would be as local as possible. Letters flew (there was no email); conference calls were held, and the details were worked out. Quaker House was initially assigned the calls from eight southeastern states (several more were added later). By the summer of 1995, they were ready to go.

Doty, Diener and their colleagues initially thought of this "GI Rights Hotline" as a way to be prepared for the next big buildup, and its accompanying surge of calls. Sam Diener wrote that, "As the US Military once again occupies another country [Haiti], we know that most members of the military are the last to want war. Whenever military personnel are ordered overseas, many have crises of conscience. They vitally need to know their options."

As for the "surge" expectation, "It didn't work out that way, of course," Doty said. Two things didn't fit their scenario. One was the character of the coming wars: The Haiti occupation was relatively brief and bloodless; but fighting in Iraq and Afghanistan has, at this writing, dragged on for six years.

"The other factor was the arrival of the Internet and the web," Doty said. "The GI Hotline soon had a simple web page up, with the phone number on it, visible all over the country, and around the world. And it was visible not just to GIs reading a base paper, but to families at home too."

The Hotline officially went live for receiving calls on September 22, 1995. Sweitzer said, "We were all absolutely terrified at the idea, quite honestly. I was sure ...we would be inundated with calls." That didn't happen, at least at first. "So we opened [the Hotline] and there was this deafening silence, because nobody knew about the number!" she laughed. "That's why we started doing advertising in newspapers and various places."

Advertising in military newspapers like Fort Bragg's *Paraglide* at bases around the country brought callers in. Once the number was out there soldiers could stumble across it anywhere. "I remember a guy calling me from basic training," Doty said. "When I asked how he found the Hotline number, he said it was written on the bottom of a mattress in the barracks."

"The soldiers called with a wide range of problems," Sweitzer explained in the Quaker House Newsletter. "Our basic guideline was that we helped people who were trying to get out—for whatever reason. Those we could not help we referred to more appropriate places."
The process began when counselors screened cases during the phone interview. Sweitzer then mailed materials to the caller, and if the person called back after reviewing it, which less than one-third of them did, Sweitzer then agreed to help them fill out forms, or possibly accompany them to a hearing, or be present for support when they turned themselves in from being AWOL.

And if there was not a flood of calls, at first, there was soon a steady, increasing trickle. As different organizations came into and left the Network, the remaining groups would scramble to make sure particular area codes were covered. In its first full year, the Hotline received more than 1800 calls, and at least half of those came to Quaker House.

"Talking to soldiers was a really powerful experience for me spiritually," Sweitzer said. There was a period when she was receiving a lot of calls from new recruits going through basic trainng at Fort Benning, Georgia. "They sounded like these big burly 18 year-old guys calling in tears because they were so homesick," Sweitzer said. "That was very difficult."

The opening of the GI Hotline also had internal significance for the project. "The late nineties were a real turning point for Quaker House," Sandy reflected. "When we arrived there hadn't been a Director for about nine months, and for a good six months to a year, a question that came up at pretty much every Board meeting was, 'Do we need Quaker House? Is there still a need for these services?'

An early GI Rights Hotline poster (the number is updated).

"And then . . .we got a call from Alex Doty at CCCO in Philadelphia, asking if we were interested in being part of a GI Rights Network." And once the Hotline was launched, and calls began their steady, urgent increase, the questions about whether there was still a need for what Quaker House offered began to be answered, indeed drowned out, by the frequent ringing of the phone.

"It can be sort of daunting to live at the house with the phone always ringing," Sweitzer remembered. Knowing as well as she did what was on the line for each caller, "You don't want to miss a call." The information that Sweitzer and other Hotline counselors provided could mean the difference between an overseas deployment for a son with a dying parent or a compassionate reassignment. It also made a big different to the counselor themselves.

Although Sweitzer almost always had some clients seeking conscientious objector statues, she mainly dealt with other sorts of problems. Service members who were AWOL and needed support returning to their units called often, as well as new recruits who had problems with the Delayed Entry Program, or DEP. This recruitment device permitted a person to sign up for inactive reserves for up to a year with a promise to report for basic training on a specific date.

Trey Rogers from Columbia was not the first, nor would he be the last, young person who came to Quaker House with questions about the DEP.

"The visit to Quaker House had an impact on him," Rebecca said. "He got to hear the things they were saying to him and the emotions...but heard it more objectively." Sweitzer showed Trey some materials and soon afterward, he wrote the Marines a letter and canceled the deal.

This was entirely legal – though many recruiters tell their prospects that it is forbidden, and they will go to jail if they drop out of the DEP. Had Trey not had the counseling at Quaker House, he could have been left like many others, feeling he had made a mistake, but had no option.

Instead Trey joined the City Year program, a volunteer service corps which Rebecca Rogers recommends as an alternative to young people who are unsure about joining the military. "Providing information about where they can earn money for school and receive job training outside of the Armed Forces makes a big difference [to them]," she said.

When seeking a successor for Stephanie Atkinson, the Board of Overseers of Quaker House sought a staff person who would grow the Fayetteville Friends Meeting, a key component of the Quaker House program. Sandy Sweitzer filled the bill: a birthright Friend whose warmth and sense of humor combined with a strong social witness, and a mom besides, Sweitzer drew people to weekly Meeting for Worship.

Sweitzer and Lamme also needed the spiritual and emotional support the Meeting gave them. They averaged ten people at meeting for worship with a few attenders asking for membership. A First Day School–Quaker parlance for Sunday School for kids–met regularly. The open atmosphere they fostered attracted people who were searching spiritually, which Sweitzer said was an indication that she was doing the right thing.

Once the GI Rights Hotline was up and running, Sweitzer and her counterparts around the country worked to advertise the service, and the total number of calls on the network kept growing. From 1800 calls in 1996, it jumped to almost 3300 in 1997. At the same time, there was continuing demand for Sweitzer's diversity and prejudice reduction training. Quaker House was booming.

But with two small children–their daughter was born in 1995–they felt it was time to move on.

"We had never intended to stay as long as we did," Sweitzer said. "We thought that if we survived two years we'd be lucky."

Another major element of continuity also ended in these years, when in mid-1997 Bruce Pulliam quietly retired and moved to Murfreesboro in the far northeast part of the state, four hours away. He had been a central pillar of support for almost every Quaker House staff person to come through. "He was very much the key person in Fayetteville," Bob Gosney said about him. Sandy Sweitzer remarked, "[He] was just crucial to our sanity."

Pulliam also played an important role in the founding and growth of Fayetteville Friends Meeting. He came from a family with Quaker roots, although the Fayetteville Friends Meeting was where he reclaimed this distant Quaker heritage.

Ann Ashford said, "When I started attending he asked me to be Recording Clerk for the meeting." She doubted her abilities, but Pulliam persuaded her to do it. "He was very encouraging of people, whatever their abilities," she said. Pulliam, though new to the sect himself, was one of the reasons she became a Quaker.

As critical as Pulliam's emotional support was to the residents of the house and the Meeting, his position as a respected member of an array of influential circles in town also helped the project immensely. Appearances mean a lot among these close-knit social groups, and Pulliam's face was a lot more familiar to them than some of the staff people.

He knew everybody and did his best to help Quaker House directors become part of the community. When new staff arrived at the house, Pulliam would be ready with a welcoming gift of a membership to the art museum or season tickets to the Fayetteville Symphony Orchestra–he served on the boards of both groups.

His departure in mid-1997 left the project on shakier ground. Subsequent residents of the house missed out on the stalwart friendship of a weighty Quaker that their predecessors had benefitted from.

Yet Fayetteville is a city of transients and transplants. Despite the recent highlighting of what local boosters call its "hometown feeling" it feels like most people are merely passing through, as far as the military goes, that's often true. So in this way, Quaker House fit right in.

113

There had been some positive changes in the neighborhood: in the Nineties, the city cleared out the Hay Street Strip, banishing the bars and dives in an effort to reclaim and spruce up the downtown area. (The sleaze didn't disappear, of course; much of it moved a half mile or so up Bragg Boulevard.) In these years too, local history buffs petitioned the city to declare downtown and an adjoining area of Haymount Hill a Historic District; and Hillside Avenue was part of it.

Sweitzer got a job doing development at the Durham Public Library, and her husband found a post in public relations. The Sweitzer-Lamme family left Fayetteville in the summer of 1998, five years after they arrived. "It was hard to leave when we did," Sandy concluded.

Bruce Pulliam at Quaker House.

11. 1998-2001: A Bridge In Crisis

Sandy Sweitzer's initial ignorance of military culture and personnel was not simply an individual foible. Since World War Two, the cultural gap between "Military America" and "Civilian America" has been steadily widening and deepening. In a fine 2007 book, *AWOL: The Unexcused Absence of America's Upper Classes from Military Service – And How It Hurts Our Country*, authors Kathy Roth-Douquet and Frank Schaeffer show in irrefutable detail what has happened: most Americans with higher levels of income and education now complete their education and live their lives without any direct contact with military personnel or institutions.

With a moment's reflection, the global significance of this gap in experience is glaringly obvious. In Congress, for instance, the percentage of members who are veterans is lower than in many decades. Yet Congress is essentially the board of directors for a military establishment that spans the globe and spends at least half the federal budget. But when the board members of an enterprise know next to nothing firsthand about what the company really does, what kind of meaningful policy guidance can they provide? What sort of oversight and accountability can they hope to enforce?

There's been a parallel impact at the much more down-to-earth level of a small Quaker project in North Carolina. Some Quaker House staffers, like Bill Sholar and Stephanie Atkinson, have been veterans, many others, like Sandy Sweitzer, have had to make a huge cultural adjustment to life in Fayetteville, with its pervasive military presence. Whether it was listening to the windows rattling during artillery practice on post, the strong pro-war sentiment in the city, or the sleaze of the Strip, much of it seemed foreign, even alien. This has clearly been an obstacle to maintaining staff over the years.

For Phil Esmonde, however, who was hired a few months after Sweitzer left, Fayetteville was actually a quieter, less militaristic place than his previous job, which had been in a war zone. Say what you want about Fort Bragg's impact on Fayetteville, but without the bombed villages, refugee camps and open violence, it appeared down-right peaceful to Esmonde and his wife, Kaushaliya when they arrived in October of 1998.

Esmonde came to Quaker House after living and working in Sri Lanka, in the midst of a decades-old civil war that has left over 60,000 dead. First as a representative of Quaker Peace and Service (an arm of Britain Yearly Meeting) and then as an advisor to the Canadian High Commission, he spent over seven years traveling the island, fostering reconciliation between the complex web of groups locked in battle. His efforts involved off-the-record meetings with both sides as well as teaching, facilitating and strengthening non-violent approaches to resolving the conflicts.

Esmonde was born in England and spent part of his childhood in Canada, but enlisted in the US Air Force in 1968, at the age of 17, while living in Raleigh, North Carolina. It was naivete that led him to sign up, he said, so he wouldn't get drafted.

"Quaker House and its important work seems a natural cycle of return for me," he told supporters in a 1998 letter. "I can very much relate to the young men and women who are struggling with deep questions concerning violence with little or no support."

"I went through a very lonely process with my [Conscientious Objector] application and had no outside counseling or other support," he said. Before ultimately being denied conscientious objector status, Esmonde had letters of recommendation and support for him torn up by commanding officers and was refused access by the Air Force to certain documents that the lawyers from the ACLU who were helping him needed. He was told to state in writing why he wanted the documents so that the Air Force could decide whether or not to provide them. "That was a few days before I was slated to go to Vietnam," he remembered. "I came very, very close to deserting, but instead felt compelled to go to Vietnam."

Once there, he refused to fight and was assigned to do maintenance on the Air Force telephone system. "The process of fighting the system before going (to Vietnam) as well as while there, turned me into an activist," he explained in a letter to the Board.

He first encountered Quakers while in college at the University of Victoria in Canada, meeting some British Quakers who gave a talk about their opposition to the war in Thailand. "They were trying to go onto a base to prevent it from being bombed," he explained. "I may or may not have agreed with what they were doing...but what struck me was their strong faith and inner conviction." He didn't feel that his own religion, Catholicism, supported his position on war and violence and eventually became a Quaker.

One morning in late 1998, while Sandy Sweitzer was helping Phil Esmonde settle in at Quaker House, a letter arrived from Fort Benning, Georgia. It was from a soldier in basic training there, complaining of the harassment he was receiving as he awaited discharge. He felt so isolated he had even considered suicide, he wrote. Later they answered calls together on the GI Rights Hotline and within three hours they had spoken with three soldiers, including one who was preparing a conscientious objector application and an AWOL soldier looking for advice on turning himself in.

"In that one day I was able to get a deeper glimpse of the need for Quaker House and also the deep gratitude with which GIs receive Quaker House's work," Esmonde recalled.

By the time Esmonde arrived, most new counseling cases came in via the GI Rights Hotline. By 1998, total calls reached 2800, Of all the Hotline calls during this period, 45 per cent or 1,872 calls were channeled to Quaker House. That was an average of over five calls per day. Hotline phone charges for Quaker House that year totaled $2,100. This was a significant budget item, and represented a 52 per cent increase in call volume and cost over the previous year.

Although Quaker House and other network groups continued to advertise the Hotline in military newspapers like Fort Bragg's *Paraglide*, it was the Internet that facilitated the boom in calls. The new technology made the free, private counseling relatively easy to find.

Esmonde answered calls coming into the Hotline from area codes in eleven states, providing coverage during daytime and early evening hours five to seven days a week. A message machine picked up calls at non-answering times and he would follow up with a phone call back or information through the mail.

Gone were the days of fretting about whether there was still a need for the project. Instead, the rising tide of Hotline calls was by now beginning to swamp everything else. Esmonde found it increasingly difficult to maintain the diverse program Quaker

Phil Esmonde, right, with Thomas Mayfield, an Army CO discharged from Ft. Bragg in 2000.

House was accustomed to having. Of particular importance to Esmonde was visiting high risk prisoners in the brig at Camp Lejeune. As official visitors sanctioned by Prison Visitation and Support, he and his wife Kaushalia, whom he had met in Sri Lanka, relished their opportunities to relieve some of the isolation and loneliness the young men suffered.

"The Board does not want the director to spend all of his or her time just on calls," the Overseers instructed, "but to also respond to other leadings as able." In hopes of giving Esmonde some space for other work, in early 1999 the Board put out a call, seeking Friends and others around the Southeast willing to be trained as volunteer Hotline counselors.

When the call for volunteers went out, Lenore Yarger was serving on the Board of Overseers as a representative of Durham Friends Meeting. She regularly heard Esmonde talk about the counseling in his reports to the Board. "I really liked listening to [him] talk about the cases he was handling," Yarger remembered. She was impressed by his ability to counsel people. "He was very personable and easy to talk to," she said.

Answering the call for volunteer counselors, Lenore and her partner Steve Woolford soon began making regular trips to Fayetteville to answer calls on the Hotline with Esmonde. Others in the GI Rights Network gave them additional training and soon they were able to cover a few hours a week.

Even with training, they were still learning on the job. "I remember being very insecure and not knowing what to say, trying to think really fast on the phone," Yarger said. Over time she learned to be comfortable with telling a caller, "I'll look this up and call you back" when she couldn't answer a question.

Lenore Yarger & Steve Woolford, at home in rural Silk Hope NC. Despite the rustic appearance, chances are one of them has a cell phone in a pocket, ready for the next GI Hotline call.

Doing military counseling on the phone began as part-time volunteer work for the couple, but in less than a year's time they would come to play a much larger part in the work of Quaker House.

"About half of the calls coming to Quaker House are from new recruits at Fort Benning, Georgia," Esmonde reported in the Quaker House Newsletter in early 1999. "Our existence is one of the hottest topics and pieces of information in circulation." The reports from Fort Benning, where many new recruits were in basic training, told of high levels of harassment, physical and mental abuse resulting in high numbers of AWOL soldiers. The parents of one soldier at Fort Benning who was a potential suicide asked Esmonde for help in contacting their congressman.

"Quaker House is trying to get better documentation of the abuse that is taking place in hopes of passing it to those who can do something about it," Esmonde wrote.

The majority of new recruits that Esmonde spoke with entered through the Delayed Entry Program, or DEP, which was notorious for trapping young people, like Trey Rogers, before they had a chance to consider their options. One common problem with the DEP that counselors saw frequently involved recruits with identified prior health problems being told by recruiters not to say anything about them on enlistment forms. Once in the military, when such problems surfaced, the enlistee was subject to being court martialed for falsifying the enlistment application – and the recruiter would by then either be long gone, or would deny everything.

Esmonde began checking with some of the counselees to see if they would be willing to speak to the media once they were discharged. With the help of the CCCO based in Oakland, California, Esmonde sent out a press release about the situation at Fort Benning and by that summer he was in touch with a producer from one of the national TV networks in Atlanta. The resulting media attention focused on the DEP. The two-part series, "GI Lies," aired in early November, 1999 on Fox 5 in Atlanta, Georgia.

Using stories from Esmonde's counselees, the news programs showed how many young people were maneuvered into the DEP by recruiters' promises. Discovering later that they'd been misled or lied to, many tried to drop out of DEP.

Although it was in fact legal and easy to quit DEP, many were falsely told by recruiters that quitting was illegal and they would end up in jail if they did so. Thus many went on to boot camp, and once sworn in there, it was a crime under military law to leave, or be Absent Without Official Leave (AWOL). Esmonde put the Fox News producers in touch with several individuals who had been falsely threatened with jail time, dishonorable discharges, and cutting off of scholarship money if they quit the DEP and failed to report to boot camp.

The program also featured an ex-recruiter speaking out about the pressure tactics used to keep individuals in the DEP. He had concern for the legality of such tactics and noted for the need for groups like Quaker House to support these recruits.

The program reached the conclusion that recruiters "intimidated, threatened and even outright lied to young people in an effort to bully them into enlisting." Georgia Senator Max Cleland, a vet and member of Senate Armed Services Committee, publicized the report saying that he had sent copies of the program to the Pentagon. Esmonde remembered the expose as one of the highlights of his work at Quaker House.

As Trey Rogers found out, recruits can be discharged from the DEP. The main requirement being the completion of a letter stating the reasons for desiring the release. Rogers was one of the lucky ones, however. Abuse of the DEP by recruiters would be a continuing problem, which GI Hotline counselors grappled with through the coming decade, and after.

Over the next year, growth and change were rapid at Quaker House. Hotline calls continued to increase, taking up all the volunteer time Steve Woolford and Lenore Yarger could spare.

The pacifist anarchist Catholic Worker (CW) movement had been important to them since their college days in the late 1980s. This lay movement of Catholic radicals was founded by Dorothy Day and Peter Maurin during the Great Depression, by the late 1990s it had grown to include over a hundred communities across the US Many were in cities, but the founders also encouraged the settling of farm colonies.

At Duke, Lenore was very moved by Dorothy Day's memoir, *The Long Loneliness*. At Notre Dame, Steve caught the bug during a summer at a CW house in Illinois. This common interest led them to a CW-related house–and each other–in Phoenix Arizona, in the early 1990s. In 1997 they came to Durham, NC, to be nearer their families, and hoping to start a CW house of their own. "We wanted something big enough to offer hospitality," Lenore said, "but also rural enough so we could do a large garden."

"And we needed to be able to afford it," Steve added.

Silk Hope, in rural Chatham County, an area beset by the collapse of the Carolina textile industry, fit the bill.

While in Durham, though, they often attended the Friends Meeting there. "We're Catholics," Steve noted, "but with a fondness for the Quaker way of worship." Lenore added, "We've met lots of Quakers through various peace actions." In one such action Lenore was arrested at Fort Bragg. And maybe, she mused, it was this that moved Durham Meeting to ask her to be their representative on the Quaker House Board.

Lenore was drawn to Quaker House, but found GI counseling more compelling than Board work. "Usually I was on the other side of the fence from the GIs, at protests," Lenore recalled, "but I wanted to have a positive form of contact too. So many GIs are victims of military culture, and they're desperate for helpful contact with someone on the outside."

Woolford agreed. "It seemed awkward to me that we'd be standing outside a base [protesting] and there were people going in to work there," he said. The workers on the base weren't the decision-makers who were culpable for the things Woolford opposed, they just needed a job. "We weren't condemning them," he explained. "It's important to fight injustice in the abstract. But when you can also connect that to an individual human being, and help them out, it's very rewarding."

Such personalism is an integral part of the CW spiritual path. "I think there's a real bridge in the counseling we do," Woolford said. Working through Quaker House gave them a chance to connect both sides of the fences around the bases where they went to protest.

Their involvement with GI counseling took an unexpected jump in late 2000. Early that year Phil Esmonde was offered a position with Oxfam. The London-based NGO asked him to direct their programs in Sri Lanka. Although he had signed up for a three-year stint at Quaker House, this was an offer he felt he could not refuse. It would allow him to get back to work he had grown to love while living in his wife's home country. And though the work at Quaker House meant a lot to the couple, especially the counseling and the prison visitation, in truth Fayetteville seemed not to suit them. For one thing, the lack of public transportation frustrated Kaushaliya, who didn't drive. Friends also noted that she was homesick. Here was a situation where the absence of Bruce Pulliam's ability to smooth the adjustment was almost palpable. The Board accepted their sudden departure with regret, but recorded appreciation for their contributions to Quaker House.

At the time, Quaker House was receiving close to 100 calls a month from the GI Rights Hotline. During one particular week in late July of 2000, Esmonde fielded 27 calls. The GI Rights Network web page was getting 75,000 hits per month. Quaker House was covering area codes for a huge swath of the country, and its closest neighbor in the military counseling sphere–Norfolk Quaker House, a small project organized by a couple from North Carolina Yearly Meeting Conservative–had recently ended its counseling program. Where would those soldiers, sailors and airmen get the information they needed?

Yarger and Woolford had become passionate about the counseling work, and when Phil Esmonde left, they stepped in to keep up with the telephone counseling, from their Silk Hope home, at first as volunteers. Their hospitality work, Lenore explained, along with the demands of their farming, meant that they spent a lot of time at home. "Counseling on the telephone fit well with our lifestyle," Yarger said. But soon the call load was taking up so much time that they asked the Board to pay them enough to keep going.

"We see our job as presenting people with as much information as possible," Yarger explained. "We're not attorneys, so we're not advising people on what to do." The military has control of most aspects of a service person's life, and much of this control is over access to information. By providing information many GIs are unable to find on their own, counselors can help combat that disempowerment.

"I think it's very important to practice a form of counseling that allows [soldiers] to take control of their life," Yarger said.

For the soldier, it might mean the difference between a complete dead end, and navigating the regulations to get properly treated for post traumatic stress disorder. For Yarger and Woolford it was a step toward subverting the dehumanizing military paradigm. It can create a bridge between people who worked to demobilize the warmaking machinery and the people who were the work force for the US military.

The bridge metaphor is apt in more ways than one. The counseling work that Steve and Lenore undertook would also span the widest gap of time that Quaker House went without a Director in its existence. As they were not interested in moving to Fayetteville, the Board contracted with them as a stop-gap until a new director was hired for Quaker House. As it turned out, that wouldn't happen for well over a year.

Thus through much of 2000 and almost all of 2001 the project was again without resident staff. The House on Hillside Avenue was still used by the Fayetteville Friends Meeting for their weekly worship; but mainly it stood vacant behind the "Quaker House" sign in the front yard.

In the meantime, applications for the Director's post were few and unimpressive. Before long, despite the growing demand for the GI Hotline, the old questions re-surfaced in the Board's deliberations: was Quaker House still a valid witness to the Quaker peace testimony?

Aside from the evolving character of the work, the difficulty of finding and keeping staff at the house in Fayetteville left some frustrated Board members unsure that it was necessary to maintain a peace witness there. Quaker House was an organization of outsiders in that army town–it was staffed and overseen by people not from Fayetteville and, mostly, not familiar with life within the military, the city's dominant dynamic.

Directors have come from many different places, but have always been much more likely to have a master's degree than to have served in the military. The same is true of the Board of Overseers.

Young, single staff persons had had trouble finding a social group of peers because in Fayetteville, their demographic is almost exclusively oriented towards life on the post. As a result, none have stayed long. For that matter, Fayetteville natives who did not join the service or one of its local satellites mostly left town for school or jobs elsewhere.

The families that have come to Quaker House seemed to have fared slightly better and stayed longer than their younger counterparts. They had concerns about how their children would fare in the midst of constant war preparation, in a city with high rates of crime and drug use, and low levels of school spending. But ultimately, raising a family in a small, semi-public house, combined with emotionally demanding work, took its toll on the parents of Quaker House families as much as anything else.

When Esmonde left and the empty months began to add up, one point of consideration was that to the extent that the military counseling was at the core of its mission, the project could presumably be run from anywhere. Why not the Triangle with its liberal Quaker communities associated with the colleges and universities that had supported it from its inception? Why not Greensboro, with its deep Quaker roots manifested in New Garden Meeting, founded before the American revolution, and Guilford College? Either of these locations were sure to attract and maintain staff better. And after all, as a stopgap the Quaker House Hotline was being operated from a farmstead in rural Chatham County, far from any of these, or from any military bases.

As the Board searched for the way forward following Esmonde's departure, they contacted Sandy Sweitzer in Durham for her input. They asked if she thought it was important for the director of Quaker House to live in Fayetteville.

Her answer was a definite yes – the presence of Quakers in Fayetteville was an important part of the program that shouldn't be sacrificed. The experience of living there was invaluable to the director, she told them.

Some Board members agreed, and still felt there was a continuing need to maintain a peace witness in Fayetteville. But others were not so sure. One proposal was to lay the project down, sell the property and donate the proceeds to Guilford College to endow a chair of Conflict Resolution. This idea did not carry the day, but those who wanted to keep Quaker House alive had to admit that the search for a new director was not going well.

"What few applicants there were, were clearly totally unsuitable," remembered Anne Matthysse, a member of the Board who served on the search committee. "They were young kids who had never done such a thing before and knew nothing about Quakers.

" As the months stretched out, she said, "It was clear that Quaker House was again in a real crisis."

The issue now went beyond the old concern about whether it was needed. Even if it was needed, was it sustainable?

12. 2001-02: "Time To Get Ready For War."

A resolution of the crisis faced by Quaker House in mid- 2001 was made possible by two obscure and outwardly unrelated events, which were leavened in turn by a much larger and inescapable crisis.

First, Chris Olson-Vickers, a Quaker living in Richmond, Virginia, visited her aged mother, in Fayetteville. There she learned about Quaker House and its plight. The news troubled her. Olsen-Vickers had been raised in an Army family there. She understood why Quaker House was needed in Fayetteville, and carried this concern back home.

Secondly, more than five hundred miles north, in Bellefonte, Pennsylvania, a Quaker was laid off from his part-time teaching slot at Penn State University.

In early August, Chuck Fager, the now-unemployed Quaker, attended the annual session of Baltimore Yearly Meeting, which in 2001 was held on a college campus near Richmond. He asked if a local Friend might offer hospitality, to save on room fees.

Chris Olson-Vickers took in her impecunious co-religionist. And over dinner one evening, she brought up the opening at Quaker House. "You should apply for it," she urged.

Fager demurred. "I told her, 'Definitely, no thanks,'" he recalled. "I had lived in the south for many years already, and was happy to be away from it, up in Pennsylvania."

But Olson-Vickers persisted. She knew he had been among Friends for a long time, and active in various peace projects along the way. She drew out of him that, like her, he was a "military brat," who had grown up in an Air Force family, almost attended the Air Force Academy, and won medals in ROTC, before ending up as a Vietnam era Conscientious Objector. All this background would be directly useful at Quaker House.

Still he declined. "I told her North Carolina was a '4-H state,'" Fager said. "It had Heat, Humidity, Hurricanes, and [notoriously conservative Republican US Senator Jesse] Helms. I felt for the Quaker House Board, but again, no thanks. I didn't like being out of work, but figured something would turn up in Pennsylvania eventually."

Olson-Vickers shrugged off his objections. Without new staff, she said, the project would have to close down. And that would be a shame, because there was still plenty for it to do.

"But I've been too controversial among Quakers," he said. As a writer and reporter, he had published an independent gadfly monthly, "A

Friendly Letter," for more than ten years. The newsletter had printed provocative articles on many hot Quaker topics, some of which had upset applecarts and stepped on toes.

Again, Olson-Vickers was not deterred. The Board could get past that, she said. And Fayetteville was hardly a place where Quaker controversies bubbled; too much actual work needed to be done.

After an hour of such sparring, Fager yielded a bit. "To get Chris to leave me be, I agreed to send Quaker House a resume," he said. "And when I got home, I did. I figured nothing would happen and promptly forgot about it."

For the rest of August, he did contract work, and then took a trip with his son, who had recently graduated from high school. They drove up to Canada, then east and down to Maine, where they again found hospitality with a Quaker acquaintance.

On a bright Tuesday morning, they were just about to leave, headed for New York City to visit Fager's brother, when their hostess urged them to come back into the house to see something awful unfolding on her television screen.

That morning, September 11, 2001, the two travelers did not go to New York. As traumatized as everyone else, they headed back to Pennsylvania.

"Watching the towers fall, I felt I knew two things, as surely as I knew my name," Fager said. "First, that my country was going to be at war soon; you didn't have to be much of a prophet to see that. And second, that one way or another, I'd be involved in efforts to try and stop it."

Just a day or two later, he received an email from Bonnie Parsons. A school official in the Greensboro North Carolina system, Parsons was a member of Friendship Friends Meeting. She was also the Clerk of the Quaker House Board. She wrote that the Board would like to talk to him.

"When I read this email, so soon after the attacks," Fager said, "everything seemed completely different. I felt like an old reservist being called back to active duty. All my complaints about the south were now just, so what? There was a war on, or soon would be. In wartime, soldiers follow orders and do their duty. Being comfortable is incidental. I knew that if the Quaker House Board really wanted me, that's where I'd go.

The Board did want him. And after a trip to Fayetteville, the deal began to take shape.

Following the September 11th attacks, the attenders at Fayetteville Friends Meeting, who were "holding the fort" at the otherwise-unoccupied 223 Hillside, told the *Fayetteville Observer* that they backed the pursuit of justice against the terrorists, but opposed the violent retribution taking place in Afghanistan. In the meantime, the telephone counseling by Steve and Lenore from their home more than an hour away was the only part of the Quaker House program that continued uninterrupted. Predictably, calls spiked following 9/11.

It was clear that the new "war on terror" would be very different than the Vietnam War, which shaped Quaker House initially. Now, everyone was a potential target. After the attacks, public support for a military response was overwhelming. Friends and peace activists were very much on the defensive. The Board of Overseers felt increasingly at a point of crisis: Quaker House needed to be reinvigorated, even reinvented if it was to survive. But how could that happen without a Director?

Thus, after such a long hiatus, the Board was inclined to be flexible: if a new Director chose not to live in Fayetteville, they offered to increase the salary to help cover rent somewhere else, say in the seemingly more desirable Triangle region, where most Board members were from.

Fager kept the option open, but said he'd move into the house for at least six months before making a definite decision. The most important factor, he told them, would be how it affected what he saw as the Quaker House mission. And that mission was now, as he put it, "To get ready for war."

Further, they could expect to do so in an atmosphere very different from the heady days of 1994, when Quaker House was toasted by officers from Fort Bragg on its 25th anniversary. Then the army was shrinking; now it was expanding, or trying to, hanging on to every soldier it legally could, and then some. And the drumbeat for war was rumbling louder with each passing week, along with scorn for dissenters, and blatant attempts to shape the news, as much with falsehood as with facts.

However, as the discussion continued, Fager recognized an "elephant in the room," one of those unspoken questions which needed to be faced: if he was to become Director, what would happen to the arrangement with Steve and Lenore?

Quaker House had always been a one-staffperson, one paycheck operation, even after the Hotline began in 1995: Sandy Sweitzer and Phil Esmonde had answered almost half the steadily growing number of calls for the entire GI Rights Hotline network, in addition to their other work. The latest statistics indicated that the 2001 total for Quaker House would likely pass 3000 calls.

The default modus operandi would have meant that, with a Director in residence again, GI Hotline work would shift back from Silk Hope to the house in Fayetteville.

But was this really workable? Fager asked the Board. "You want me to learn about and take over the program, get ready for the war that's coming, raise funds for the budget, keep up the house – and answer 3000 phone calls too? I'm not crazy – that's a recipe for quick and total burnout, and you'd be right back where you are now. There's got to be another way."

And another way seemed possible, right there in front of them: junk the traditional model. Keep Steve and Lenore, who liked what they were doing and had lots of experience, increase the budget to cover their modest pay, and raise the funds to cover the difference.

Yet some Board members were made nervous by such ambitious talk. Quaker House had always been a shoestring operation: low pay and free rent for one resident staffperson (and their family), supported by donations from supporters mainly in central North Carolina's handful of liberal Friends Meetings. The budget for 2001-2002 was barely $30,000.

Fager argued it was time to think bigger. Not massive, just bigger. "We're not trying to build an empire here," was his frequent mantra, "but we're going to be called on to do more. A lot more." Combat had already started in Afghanistan; a major buildup for war against Iraq was underway; and the White House was making threats against Iran and North Korea as well, as part of what it called "the axis of evil." Fort Bragg would be deeply involved in all of it. And of course, there could be more terror attacks – repeated alerts kept the public jumpy, and domestic repression was on the rise: already the sweeping, so-called PATRIOT Act had opened the way to stepped up surveillance of American citizens, in more ways than the citizens then knew.

Reserve and National Guard units were being called up. Rumors persisted that the military draft might even be revived. GI Hotline calls kept increasing. New antiwar actions were also being organized. And Quaker House had more than thirty years of experience with most all of that. It was time to get it mobilized too, ready for an increased workload. To do that, Fager wanted to raise the project's profile, extend its reach and widen the circle of its support.

Some Board members remained nervous, but agreed to let Fager give it a try. He signed up for a three-year hitch. He was to start on December 1, 2001, from his home in Pennsylvania, and move in by the end of the year.

Fager did start in December, and his first task was to write a fund appeal letter. Feeling that time was short for end-of-the-year donations, he wanted to send the appeal by faster, but higher-priced first class mail. Again, the price tag of several hundred dollars for stamps caused butterflies for some Board members, so Fager offered a deal: "I said I'd pay for the first class stamps myself," he recalled, "and not ask for reimbursement unless the returns covered all the expenses and put Quaker House ahead."

Adding his own mailing list from the days of his Quaker newsletter to the in-house names, about 2000 envelopes were soon in the mail, and everyone held their breath.

Former Treasurer Bob Cooper, a Fayetteville resident, kept an eye on the returns. "But when they passed $6000," he said, "I quit worrying."

In the world of non-profit groups, this was a tiny sum. But it was big for Quaker House; Fager got his stamp money reimbursement. More important, the goal of keeping Steve and Lenore on the Hotline now seemed within reach. In a real way, the success of this mailing marked the beginning of a more public era in the history of Quaker House.

From there, Fager asked the Board to reconsider its allotment for travel. To raise more funds from Quakers, the new Director argued, Quaker House had to be seen and heard among them, not just be on paper. That would mean travel, especially to Yearly Meetings, which mainly met in the summer months.

Moreover, his plea was about more than marketing. Preparing for war was not only for Quaker House, but for Quakers generally. They needed to be mobilized like the reserves, encouraged, presented with options and resources – that is, the benefit of thirty-two years of "Front-Line Peacemaking" that Quaker House represented. As the one survivor out of all the Vietnam era antiwar projects near military bases, surely something had been learned in all these years. It was time to formulate that learning as a resource, and share it, with Friends first, and others as way opened. Fager was convinced that this would be a big part of Quaker House "getting ready for war."

"But that year the 'travel budget' was only enough to cover one trip to Greensboro and back, per month," Fager said. He argued that it was an investment which would pay off concretely as well as in terms of the mission. Finally he won an increase, contingent upon raising the revised budget target of $47,400, a total which seemed hefty to some.

Yet by the fiscal year's end on June 30, 2002, that target was met and surpassed by several thousand dollars, and skepticism on the Board began to recede.

"It's not that I'm some great fundraiser," Fager said. "But I learned an important lesson a few years earlier, working for another Quaker group. My job then was to create and run a social issues program, while the group's fundraiser was to bring in the money to keep it going. I designed and set up the program, worked very hard on it. But the fundraiser couldn't find the right appeal, and more funds didn't come in. After a couple years, the program was dropped, and my job went with it."

Point taken. "So when I came to Quaker House," Fager continued, "I was clear that keeping the donations coming to ensure the project's survival – and with it my future paychecks – was up to me and nobody else, no matter what the paperwork might say." This focused awareness has served Quaker House well. Through 2008, it had met each year's budget target, in a time of war when the total budget amount more than tripled from 2001.

Fager likened the work of fundraising to riding a bike uphill–if you have a good set of wheels (which Quaker House is) and keep pedaling, you can get somewhere. "But you can't coast very far. If you slack off and think it will happen by itself," he explained, "you start to slide backwards."

Whether that can continue in the time of deep recession and worse that Quaker House and everyone else faced as 2008 ended is another story, which will be told elsewhere.

Fager still did some counseling, when the need arose, as he described in the Spring 2002 Newsletter:

> One Wednesday afternoon at Quaker House, I was digging into the pile of papers on my desk, when the doorbell rang, and a young man was on the porch. His name was Thomas Mayfield.
> Turns out he was a former QH client: he had a QH Newsletter

from March 2000, and he was pictured there, with a shaved head and a broad smile, shortly after being discharged as a CO from the army at Fort Bragg. He was looking for my predecessor, who worked with him for the 10 months his CO process took, doubtless to catch up. Seems he's on something of a spiritual journey, or maybe just wandering, having spent time in an ashram in Florida. (He also has much more hair now!)

We settled on the front porch and watched the warm rain come down, and before long he had retrieved his CO file, which he carries with him, and I had an idea. There's a soldier now at Fort Bragg, I'll call him Alex, with whom I've been working, who's moving toward filing his own CO claim; and it occurred to me that Tom had experience which might be useful.

So a phone call and an hour later, Tom and Alex were sitting on the couch, looking over Tom's paperwork and talking in abbreviations ("MOS", "FSB," etc.) which "TOC" ("This Old Civilian") had to struggle to keep up with. We all spoke about our various experiences with CO forms and procedures, and I think Alex both learned a good deal, and gained some encouragement from this.

One suspicion I think we all had, but only talked about a little bit, was that the Army might not be as accommodating to Alex's claim as it was to Tom's (if 10 months and several cases of "lost paperwork" can be called accommodating).

At one point, Alex looked over at me and said, "I suppose we're keeping you from your work, sitting here."

I just grinned at him. Yes, the paperwork was still waiting, and probably quietly reproducing the way it seems to do. But this conversation was "work" too, indeed part of the original work of Quaker House.

Soon they were on their way. Tom Mayfield may or may not drop back by, as the spirit moves, before he heads further north and west. But I'm confident I'll be hearing more from Alex, one way or another. And I'm back among the paperwork, until the next such "disruption" occurs.

Another continuing concern was aggressiveness and frequent deceptiveness in recruiting. As an educator, Board Clerk Bonnie Parsons had a special concern about this. She was astonished to learn in 2002 that the new "No Child Left Behind Act" contained an unheralded section that waived privacy restrictions and gave recruiters automatic access, not only to schools, but also to students' contact information, unless parents specifically filed a notice refusing permission. In the rush of patriotism, many schools did not inform parents about this right to "opt out."

Thus far, the elements of the Quaker House program were familiar, even traditional: peace actions, GI counseling, recruiting – there was just greater demand and intensity in the face of the war fever and military buildup. But as 2002 unfolded, new elements began forcing their way onto its agenda.

One came not from the future but from the past. Early on in his tenure, Fager drove to Guilford College in Greensboro, two hours northwest, to look at the Quaker House archives, which were stored there. While he was leafing through early minutes and newsletters, the archivist, an earnest petite redhead, brought in a large flat box of library gray cardboard, and set it down on the table. "I think you'll like this," she said with a smile.

Fager's eyes widened when he lifted the lid. Inside was a stack of copies of *Bragg Briefs*, many brown and stiff with age, flyers from GIs United, posters for shows and rallies, including Jane Fonda's FTA troupe at the Haymarket Coffee House, and more, what librarians call "ephemeral materials." He'd heard of these things, but hadn't seen anything like them in years, decades.

"You're right – this is a treasure trove," he said to the archivist, who was Gwen (neé Gwendy) Gosney Erickson, daughter of Bob Gosney.

The Quaker House archives were in good hands, under the care of one who had spent much of her youth there. They also included, Erickson said, the most extensive such collection of GI resistance items that she knew of.

But who collected them, Fager wondered,? And how did they come to be this far from Fayetteville?

Gwen Gosney Erickson explained: Bruce Pulliam had gathered the materials. He had been, after all, a history teacher, and as the GI movement grew, he did what an alert historian would do: he collected its publications. But then, as the Vietnam War ended and the collection was completed, he offered it to his school, and to the local history section of the Cumberland County Library in downtown Fayetteville.

No one there wanted anything to do with it. This episode was evidently regarded as disreputable and disloyal, even shameful, nothing to be remembered and certainly not celebrated. Pulliam had to go to Guilford, a Quaker institution over a hundred miles away, to find a library ready to accept his compilation.

What Fayetteville wanted, instead, was the Airborne and Special Forces Museum, which had opened with much fanfare only a few months before Fager arrived. It was just down Haymount hill, taking up a whole block of what had once been the most notoriously disreputable stretch of the Fayetteville "Strip." He had visited it and was impressed by two things: first, the careful, meticulous attention to details of equipment and weaponry – and second, by the absence of any significant representation of the cost of all this combat: from World War Two through Vietnam, the Gulf War, and many other battlefields in between.

Beyond a couple of fuzzy black and white photos of indistinct lumps in a gray European meadow, he had seen no sign of the mountains of dead left behind, US or foreign. Nor amid all the celebratory battle narratives had

BRAGG BRIEFS

VOL. 5 no. 2   MAY 1972   DONATIONS

THIS IS YOUR PERSONAL PROPERTY (AR 210-10)
ANYONE WHO TRIES TO TAKE IT FROM YOU IS COMMITTING A CRIME.

Make Your Own
History or

They'll
Make It For You

A remarkable cover from *Bragg Briefs,* in 1972, part of the Bruce Pulliam Collection in the Quaker House archives.

he found any actual casualty figures. One left the exhibit hall, a recorded GI choir's refrain echoing in one's ears, with the clear sense that airborne war was glorious, exciting, necessary, good for the world – and evidently almost painless. The effect was downright eerie.

With this larger exhibit in mind, Fager at once knew what had to be done with Pulliam's cache. "We can't just leave all this here in the shadows," he said. "We've got to make it visible again." The collection was a prime example of the kind of resource Quaker House had to offer a wider audience.

Within a few months, together with an intern from Guilford, Sally Stevens, an exhibit had been assembled, titled "Make Your Own History." It was on folding display boards set up on the dining room table and full-size color reproductions taped to the walls. Many of the images were also uploaded to the Quaker House website, where they remain in 2008.

"The 'proof of the pudding' for me was when a military reporter from the *Fayetteville Observer* came to look at it," Fager said. "She was young, definitely post-Vietnam, and she was preparing a series, 'From Hanoi to Hay Street,' on Fayetteville and Fort Bragg during the Vietnam war. She came into the house as if she was walking into an ambush. As she looked over all the copies of *Bragg Briefs,* the photos of protest marches through the Strip and Jane Fonda in Rowan Park, her initial reaction was mainly disbelief. She had never heard of any of it, never seen any of these items. I think she figured we had faked it all, even though it included several articles from her own paper."

The veteran reporter in Fager was amused by the skepticism. "Hey, don't take our word for all this," he told her. "Check it out."

She did, and her series included a section of the GI resistance. Which to Fager meant the Quaker House exhibit was a success – even though the articles made no mention of it.

Another element that crowded onto the Quaker House horizon was military-related domestic violence. This phenomenon was a kind of continued background noise, like the booming of artillery that regularly shook the house and rattled the windows. Barely two weeks after moving in, Fager opened the *Fayetteville Observer* on the morning of Monday, January 14, 2002, to this headline:

Victim Stabbed Outside Eatery

A Fayetteville woman died Sunday afternoon after being stabbed by her estranged husband in front of the Mi Casita restaurant on Raeford Road, police said.

Shalamar Franceschi died at the scene, Fayetteville police said. She was 24.

Officials said her throat was cut and she was stabbed multiple times.

A warrant has been issued charging her estranged husband, Damian Colon Franceschi, 26, with first-degree murder. Authorities were looking for Damian Franceschi on Sunday night. He is considered armed and dangerous . . . .

The husband, who had just been bailed out of jail after repeated physical and sexual assaults on his wife, had also been discharged from the army only days before. He was captured several days later, and is serving a life sentence.

"Jesus," Fager thought, reading the report. "Welcome to Fayetteville."

However shocking, the Franceschi killing was not Quaker House business. Even so, busy as he was with other work, he was haunted by the story, as were other local citizens he got to know. And the ugly fact of military-related domestic violence, however peripheral in program terms, refused to go away.

Shalamar Franceschi, with her son. She was murdered by her estranged husband, who had just been discharged from the Army, in Fayetteville, January 2002.

The Franceschi murder was not reported widely outside Fayetteville. Yet it was one of a long series of similar crimes, some of which did attract national attention, like the skinhead killings in 1995, and the Jeffrey MacDonald "crazed hippie" murders of 1970. Such lurid cases were big contributors to the "Fayettenam" image which local boosters so despised.

More bizarre, but widely noted in the region, was an incident a month later. On February 23, 2002, in adjoining Moore County, a deputy sheriff pulled over a pickup truck he saw speeding suspiciously through a rural area. When the two men in the truck first tried to bribe him, then came at him with weapons, the alarmed deputy pulled out his service revolver, warned them to put their hands up, then sprayed one of them with mace. Still they kept coming.

It turned out that almost all of what happened next was supposed to be a game. While not in uniform, the two men were actually Special Forces trainees from Fort Bragg, taking part in their "final exam" before winning the coveted Green Beret. This exam, however, was a two-week long war game called "Robin Sage," which is played out over a ten-county area of central and western North Carolina several times a year.

In the "Robin Sage" scenario, the fictional country of "Pineland" is occupied by evil invaders, and the Green Beret trainees carry out guerilla missions to free the oppressed Pinelanders. Each Robin Sage involves a couple hundred soldiers and scores of civilian volunteers, who play various supportive roles.

The exercise entails lots of derring-do, wrestling, running through the woods, screeching up and down secluded roads, and firing off blanks from real weapons. So when the two trainees were pulled over by the deputy, they thought he was part of the action, and tried to "take him prisoner."

Except the deputy had not been notified about Robin Sage operations, and as far as he knew, the guns these two roughnecks were pulling on him were loaded with real bullets.

His was at any rate, and when they still came for him, he started shooting, killing one and wounding the other.

The deputy was exonerated, having followed procedures for dealing with an attack by superior numbers. And no doubt tons of reports were generated within the Special Forces and the Army. The *Fayetteville Observer* covered it all with gusto and in detail, and the green newcomer Fager lapped it all up, slack-jawed. Although the whole thing could be written off as a regrettable accident, it did nothing to help Fort Bragg's image.

No wonder then, that as spring of 2002 came on, the city's leaders resolved to do something serious about "Fayettenam," by giving Fayetteville a public relations makeover. A high-powered advertising firm was hired, meetings were held, surveys taken, ideas generated. The outcome was an ambitious plan for a major advertising campaign, all built around a new, carefully-crafted slogan, "Fayetteville: History, Heroes, and a Hometown Feeling." A roll-out ad blitz was set to kick off in early summer.

But then a different kind of blitz got in the way.

On June 11, Special Forces Sergeant Rigoberto Nieves, who had just flown home to Fort Bragg from Afghanistan, to deal with what he told his comrades were "personal problems," shot and killed his wife Teresa, and then himself.

Two and a half weeks later, on June 29, Special Forces Master Sergeant William Wright clubbed his wife Jennifer to death with a baseball bat, and buried her body in a wooded area near Fort Bragg.

On July 9, Sergeant Cedric Griffin of the 37th Engineer Battalion stabbed his estranged wife, Marilyn, more than 50 times. Then he set her corpse on fire, while her two young daughters slept in an adjoining room. (The girls heard a smoke alarm and escaped.)

Ten days later, on July 19, Sgt. William Wright agreed to lead police and MPs to the spot where he had buried his wife's body. While investigators were still there, a police cell phone rang, and an investigator called out: "We got another one."

Another two, to be precise. East of Fayetteville, in their new "dream house," Delta Force Sergeant First Class Brandon Floyd, also recently back from Afghanistan, had just shot and killed his wife Andrea, and then himself. Neighbors had referred to the outwardly happy and attractive couple as "Barbie and Ken."

And still it wasn't finished. Four days afterward, Special Forces

Major David Shannon was shot and killed while he slept. His wife Joan at first said an unidentified intruder was responsible, but a week later, on July 29, police charged her with murder and conspiracy. On August 2, their fifteen year-old daughter Elizabeth was also arrested.

Thus in the space of barely six weeks, seven military-related murders and suicides occurred on and around Fort Bragg. (And that wasn't the end of the series; nine months later, in March of 2003, Sergeant Wright hung himself in his cell while awaiting trial.)

The first four cases made orphans of a total of nine children. The only survivor of the four male shooters, Cedric Griffin, was sentenced to life in 2005. Both Joan Shannon and her daughter are likewise in prison; the daughter testified that her mother persuaded her to pull the trigger, for insurance money; at trial, Joan Shannon denied this, but did admit that she and her husband had taken part in group sex parties, complete with explicit photos; she was convicted and sentenced to life.

Two other lesser casualties fell by the wayside of this trail of mayhem: one was the "get-rid-of-Fayettenam" re-branding campaign. The city garnered plenty of national publicity that summer and fall, but of exactly the kind it was trying to overcome. When the dust settled, a dozen or so small signs bearing the "History, Heroes and a Hometown Feeling" motto, standing forlornly on roads entering the city, were about all that was left of the grand campaign put together with such hope a few months earlier. The "Fayettenam" label was stuck to the town's image more firmly than ever.

And as if this travesty was not enough, a touch of farce was added on July 25, when the President of the Chamber of Commerce, one of the key figures in the makeover effort, was arrested near downtown, charged with soliciting an undercover female police officer to perform what was euphemistically called "a crime against nature." He said it was all a "mistake," but resigned less than a week later.

All this murder and its fallout were gripping and tragic, but again, not something Quaker House was prepared to deal with.

Or was it? For Fager, a former journalist, yet another side of the story was visible, mainly from close up, which was connected with something he was trying to get a handle on: in the wake of the killings, he watched a full-spectrum military effort at damage-control and news management click into gear. A piece he wrote in the Newsletter described this process, and an unexpected reaction to it:

> There was something surreal about Fayetteville's community meeting on domestic violence on August 21, 2002. The mix of victims, civilian and Army professionals were to talk about how to prevent more domestic homicides. We were all there, of course, because seven corpses had been hauled from local homes in the space of five weeks that same summer, the deadly result of murders and suicides by military family members.

This bloody outburst brought national media attention, as well it should have. It also aborted the city of Fayetteville's latest PR campaign to change its unhappy "Fayettenam" image. But all this was muted nearly into invisibility that morning. A Colonel Tad Davis, Fort Bragg's garrison commander, spoke, but his rhetoric was almost as hard to make out as the nametag sewn on his camouflage green uniform.

This was a "great day," he declared, in which to "come together" and "move forward" to increase "awareness" and "outreach" to "people who are hurting." Pausing to praise Fayetteville as an "All-American City," he insisted on "accountability" for people involved in "these situations " as the Army worked for "more productivity" on the "issues at hand."

He could have been talking about diabetes or drunk driving. Only when announcing a newly-scheduled seminar on post did he actually speak the "DV" words, hurrying past them to wrap up with a promise that this was not "a short-term thing." He finished to warm applause.

Most of the rest of the session was carefully focused on domestic violence away from Fort Bragg, as a statewide problem in North Carolina, and on pleas to get more information for families at risk, about counseling and other services. The oblique character of the event was probably unavoidable; certainly spousal murders are a scourge across the state, occurring almost weekly. But that wasn't why we were there, nor did it explain the gaggle of reporters and TV cameras outside the door collaring anyone willing to call herself a victim or an expert.

Only in the back of the room, little-noticed on a literature table, was there a discordant, more revealing note: a stack of reprints from a newsletter, *Domestic Violence Report,* which presented data on the real issue, the 900-pound guerilla everyone was stepping so carefully around: the epidemic of domestic violence in the US military, and the blatant, chronic inadequacy of its responses.

One speaker could have cut through the fog of phony optimism: Deborah Tucker, who is Co-Chair of a task force on DV that was forced on the Defense Department by Congress in 1999 after earlier searing exposes of "The War At Home" on TV's *60 Minutes* and elsewhere. Tucker's task force has issued two reports which, within reams of carefully modulated bureacratese, deliver a damning indictment of systematic denial and coverup of rampant family abuse in the military. But Tucker too pulled most of her punches, offering only the mildest of criticisms, carefully wrapped in praise for the good intentions of the Pentagon brass.

As an exercise in Army damage control, the meeting was a success: I watched a uniformed officer shrug and tell a TV reporter that there was nothing special about the recent killings: "They were just an anomaly." And the *Fayetteville Observer*'s report dutifully headlined the event with a distinctly upbeat slant, portraying it as somehow marking the turning of the tide. The issue has since been receding from Fayetteville's public consciousness—at least until the next bodies turn up.

Given the institutional and cultural realities here, the meeting probably went as well as could be expected. But what was not said, and has not been acknowledged, is that the real news about this rash of killings and what it represents is—that it really isn't news at all.

In this regard, the experience of the *Fayetteville Observer* is revealing: The *Observer* has the makings of a good paper, but its coverage has a predictably ingrained pro-military bias. Thus its early stories on the killings reflected spoon-fed Army PR, with spokesmen expressing shock, bewilderment and the "just an anomaly" line.

But then something truly anomalous happened: the *Observer*'s phones began to ring, and wouldn't stop. On the other end were military wives, dozens of them, spilling out gruesome tales, not only about beatings and abuse, but of a military culture that, despite PR protestations, remains deeply and systematically indifferent to their plight. The recent killings, these witnesses made plain, were just the bloody, impossible-to-ignore tip of a very large and otherwise submerged iceberg.

This outpouring must have been difficult to listen to, but the reporters, to their credit, paid attention. While the *Observer* still ignores or downplays the plentiful evidence that DV rates are much higher in the military than the civilian population, it chose not to ignore the anguished testimonials of dozens of its local neighbors.

The Army clearly hated that. It works nonstop here and elsewhere to project a wholesome, family-friendly image, for various reasons, not least as an aid to recruiting. And to be sure, many Army families are perfectly normal. But too many are in serious difficulty. Nor is this epidemic confined to "families": the *Army Times* reported on August 19 that there had also been five GI suicides on Fort Bragg since January. A strong case could be made for adding them to the tally, but this report has not made it into the local press.

The intertwined issues here: domestic violence, *and* military efforts at news management, information control, and "spin," made for a combination that Fager found unavoidable. The fact that the military had acted skillfully to prevent a common definition of domestic abuse from being formulated or accepted across the services was especially telling: without a common definition, no one could assemble or analyze case statistics into a coherent or reliable account of the phenomenon.

That left the public, Congress, reporters, and any other would-be reformers with only a mass of incomplete and incommensurable "anecdotal evidence." It also left the military able to deny that the existence of any real problem in military culture, and repeat its mantras about how the outbreak at Fort Bragg was simply a "fluke" and an "anomaly" – very regrettable of course, but there you are.

In the coming months, Fager was to see such treatment applied again and again, and to much more than this plague of domestic violence. In fact, the technical term for this process, "psychological operations," (or, depending on the context, psychological *warfare*) was the mission of a large unit right at Fort Bragg. How to identify this, how speak of it and act on it, was a problem he pondered often.

Behind the media firestorm evoked by the murders, the buildup to war, at Fort Bragg as elsewhere, continued quietly but relentlessly. One important piece of this buildup, which would not come to light for several years, began on September 16, 2002.

That day a conference opened at the Special Warfare Center on Fort Bragg. At the session, the staff of the rapidly filling detention camp at Guantanamo were treated to detailed "demonstrations" of the Special Forces' SERE techniques.

SERE – Survival, Evasion, Resistance and Escape. It's the part of Special Forces training where aspiring operators are "captured" and then abused, under controlled conditions, to see how long they could resist breaking down and signing false confessions.

Reports are that the techniques, which grew out of responses to the abuse of US POWs in the Korean War, can include waterboarding, religious assaults, sensory and sleep deprivation, and extremes of heat and cold. Reports also say they are extremely effective at breaking down the trainees' will to resist, usually quickly.

The goal of the Bragg demonstration, according to Army investigators and later journalistic disclosures, was to show the Guantanamo officials how to get their prisoners to talk. Until then, the complaint from Pentagon higher-ups was that the hundreds of detainees there were producing very little useful information, or "actionable intelligence."

From that fateful September 16 meeting, the SERE techniques, said investigators, "migrated" from Fort Bragg to Guantanamo. And then to Afghanistan and Iraq, at a prison once run by Saddam Hussein called Abu Ghraib and elsewhere. And then to proliferating the "black sites" operated by various OGAs, or Other Government Agencies – read CIA.

With this "migration," evidently many detainees started to talk, and didn't stop.

That's not surprising, because these techniques were not really about interrogation. They were about torture. So yes, those subjected to them talked. They spewed reams of confessions and detailed "intelligence."

But over time, as numerous investigations were to show in chilling detail, little of this "intelligence" was proven authentic.

And hundreds of the detainees, after such abuse, were released without charges – because they had no involvement with terrorism.

That is, they were not only innocent, they were also ignorant of terror plots. Their confessions were mostly fabricated, to stop the torture.

Years later, reporters were to discover that many administration officials–solid anti-terror conservatives and high military officers– came to see this "migration" as a tragic wrong turn and tried to stop it.

Without success.

And if most of the coerced testimony was false, it was nonetheless useful, to those at the top who were determined to go to war with Iraq.

Although local peace activists knew nothing of this "migration" at the time, Quaker House was still very busy with its traditional work. Hotline calls continued to increase. And Fager was soon working with an active duty paratrooper from Fort Bragg named Jeremy Hinzman, and his Vietnamese-born wife Nga.

Jeremy Hinzman, Nga Nguyen & their son Liem, Fayetteville 2003.

From small-town South Dakota and with no money for college, Hinzman had joined the army from a typical mix of motives: he wanted to travel, and did. He was very interested in the promised $40,000 bonus of college money once he finished his enlistment. He also had a real enjoyment of the physical rigors of paratrooper training – he said he loved jumping out of airplanes. And there was no denying the allure of a regular paycheck and other benefits; he said they had enabled him to marry Nga, who had also grown up in South Dakota, her family accepted as refugees from postwar Vietnam.

Hinzman also enjoyed the camaraderie and "unit cohesion" that the 82nd Airborne was so proud of. In fact, he liked most things about the

Army. "The Army did give me focus and structure in my life," said Hinzman, who enlisted early in 2001. At the time he expected to be called to fight and assumed he could do it. "But I was ignorant, probably stupidly, of an ingrained inhibition to killing another human being."

The initial naive euphoria and air of adventure were shattered during infantry training, he said later. "When we were marching around chanting songs like, 'Train to kill. Kill we will,' or during bayonet training they'd ask, 'What makes the grass grow?' and we'd say 'Blood, blood, bright red blood.' When we would thrust [the bayonet], the drill sergeant would yell that, and we'd have to scream back. People would actually get hoarse yelling this crap. I could never really get into that stuff. Some people ate it up because I think there is an opportunity in groups to kind of let go of your inhibitions and do wanton things... "It's all presented, at least on the surface, as, 'Oh, it's just in humor, and no one's around listening to it,' but I think that really does put that mindset in a soldier that they're killers."

Hinzman was widely read, especially in the field of religion, and was drawn to contemplative spiritualities, including those in the Buddhist, Catholic and Quaker traditions. This seeking led him to give up eating meat and dairy products. He and Nga, hugely pregnant when they met Fager not long after he arrived, also often attended the Fayetteville Friends Meeting.

As he reflected on his training for combat, the prospect of killing became less tolerable. At Quaker House, Hinzman began talking about possibly submitting a conscientious objector claim. But he didn't really want out of the army entirely, he said. Fager explained that he could apply to be classified as a noncombatant CO, which would enable him to stay in uniform, without having to carry a weapon.

Hinzman mulled over this option for several months, during which his son, Liem, was born. By August, after many conversations and much reflection, he had written his claim, and submitted it to his First Sergeant.

Three months later, he asked the Sergeant about the status of his CO application. He reported that the sergeant retorted, "CO application? What CO application? We don't have any CO application from you."

This was significant, because his unit was preparing to ship out to Afghanistan, and a pending CO application would likely have meant Jeremy would be kept "in the rear," at Fort Bragg.

It was also a lie. Much later, Hinzman obtained his file, and the CO application was in it, right where it was supposed to be.

But he had no proof at the time, so he was obliged to re-submit the letter, and start the clock again. And he was soon sent to Afghanistan. There, his unit was kept in an isolated area and saw no actual combat. He used part of his brief email access to write to Quaker House:

> I've been here for about a week now. Despite the fact that I was told that I'd be cooking, it seems as though I was mislead. Instead, I've been washing pots and pans for the last week. Go figure. Because of the way the water is treated or the harshness of the soap

or some combination of the two, my hands already feel as though they are perpetually burning. . . .

It's not all bad though. Being away from everybody and most everything is allowing me to gauge what was meaningful in my life and what was merely superfluous. Silence is very hard to find, for everyone seems as though they're on a constant quest to be distracted.

I spoke to Nga on the telephone a few minutes ago. She is racked with a cold, but is glad to be home [in South Dakota]. Liem [then nine months old] has his two front teeth and, as can be expected, is being spoiled by the family.

This camp could just as well be in Arizona. There are virtually no locals to be seen. We are strongly discouraged from associating with the soldiers from the other country who has soldiers here, which is that pest of Europe, Romania. The higher-ups must be horrified at the prospect that they would sell us vodka, speak a language other than english or spanish, or generally show us that there is another culture in the world that may be just a tad bit different than ours. . . .

From talking to soldiers who have been here for a few months, I was surprised to hear how many are questioning why we are here, and some even voicing criticism at America's motives. Ayotollah [US Attorney General John] Ashcroft's henchmen are probably reading this as I write, so . . . . .watch out. Anyway, I'm sure 80 percent of it is simply bitterness from being away from home, family and automobile rather than genuine dissent. Perhaps I'm too cynical in my assessment of this.

Because his CO claim was pending, Hinzman was ordered to stay in the mess tent, where he wound up washing pots all day, every day, for weeks on end. Also, during the deployment, he was called before a hastily-assembled hearing on his claim, which he felt was run like a kangaroo court, and probably violated the Army regulations for processing CO claims. Persuaded that he couldn't get a fair hearing, he angrily withdrew the claim. But he was still stuck washing pots, through the winter and spring of 2003.

Back in Fayetteville, not long before Christmas, a curious envelope arrived at 223 Hillside. The smudged postmark indicated it was sent from an "APO (Army post office), and it was addressed by hand simply, furtively to "House" and the number.

Fager opened it and found a single sheet of lined notebook paper:

To whom it may concern,

My name is David, I'm writing from Afghanistan. On Nov. 1, 2001 I started my experience in the military (Army). At first, I was inspired by the goings on of Sept. 11. I felt it was a way I could contribute to my country. So I enlisted.

After 23 combat missions, serving with the 82nd Airborne, I have come to a different place. I find my feelings have changed about the best way to make a difference.

"I graduated from the Infantry School, Fort Benning. from there I graduated from Airborne School and moved my wife . . . and two children to Fort Bragg. Then I was still a believer in my decision to join the Army. In June 2002 I was deployed to fight the war on terrorism in Afghanistan.

The change occurred after the combat missions. Just seeing the people and children's faces I realized that I can't pull the trigger. I'm writing to request a copy of the Conscientious Objector regulations for the Army.

I hope to talk to one of your counselors when I get back to the States, around December 10. Thank you.

Fager talked with the soldier, David Bunt, a few days later, and over the coming months accompanied him through a long and frustrating process of trying to get the military to acknowledge his convictions before he was finally discharged, two years later.

The counselors Steve and Lenore were busy with many other cases as well. But Steve took time out in December for a special memorial. Philip Berrigan, the radical Catholic activist and former priest, died on December 2, 2002. Berrigan had been a mentor and inspiration to many Catholic Workers and other, and Steve joined in a special tribute in his memory shortly thereafter. Characteristically, the tribute took the form of a protest in Washington DC, in which Steve and others threw their own blood on a door into the Pentagon. Several were arrested, and a court date was set for March.

The blood left only a few marks, and was quickly scrubbed off. Steve may have been expecting a fine, or at most a few nights in jail. Instead, in court he faced a US magistrate who was a close relative of a well-known reactionary columnist and political operative. The magistrate summarily gave Steve the maximum six-month sentence and had him bundled off to jail.

This sudden sabbatical left Lenore to deal with the growing load of Hotline calls largely on her own. She held up gamely. But when Steve was transferred to the federal prison at Butner, north of Raleigh, Fager paid him a visit. As his putative supervisor, Fager counseled against any further civil disobedience that resulted in jail time – not on grounds of principle (Fager had collected five arrests himself for civil disobedience earlier in his career), but simply as a matter of practical Hotline call management. Steve agreed. He was released in early September 2003.

By then, the gathering storm had broken.

13. 2003: The Mission After "Mission Accomplished"

In January of 2003, Lenore Yarger visited Iraq along with a delegation from Peaceful Tomorrows, an antiwar group whose members had lost close family in the September 11th attacks. Their mission was to bear witness to the suffering of Iraqi people from twelve years of interwar economic sanctions and, in recent months, increased US bombing–two and a half months earlier the US Congress had authorized the use of US military force to topple Saddam Hussein. The devastation already wrought by years of economic sanctions was well documented.

"I found it wrenching to say goodbye to people we met in Iraq," Lenore wrote in an opinion piece in the *Fayetteville Observer* after she returned. "The reality that they could be dead–in two weeks, a month, six months–because of a US invasion stood like an icy pillar between us."

Back in Fayetteville, a similar barrier divided a small but growing peace constituency that was speaking out against the push for war, and those who sought to discredit them. Around the country, around the world, marches and rallies denounced the plans for war. They failed to stop it, but the unprecedented size and vigor of the outpourings were inspiring to many, participants and observers alike. They also left those in command of the war machine unmoved.

In Fayetteville, this spirit took the form of small vigils around the historic Market House downtown every few weeks. They were organized by Fayetteville Peace with Justice, an informal network of local dissidents that formed shortly after the September 11th attacks, along with Quaker House. Compared to the millions of protesters tramping through the streets of London, Paris, Rome, Montreal and many other cities – plus Washington DC, these vigils were hardly a speck on the map. Yet as was true in the Vietnam years, such actions were daring and dramatic in this military town.

When the actual invasion began on March 20, many antiwar groups around the US took to the streets and sat down, hoping to physically disrupt the war machine with their bodies. Many were arrested, but the invasion rolled on unhindered. In Fayetteville, the consensus was that such symbolic civil disobedience would only muddy the waters. But some escalation was necessary; so the downtown vigils were increased to weekly events.

Although attendance hovered between six and a dozen, the quiet assemblies attracted attention, mostly negative. They also attracted counter-demonstrators. "Their mantra was 'These antiwar people hate soldiers, hate their families and want them to die,'" Fager remembered. But hard

143

experience as an activist during and after the Vietnam War had taught him to be aggressive in countering such negative framing. His handmade sign read, "YES to the Troops. NO to the War." Others said, "Support the Troops: Bring them Home."

The Rivalry did not produce any violence. The worst the vigilers had to endure were some catcalls, obscene gestures and a plastic soda bottle that flew out of a car window. But few could forget the accounts of the mysterious arson attack on the original Quaker House, which had stood but a few blocks away.

"It's very much a struggle for me," peace vigiler Darlene Hopkins said one afternoon that spring. A psychologist and counselor at Methodist College in Fayetteville, she had worked with soldiers returning from the first Gulf War. She also attended Friends Meeting at Quaker House.

"I don't want to make anyone's pain any worse," she said, "and yet I feel I have to tell the truth. This war is not the answer." Standing beside Hopkins was a 19-year old active duty Navy sailor, a city councilwoman and a woman veteran whose son was stationed in Korea.

At a downtown vigil just a few weeks after the invasion began, peace protesters were out numbered 5 to 1. In a scene played out across the country, police officers kept the groups apart, with American flags and prayers for God's blessing on both sides.

On May 1, 2003, the president flew in a jet fighter to a aircraft carrier anchored off the California coast, to tell the world that the US mission in Iraq had been accomplished, successfully.

It was not true, but at that carefully choreographed moment, with the flags waving and the sailors in their whites cheering, it seemed so: Baghdad was occupied. A large statue of Saddam Hussein had been felled while the TV cameras rolled. The Iraqi dictator himself was in hiding, the quarry of many soldier-hunters. In this seemingly quick conquest, US forces had reported a death toll of only 139 military personnel.

In Fayetteville, the beleaguered vigilers felt defeated. "We did our best," one said dejectedly, not daring to add out loud, "And for what? We said, 'Don't go to war,' but they did anyway. We said it would mean terrible loss of life, but really, there hasn't been that much. We said it would be a quagmire, but now it's over." They called off the vigils and considered what they could do next, if anything.

Yet as the summer months of 2003 unrolled, the hollowness of the "Mission Accomplished" bravado became plainer by the day. Attacks on US troops continued and increased. On July 3, the president upped the ante with a remarkably arrogant boast from the White House: "There are some who feel like the conditions are such that they can attack us there," he told a press conference. "My answer is, bring 'em on."

The burgeoning insurgency did just that. And when the small circle of Fayetteville Peace With Justice gathered for their monthly meeting in late July, one activist looked around the group and said, "They told us it was all over. But you know, I don't believe it is." The others around the table nodded in grim agreement. In response, they resolved to resume their weekly late afternoon vigils at the Market House, and keep them up until the end of October, when early dusk made them impractical.

When they returned to their outpost, however, they found that some important changes were in the air. For one thing, the counterprotesters did not re-appear. And for another, the reactions from passers by shifted markedly. They still heard some catcalls and saw middle fingers. But week by week, there were far more thumbs up and honks accompanied by smiles. Beneath the surface, in troop-supporting Fayetteville, many more who felt unable to join the protests openly were expressing sympathy for them.

And one day, a new vigiler joined the regulars. When a reporter asked who she was and why she was there, her reply was straightforward. Her name was Pam Nolan, and she said, "My husband, who is deployed in Mosul, has been assigned to an occupation that's illegal, immoral and unjust." He was proud to defend his country against a real threat, she said, but unfortunately that's not what he felt he was doing in Iraq.

Although Nolan was not the only spouse of an active duty GI among the peace protesters, few spoke out like she did for fear of reprisals against their spouses. She told the reporter that she was not afraid. "Isn't this what America is about?"

The much-vaunted "weapons of mass destruction" were nowhere to be found. Further, the initial welcome by ordinary Iraqis had vanished, and US troops were now increasingly targeted, it seemed, from all sides. In addition, signs of a confusing and dangerous civil war were cropping up. An array of emerging insurgent groups defied all simple explanations of who the enemy was and who US involvement was aimed to help. Was it the Sunnis or the Shia the US were supposed to save? Which factions? Or was it to keep them from killing each other? If the US came to help Iraqis, why was the military spending so much time protecting American contractors from Iraqis who were trying to kill them and the troops? Wouldn't it be a big help to the Iraqi men who were looking for work if they could do those jobs instead of American contractors anyway? Then US troops could get out of here!

Morale plummeted. When a general visited a troop unit with TV news cameras rolling, and asked several enlistees how they were doing, the replies rang out loud and clear: "Ready to go home, sir! Ready to go home!"

For Quakers and others who opposed war and military violence on a spiritual basis, the altered combat situation was a change of conditions, not of principle. They were against the invasion before it began and worked to end it no matter what character it took. But continuing war meant something different than one that was all over. And to military families, who had supported plans for a swift invasion in the interest of national defense, things had changed even more dramatically.

Military families supported sending their loved ones to combat to protect Americans at home, and if that meant removing Saddam Hussein, they were behind it. But then the weapons of mass destruction were not

145

found and the links to the plotters of 9-11 proved equally elusive. By late 2003, it wasn't just the French who opposed the war in Iraq, it was a growing number of military families across the US.

Some of the first were the wives of troops serving in the Third Infantry Division, based at Fort Stewart in Hinesville, Georgia. They weren't against the war, they explained. But the Third Infantry Division had deployed early, and now that the fighting was over, its return had been promised then delayed, promised but delayed, and delayed again.

By midsummer, many wives of Fort Stewart were fed up. Public protests erupted, demanding – not an end to the war exactly, but the immediate return of the Third Infantry Division to base. They said their men agreed. One wife angrily read from a letter she'd received from her husband, while a TV news camera rolled, "Our morale is not high or low," the missive declared, "our morale is non-existent." When a colonel tried to placate a roomful of restive spouses, the reaction was so hostile that, according to reports, he had to be escorted from the building under guard.

These protests shocked their small community and the ripples spread widely when the media began to notice. The furor only died down when the Third Division actually did come home, in late summer. But by then, it was clear that "mission accomplished" was the lie it had been from the moment it was uttered. The war was not over; the troops of the Third Infantry Division would have a break, but soon enough they would be going back to Iraq.

Calls to the Quaker House Hotline phone totaled 6,187 by the end of 2003, double that of 2001. The GI Rights Hotline as a whole experienced almost as dramatic an increase, with a total of 28,822 calls that year. "Many of the stories we hear from callers are troubling and reflect the difficulty of the Iraq occupation," Lenore Yarger wrote to Quaker House supporters in the Newsletter.

The peak number of calls was in March 2003, corresponding with the beginning of the invasion. As the length of deployment and the number of casualties rose, so did the number of calls. Reservist mobilizations meant a jump in callers later in the year. Calls from soldiers who were AWOL or thinking of going AWOL increased by about 25 per cent per month over the previous year. Three times as many members of the National Guard and the Army Reserves called the Hotline in 2003 as in the previous year.

Yarger and Woolford reported that eight soldiers who had sought help from Quaker House in becoming conscientious objectors in 2003 were discharged by the end of the year. Conscientious objector status was the most commonly asked about discharge that year, followed by medical discharge, hardship discharge and entry level separation.

One phrase counselors heard on the phone a lot was "stop-loss." Stop-loss orders from the Pentagon prevent servicepeople from leaving the military or the reserves when their enlistment expires or when they are eligible to retire. Many GIs expressed shock and outrage when this happened, and a few even tried to challenge the orders in court.

But they lost. Buried in small type in the "enlistment agreement" that each recruit signs is the giveaway phrase:

> "In the event of war, my enlistment in the Armed Forces continues until six (6) months after the war ends, unless my enlistment is ended sooner by the President of the United States."

The potential impact of this option became especially ominous in the context of the "war on terror": the battlefield, we have repeatedly been told, is everywhere. The enemies are mainly faceless and stateless. And the "war" could go on for generations. So how will we know when it ends, if it ever does?

That is, in the new war, an enlistment could potentially be involuntarily extended for decades.

"Some critics have called stop-loss a kind of disguised draft, preventing soldiers from leaving the military rather than forcing them to join," Fager told readers in the Newsletter. "By whatever name, these orders are causing a lot of hardship for servicemembers and their familes."

The folly of the "Bring 'em on" boast dismayed even some on Capitol Hill. But it was the reaction of soldiers and their families that would have the greatest impact. By mid-August, Military Families Speak Out, an antiwar organization founded in 2002, and Veterans for Peace, which began during the Vietnam War, launched the Bring Them Home Now! Campaign. They chose to have two press conferences to announce their new effort—one in Washington DC and one at Quaker House.

For the first time in a long time, the front lawn was adorned with brightly colored banners and signs. News media from across the US and as far away as Australia showed up to cover the event. On the walls inside the house, the new exhibit of the history of the Vietnam era GI resistance still hung. It was the backdrop of an emotional scene as parents and relatives of service people fought back tears as they told the stories of loved ones killed or in danger in a conflict some had once supported, but no longer believed in.

Nancy Lessin, co-founder of Military Families Speak Out, told the pack of reporters and photographers crowded into the dining room, "We want to talk about three words of false bravado uttered by George Bush, from a safe and secure location, surrounded by armed guards that taunted those shooting at our loved ones...George Bush said 'Bring them on.' We say, 'Bring them home *now*.'"

"How many of Bush's cabinet members have loved ones in Iraq?" asked Susan Shuman, whose son was in combat there. (Answer: None)

Unlike the campaign by the wives of the soldiers at Fort Stewart, Bring Them Home Now! sought to bring not just their loved ones home from combat, but all of the US soldiers. This was a decidedly antiwar group, organized and promoted exclusively by military families. It would be a full year before returning soldiers would form Iraq Veterans Against the War to fight for an end to the occupation, reparations for the damage Iraq suffered and full benefits for returning service-members.

Reporters who saw copies of *Bragg Briefs* on the wall often asked if Quaker House hoped to be part of a mass GI resistance like the earlier one. Fager always answered with an emphatic "No."

"We can learn from this past," he continued, "and in many ways we need to celebrate it. But I don't live in the past. The Sixties are over, Vietnam is over. This war is different. The Army is different. I do expect GI dissent and resistance, but it will be different too. We'll support that, as long as it's nonviolent. But it will find its own forms."

How was the Army different in 2003? The draft had ended ten years earlier, for one thing. That meant each soldier was officially a volunteer, even if many had been traduced by recruiter falsehoods. The force was also older, and much more likely to be, or have been, married. Plus a substantial percentage of enlistees were at least considering the military as a career path.

Fort Bragg was different too. After September 11, commanders regarded its open character as an invitation to terrorist infiltration. Gates suddenly sprang up along the main roads there, tended first by rifle-toting soldiers in battle dress, and later by security contractors. Shiny razor wire was unrolled along brushy roadsides, with chain link fences sprouting elsewhere. Plans were announced to close the public roads that crossed the post's land. Fort Bragg was zipped up tighter than an overstuffed duffel bag. There would be no repeat of J.C. Honeycutt's quiet incursions to flip copies of *Bragg Briefs* on the grass outside the barracks.

And to the north, the Canadian government, which had welcomed tens of thousands of young American military emigres in the Sixties, was now much less friendly to immigrants generally, especially those who were deserters rather than draft dodgers.

All of which was a damper on the prospects for a repeat of the kind of large-scale resistance of the Vietnam years. To be sure, plenty of GIs still wanted to get out – the burgeoning Hotline traffic despite minimal advertising showed that. But with the personal stakes so much higher, soldiers with doubts would likely agonize more and longer. The most public early voices of military dissent came, as we have just seen, from GI family members. Fager figured actual resisters in uniform were likely to appear one or two at a time, here and there.

Jeremy Hinzman was a prime example of a soldier in conflict with himself as well as the Army. Back from Afghanistan by midsummer, he was troubled that his toddler son didn't recognize him at first. At the same time, the return to routine on Fort Bragg was mostly welcome; he got to jump out of airplanes again, and without a pending CO application, was back among his buddies as one of the gang. At home he and Nga contentedly made thrifty vegan meals and attended Quaker Meetings.

But what about Iraq? His unit was bound to be deployed there sooner or later – probably sooner–and Hinzman definitely believed the invasion was illegal and immoral. When Fager asked what he might do about going, Jeremy was noncommittal. In truth, he preferred not to think about it. Fager didn't press the issue.

In any event, another case soon landed unexpectedly in his lap. In early September, the phone rang at Quaker House. On the line was a San Francisco attorney, Stephen Collier, calling about a Marine reservist named Stephen Funk. Seven months earlier, Funk had refused to join his unit when it was called up to join the Iraq invasion. Six weeks later, on April 1 2003, after making public antiwar statements, and drafting a CO petition, Funk turned himself in at the San Jose Marine Reserve station, accompanied by friends, family and media.

His CO petition was turned down, and after months of being restricted to the base, Funk was sent to New Orleans, where he was court martialed on charges of desertion and "unauthorized absence," another term for AWOL. "Desertion" is defined in part as leaving one's unit intending never to return. But since Funk had in fact returned voluntarily to his base, the charge didn't stick.

But he was convicted of "unauthorized absence," and sentenced to a Bad Conduct Discharge (only one step above Dishonorable) and six months in the brig. Compared to many other punishments for six weeks of "UA," as it is called, the sentence was draconian; but not surprising for one of the first soldiers to publicly defy orders to join the Iraq invasion.

All this was interesting as Stephen Collier explained it, but Fager wondered why the attorney was calling Quaker House, across the country from California and more than 800 miles from New Orleans.

The answer was simple: Funk was being taken to the brig at Camp Lejeune, on the Carolina coast to serve his time, and that had Collier worried. It was a continent removed from Funk's friends and supporters. Collier had heard reports of harsh treatment of other COs imprisoned there during the Gulf War. And Funk had also come out as being gay, which also added to the risks in the super-macho Marines atmosphere. Could Quaker House help?

You bet it could, he was assured. Within days Quaker House was recruiting Quakers and others to visit Funk in the brig, and appealing by broadcast emails for others to write letters and send cards.

This effort was a success: Funk had visitors on almost every weekend visiting day of his stay; and he received over a thousand cards and letters, from several foreign countries as well as the US.

The visits and cards had a dual purpose: on the one hand, they helped Funk keep his morale up; and on the other, they let brig officials know that outsiders were watching. "The Marines wanted to keep Stephen behind bars, isolated and forgotten," Fager reflected later. "They succeeded in the first; but they failed at all the others."

Funk did his time free of sexual or other harassment in the brig as well. In fact, he became popular with other inmates, especially after he led a team to the championship of an in-house cards tournament. He was released on February 4, 2004, and he returned to the West Coast. "I can't fault the brig staff," said Fager, who visited Funk numerous times himself. "They were hardly friendly, but they were professional."

While Funk was still in the brig, Fager's attention was distracted from global matters like war, defiant soldiers, and the possibility of a renewed draft to something much closer to home: the condition of Quaker House itself. On November 9, 2003 the heating system failed, as the temperature dropped into the low forties.

Although unwelcome, the failure was not entirely unexpected. The new Director was not a "handyperson" type, but he saw early on that the house was in need of attention. The roof leaked, dripping into the bathroom during rainstorms; several of the ancient light switches did not work. Bricks were loose around the foundation; the venerable front porch boards buckled, and the railing sagged. This much was apparent even to a relatively untutored eye.

For help, he turned to a Friend from Philadelphia, Sean Crane, who had extensive experience refurbishing old houses. While in North Carolina in January 2003 for a Friends peace conference at Guilford College, Crane undertook a thorough house inspection, which had yielded a 20-page report describing a host of problems and a long list of needed repairs and upgrades.

The Board received this report with some skepticism. The repairs called for would be costly; in previous years, most work on the house had been done by Directors and volunteers on an ad hoc, minimal expense basis.

Crane's response was that these decades of amateur work had left cumulative deficiencies, which were now putting the whole house at risk. He noted in particular that the heating system looked near to giving out, and that the obsolete electrical wiring, most of which was more than sixty years old, was becoming downright dangerous.

The heating

Why is resister Stephen Funk smiling? Because he's just been released from the Marines brig at Camp Lejeune, February 4, 2004.

150

system's failure was the first major confirmation of Crane's diagnosis. Replacing it proved a challenge, and took more than two months. The old system, it was discovered, had had a ten-year warranty; it failed at ten years and six months. He urged the Board to authorize installation of a high-efficiency replacement, with a 30-year warranty, as more economical over the long term. They agreed, and with an urgent appeal, donations came in to cover the cost.

The new system was set to go online January 30, 2004, one day before the Board was to convene there for a meeting. That week was quite cold for Fayetteville, and several electrical space heaters were turned on to keep the house habitable. Sean Crane was visiting with his son Joshua. At one point the evening before, Joshua stepped outside to smoke a cigarette. But as he lit up he smelled smoke, smoke that was definitely not tobacco, and it seemed to be coming from the house. He rushed back to alert the others.

Sean Crane pulled down the folding stairs, raced up to find the attic filling with smoke, and saw a fire smoldering in a far corner. Shouting for the others to call 911, he grabbed a fire extinguisher and doused the glowing spots.

Consultant Sean Crane, at left, gives the Board some HOMEwork – a guided tour of all the renovations needed on Quaker House, as of early 2004. In this view, the porch floor needs to be replaced; the brick and plaster need repair; and there was lots more.

A fire engine was there in minutes, and the flames, never large, were quickly snuffed out. But as calm descended again, Crane explained that they

151

had had a very close call. Another fifteen minutes and the woodframe roof and attic space would have been fully ablaze, and likely a total loss. (They learned later that the lumber in the house structure was a kind of pine that repelled termites [the good news] but which also [the bad news] burned fast and fiercely.)

By the time the Board gathered two days later, the organization's situation had changed markedly. In the wake of the fire engines city inspectors had appeared to examine the damage. They immediately discovered the amateur electrical system work, noted that it had been done without permits, was entirely out of code, and technically illegal. They could have shut the house down pending repairs, but didn't.

When Sean Crane gave the Board a guided tour, pointing out all the additional needed work, he was heard with considerably more respect than before. After all, two of his major predictions, the heater and the hazards of the ancient wiring, had been confirmed in spades. The Board authorized stopgap repairs, and began a long process of preparation for what would eventually become a complete house renovation project.

In late December, while the space heaters were still glowing, Jeremy Hinzman's unit got orders: it was to leave for Iraq in early January, 2004.

The time for procrastination thus came to an abrupt end. Was he going to go or not? It was almost Christmas when Jeremy joined Fager and another friend at a nearby fast food shop to talk about his convictions and his options. As far as they could tell, it came down to three: he could go to Iraq; he could refuse to go, and face court martial as Stephen Funk had done; or he could seek refuge somewhere outside the US.

"My personal preference would have been for him to stay and make a public resistance stand," Fager said afterward. "But it's not about my preferences, is it? It's Jeremy's conscience, and his butt on the line. We said we'd support him whatever his choice was. But I don't mind admitting I prayed he wouldn't get on that plane."

New Year's Day 2004 fell on Thursday, and Jeremy's unit was given a long 4-day weekend off. A day or two earlier, Jeremy stopped by Quaker House to say he and Nga had made a decision, and he'd be back later with more about it.

The more proved to be a carload of books, CDs, and baby toys. Jeremy and his family were quietly clearing out their apartment. Then sometime that weekend, they put young Liem into their car, and drove north and west to Niagara Falls, and then to Toronto. They were across the border, and at the doorstep of the Toronto Friends Meeting before anyone at Fort Bragg even knew they were gone.

Within a few weeks, Jeremy had surfaced in Canada to file an application for refugee status. He was the first US soldier to seek asylum from the war outside the country. The Toronto Quakers, experienced at sheltering refugees, took them in; Vietnam era draft exiles rallied round, and reporters lined up for interviews. Jeremy proved to be calm and articulate, and his young, lean visage was soon visible around the world.

Only the Canadian government was stinting in its reception. While it had officially disapproved of the US invasion of Iraq, this did not translate into open arms for anti-militarist emigres, as Jeremy and many others arriving soldiers would soon learn.

14. Brave Army Wives & The First Rally: "See You Soon Baby"

"January [2004] was our highest volume of calls in any month ever," the Quaker House counselors stated in their Hotline Report. Nationally, the GI Rights Hotline received a stunning 4271 calls in January; of that total, 819 came to Quaker House.

"Often in January calls are high because service members home on holiday exodus do not want to return to military life," the report added. "The high number of calls from people absent or considering absence offenses (69, the highest ever for this category) reflects similar feelings this January, and many soldiers we spoke with felt and expressed a similar reluctance to go back. We cannot say whether more people are having problems with the military than in other years but we do know that more of them are reaching the Hotline."

Besides heavy shifts on the Hotline, Quaker House was also preparing for the largest peace rally in Fayetteville since GIs United against the War in Vietnam filled the streets thirty-five years before. An ad hoc coalition was the official sponsor, and was working in the Triangle area to attract support, but most of the logistics work fell on locals.

Fager negotiated the permits for a march and rally with the local police. "They seemed paranoid about an invasion by 'anarchists,'" he recalled, "I guess with visions of the 1999 protests against the World Trade Organization in Seattle in their minds. But being old and white, I looked relatively harmless to them. I kept reassuring them that we meant to have a legal and peaceful gathering, which we did, and any visiting anarchists would be held to that discipline.

The rally was set for Rowan Park, the same place where Quaker House had helped organize the May 1970 rally at which Jane Fonda had spoken to several thousand – just a few days before the original house was firebombed. The police agreed to terms, but insisted on searching bags and backpacks as protesters entered the park. The planners didn't like this; but in the era of the PATRIOT Act, their best counsel was that a court challenge would likely be futile. (Other court challenges to random searches in trains stations and elsewhere, for instance, were rejected by courts.)

Was the police response too heavy-handed? By the day of the march, Fager wasn't so sure. A threatening email he received a couple days before gave pause. It was addressed to Lou Plummer, a veteran working with the planners:

154

Thursday March 18, 2004 at 10:26 AM
believe me Lou, when your buddies head back to Chapel Hill, you will be regretting you ever did this.

I have a lot of well laid plans ready to be executed. You will not have the cops on your side by the time the day is over. Watch out for groups splintering off the main group. Watch for fights within your group. Watch for your people throwing the first punch at a Freeper. And it will all be documented for court evidence. (The subtle instigation of the fights will be hidden and impossible to see and prove. But the criminal acts your people will engage in won't.

I am highly experienced at this. I will not be with the regular freepers. They don't even know I will be there. But when you see the mayhem and arrests of your people, YOU will know I WAS there.

See you soon baby.

The message of the peace rally in 2004 was clear – YES to the troops, NO to the War.

Beth Pratt, her husband deployed in Iraq, speaks at the March 20, 2004 peace rally in rowan park.

Fager passed the note on to the police, and fortunately nothing came of it. Yet as worried as the authorities may have been, many who came to "Fayettenam" that day from the quieter precincts of the Triangle were equally or more apprehensive. Again and again potential participants spoke of their fear of the city, with its reputation for crime and violence.

This gap in perception was a fine corroboration of the deepening cultural gap between Military America and Civilian America. As it happened, the rally was almost tediously well-behaved: no arrests, no attacks on participants – and no anarchist mobs rampaging through downtown, torching shops or breaking windows. Volunteers even cleaned up Rowan Park after it was over.

As was intended, this absence of procedural melodrama kept the focus on the rally itself. And there, haltingly, fitfully, one soldier and family at a time, a new GI peace movement was finding its voice and even its face.

The face of this nascent resistance was Beth Pratt, a nurse whose husband Luigi was deployed in Iraq even as she spoke. Beth Pratt had come to Quaker House some months earlier, seeking advice on whether and how her husband, who like her was against the war even as he followed orders to fight it, might find a way out of the Army. Fager talked with her over the intervening months, and finally asked if she would be willing to speak her convictions at the rally.

At first she said no, and he didn't prod. But as the date approached, Pratt came to feel that she should speak and could, if it was short and she could write her text out in advance. Here is most of what she said:

> I'm Beth Pratt, I'm a nurse and I grew up in Minnesota and came here from south Florida about a year ago with my husband, who's in the 82nd Airborne. . . .
>
> The army recruiter had told him that if he was trained to drive trucks, the army would send him off to Italy, which sounded exciting and even fun. Neither of us had dealt with the military recruiters before, so what did we know? He joined up to get a steady income and be able to go to college. Now of course, we know better. At least he did get to drive trucks -- he was sent to Iraq with his unit last September and he drives trucks there, so he's constantly in danger. At least one soldier in his platoon has been killed, and some others have been wounded. . . .
>
> This whole experience has been extremely difficult. This is our first year of marriage, and even tho we knew it would happen, it's hard to be apart so much, especially in this new place,
>
> If we're lucky he'll be back home next month, and then maybe I can relax. But not for long, probably -- he's been told that his unit will be sent back to Afghanistan soon, for a year. And then I'll get to go through this again, just like thousands of other Army and reservists' wives and family members. He's due to get out of the Army on October 23, 2006 -- that's a date I've had memorized ever since he signed up. But maybe he won't be done then -- now I know that they could put on a stop-loss order and keep him in indefinitely. What kind of a life is that? It's my life, unless we can get this war stopped. . . .
>
> If I believed in this war, maybe it would be easier to deal with this separation. But I don't. I felt from the very beginning that if there really were wmds like they said, we could have taken the time to look for them, and if we had, we might not be in this whole situation. And there are plenty of other bad dictators in the world, so why here? None of the terrorists from 9/11 came from Iraq anyway. And the racist expressions I've been hearing about people of Middle Eastern origins really upsets me – it's another way this war has done damage to our culture.
>
> I want to thank all of you who have come out here today, because it takes courage to speak up about these issues. It's taken all the courage I have to stand up here myself and speak for these few minutes. If you're of a different mindset around here, you can feel very isolated and alone. So a peace rally like this one where people can speak up has been a great source of support for me, and will hopefully be to others.
>
> And as far as supporting the troops, I support my husband one hundred per cent, along with the other people who are there making sacrifices. Ending this war and bringing them all home safely would

Bill Carothers at Quaker House, March 2004.

be the best form of support that I can see. Thank you.

(Luigi Pratt did return from Iraq without visible wounds, but had trouble putting up with the Army thereafter. He wound up being discharged in June 2005, almost eighteen months early. Once discharged, the Pratts were gone from Fayetteville within 48 hours, headed back to Florida and a new life.)

A group of several dozen pro-war-demonstrators were at Rowan Park that afternoon too, kept outside the perimeter by the ranks of police. "I see them as traitors," one told the *Fayetteville Observer*, pointing to the people at the peace rally. Another said, "It's a slap in the face to the people in the military to have this here."

The March 2004 rally was deemed a success: none of the visitors from out of town were hurt, and the police who surrounded the park mostly stood around with nothing to do but listen to the impassioned speeches. Media attention was also respectful, but much of it centered on the numbers game, competing estimates of turnout. Fager resolutely refused to play: asked several times by reporters how many he thought were there, he had smiled enigmatically, shrugged, and said, "I dunno – looks like at least fifty thousand to me." More seriously, he'd added only that the organizers were "very pleased" with the turnout.

An editorial in the *Fayetteville Observer* the day of the rally validated the work of distinguishing between "supporting the troops" versus the war. It tut-tutted that the rally, "invites a reasonable suspicion that the antiwar protest might more appropriately have been transported to 1600 Pennsylvania Ave...where those policies are crafted. "But," it crucially conceded, "it is possible to oppose a war without thinking ill of those who fight it." In propaganda terms, this was a big concession.

The rally was also an opportunity for the military town to glimpse a fledgling but vocal military antiwar movement. One veteran who visited the rally certainly recognized it for what it was. A heavy-set man with a mustache wearing a baseball cap and glasses came to Quaker House after the rally and introduced himself as Bill Carothers, the GI who had bought the house in 1970 before signing ownership over to Quaker House. It had been a long time since Carothers had been a member of GIs United Against the War in Vietnam at Fort Bragg, and then a co-director of Quaker House along with J.C. Honeycutt. He and Honeycutt had later married, produced a daughter, and then separated. He had worked as a skilled metalworker for many years since. Now disabled, he still took quiet pride in his handiwork of thirty-four years before.

If the rally had gone well in Fayetteville, that did not mean it sat well everywhere else in the state. One group which was not pleased took time to send Quaker House written notice of its displeasure:

A Letter to Quaker House

May 5, 2004

Please drop Edward Hill Friends Meeting from your mailing list. We do not agree with your organization, your radical activities, and are ashamed you call your organization "Quaker."

You are a disgrace to all the Quakers who died to win you freedom to disgrace their sacrifice for your freedom.

L. Allen Bullard, Pastor
Edward Hill Friends Meeting
Bonlee N.C.

A reply was quickly forthcoming:

Dear Edward Hill Friends,

Your note was received with regret, and your name has been removed from our mailing list. Something in the letter which puzzles me, however, is the statement that you are ashamed we call ourselves "Quaker."

Our work here is, as far as we can see, fully in harmony with the *Faith & Practice* of North Carolina Yearly Meeting (FUM), of which Edward Hill is listed as a member. In particular, we resonate to the declaration on page 47 that,

"Friends feel that nonparticipation in military training and war is the only action which follows the message and example of Jesus; therefore, nonparticipation is the only way to maintain full witness to Christ's way of love." On the same page it says that *"Statements against war have been issued by Friends during practically every military crisis since the earliest days of their history."*

Given that there are various ways to interpret this Quaker Christian faith and practice, please consider this letter a request to pay a visit to Edward Hill. I hope we can "reason together" to see how you view this 300-plus year, historic stance of Quakers in North Carolina, and if we can find a basis for mutual understanding in our walks of faith.

Sincerely,

Chuck Fager, Director

(Note: as of the end of 2008, no such invitation has been received.)

The 2004 peace rally began a series of anniversary protests that continued for three more years. As an immediate followup, Beth Pratt helped initiate an addition to the Market House peace vigils, in the form of a group of trifold signboards on which were hand-printed the names of all the US troops killed in Iraq to date. When it appeared in May, the first two boards were red, the rest green. On the two red boards were the names of those killed up until the time the nation was told, "Mission Accomplished" and it was all over. The ten additional green boards bore the names of those killed since.

During the next four years, the number of green boards steadily increased, until it reached over forty-five, and the collection stretched all the way around the Market House.

15. 2004, cont.: Peace Strategy: Time To Study War Some More

While the summer of 2004 saw many in the nation absorbed with an election campaign, Quaker House began a campaign of its own. Quietly at first, with a low-key interfaith peace seminar in June to mark its thirty-fifth anniversary, and then more visibly in August, Chuck Fager undertook to put flesh on the goal of adding a kind of "think tank" resource function to the Quaker House program, making its store of experience accessible for the larger peace constituency. He regarded this as potentially one of the major contributions Quaker House could make to its supportive constituency and to the larger communities beyond it. And the principal concern of this initial foray was strategy.

Months earlier, he had been invited to give the principal presentation at Illinois Yearly Meeting in early August. He was frequently invited to conduct workshops on Quaker House and peace work, but he took the Illinois talk as a special opportunity to give order to several lines of persistent questioning:

How could the peace movement get beyond its chronic (and usually justified) sense of frustration and failure? This sense of frustration only deepened as the Iraq war sank into quagmire status. There had been record-breaking marches and rallies against it; but they were an utter failure: the warmakers had been undeterred.

A related question was, why were peace "movements" so evanescent? For instance, why was Quaker House the only survivor among the dozens of Vietnam-era projects near military bases? And how many peace "coalitions" and "projects" had come and gone, in and through North Carolina and the rest of the country, since it began?

Further, was this impermanence related to the fixation so many peace activists displayed on Washington and its constant political machinations as the central theater of action? If so, what were the alternatives? Similarly, how helpful was their parallel preoccupation with news media and commentary, particularly the "prestige" outlets favored by the highly educated?

Closer to home, did these habits also have something to do with the recurrent bouts of uncertainty in the Quaker House Board over the project's value, its purpose and mission, which had likewise puzzled directors such as Bob Gosney, Greg Sommers and Sandy Sweitzer?

Was it possible to get beyond this persistent experience of impasse and drift? If so, how? And where could the intellectual resources to work through these questions be found?

Many of the questions were all too familiar. But to approach them Fager took an unusual turn: could it be, he asked, that something important could be learned about peace work from the military?

After all, there was no denying that an outfit like the 82nd Airborne Division was very good at what it did, even if its tools of organized violence were not what Quakers wanted to use. How did the 82nd become – and just as important, stay – such an excellent organization? Moreover, the 82nd's force was deployed in pursuit of larger goals. Who set those goals, and how, and on what basis?

The answers to this last question, he soon realized, were summed up in the word "strategy." So Fager began working to learn some basics about military strategy. The outcome, described below, he regarded as one of the central pieces of his work at Quaker House.

It seemed that US strategy was laid down in levels, like rungs on a ladder. At the top was "grand strategy," which is set forth in a fifty-page document, the "National Security Strategy of the United States," issued every four years from the office of the president, and available on the White House website. It dealt with overall worldwide goals and long-term plans to achieve them. Down the ladder were operational strategies, that is, plans to meet identifiable segments of the grand strategy, and further down, more specific levels which approached the intersection of strategy and tactics, which were the work of applying larger goals in concrete situations of conflict.

A few blocks from Quaker House in Fayetteville a public park preserved a historical example of how this ladder of strategy had played out, more than a century before:

In the US Civil War, it appears that Lincoln's "grand strategy" for defeating the Confederacy had three main parts: isolate and starve the rebel states by blockading the Atlantic coastal ports; then split them in two down the Mississippi River; and finally, break them down one piece at a time.

While wars never work out exactly according to such overall visions, this is more or less what happened. And a major operational piece of the third objective was carried out by Union General William T. Sherman, who "mopped up" by burning Atlanta and then sweeping destructively east through Georgia to Savannah. Anyone who has read or watched "Gone With The Wind" knows the outline of this bloody and fiery saga.

Once near Savannah and the Atlantic coast, however, where was Sherman to go next? In the event, he soon turned north, passing near where Dean Holland had died in his car crash, and continued to burn his way across South and then North Carolina. He was headed ultimately toward Petersburg, near Richmond, Virginia, the Confederate capital, to meet up with other Union forces.

Along the way he aimed at Fayetteville, which had a large arsenal. Built by the federal government but occupied by the Confederacy, it had been busily producing weapons all through the war. In early March Sherman captured Fayetteville, and over the next several days, his troops destroyed the arsenal. (They did a thorough job, too; all that remains today are parts of the thick stone foundation, in what is called Arsenal Park.) Sherman then moved on, and within a few weeks, the Confederate armies under Robert E. Lee surrendered.

No, Virginia, This Is Not Your Daddy's Sun Tzu . . . .

Deciding which way to turn after Savannah was a question of secondary operational strategy; and once in Fayetteville, destroying the captured arsenal became a matter of tactics: Blow it up? Burn it? Batter down the walls? All of the above?

This outline was very instructive. Fager also read through a volume called *Marine Corps Doctrinal Publication 1-1: Strategy,* which laid out various principles of the discipline. But perhaps the most fruitful text was the shortest, yet one of the most central texts in the strategists' canon. It was also the oldest, at least as ancient as the Bible – and treated like it in the field: *The Art of War,* by Sun Tzu.

Sun Tzu's condensed, no-nonsense insights are highly practical; yet like the Bible, readers are often advised not simply to read them but to *meditate* on them; and the master's sayings are quoted like proof texts in strategic debates.

A few of the slim work's precepts leaped out at Fager, and became the underlying basis for a strategic approach to peace work – what he came to call, reviving an early Quaker term, "The Hundred Year Lamb's War."

The gist of this approach, which has been laid out in more detail elsewhere, is a call for peace activists to change their tune and "study war some more," learning to adapt several principles of military strategy for their own ends, including, for a start:

> Learning to think long-term and "big picture." This would entail escaping the trap of short-term reactive thinking, driven by immersion in the world of mass media;
>
> Securing our base, which among other things would mean building more long-term projects similar to Quaker House, independent yet networked and cooperative; and
>
> Training, training, training! (This is what keeps the 82nd Airborne

in top shape – and rattles the windows on Hillside Avenue.)

Minding the "tooth-to-tail" ratio; as in war, peace work is complex, involving many kinds of skills and actions; there are many important roles to be filled behind the "front lines."

One early result of such "long-term-big picture" thinking, Fager contended, was a clarification of the nature of the "enemy": it is not really the soldiers, nor even the individuals momentarily in high positions in the Pentagon and Capitol Hill, on which the media focus. Rather, the real "enemy" is more a system, the "military industrial complex," which shaped and moved them all – and most of the rest of us, with pervasive, typically small nudges that we have been trained not to notice.

An additional step was a call for a searching, unsentimental examination of the strengths and weaknesses of both this militarist system, but more importantly, the peace constituencies themselves. Sun Tzu put this imperative with blunt brilliance:

> *If you know the enemy and know yourself, you need not fear the result of a hundred battles. If you know yourself but not the enemy, for every victory gained you will also suffer a defeat. If you know neither the enemy nor yourself, you will succumb in every battle.*

The military supports professional scholars and thinkers, Fager noted, who ransack the history of past wars for insights into how to win future ones. Yet while Quakers in the US, for instance, have been doing peace work for more than 300 years, very few of them (us) know even the rudiments of this long history: what worked, what didn't, and why? That is, we don't "know ourselves," never mind the "enemy." No wonder our track record is poor.

Sun Tzu also illuminated our tactical naivete:

> *You can be sure of succeeding in your attacks if you only attack weak points. You can ensure the safety of your defense if you only hold positions that cannot be attacked.*
>
> *Hence that general is skillful in attack whose adversary does not know what to defend; and he is skillful in defense whose adversary does not know what to attack. . . . Thus the highest form of generalship is to foil the enemy's plans . . . and the worst policy of all is to besiege walled cities.*
>
> *The rule is, not to besiege walled cities if it can possibly be avoided . . . .*

What walled city do peaceworkers constantly besiege? It's Washington, the center of the media-political universe. Yet to get anywhere there, one must command huge numbers, vast amounts of money, high officials, and/or mass media. But which of these do peace folks have? None of them consistently; and one, i.e., large numbers, only in the brief moments of large peace rallies, here today and gone tomorrow.

164

Thus we reverse Sun Tzu's dicta: constantly besieging their walled city, and doing so, moreover, from our weakest, not our strongest points.

Fager, who once worked on Capitol Hill, summed up the lesson thus: "If those who run that 'walled city' gave us any thought at all, which they hardly ever do, they would most likely say, 'Keep on doing what you're doing – because it's guaranteed to keep you weak and ineffectual.'"

What was the remedy? For Fager, it began with peace workers learning to think like warriors. To study our history, examine its high and low points; to analyze the adversary militarist system, in depth beyond the often misleading media snippets; and to discern its strengths and weaknesses, looking to match these up with our own.

As Sun Tzu said: *Carefully compare the opposing army with your own, so that you may know where strength is superabundant and where it is deficient. . . .*

Then to find the places and times where our strengths (and yes, we have many), can be applied to the system's weaknesses (and it has these too).

Sun Tzu repeated the point: *So in war, the way is to avoid what is strong and to strike at what is weak.*

And to do this on a long-term, not a short-term basis.

Such an approach would shake up the typical reactive, short-term, news-driven peace posture, which has groups stumbling from one demonstration to the next election and back again. This did not mean we should never protest, or vote; but rather, that we begin to put these and all other tactical decisions into a larger strategic context.

Developing a strategic context would mean that when, recalling our General Sherman example, we occupy our version of Fayetteville, and need to decide how to demolish that enemy arsenal – we can explain, or remember, why the arsenal needs to go, and for that matter, why we're in Fayetteville in the first place. And where we're headed from there.

Speaking of where we're headed, Fager suggested three points for an American Quaker pacifist "grand strategy."

First, to make the US a law-abiding member of the international community, respectful of human rights both within and outside its borders;

Second, to move the three large monotheistic religions, Christianity, Judaism and Islam, to a place where they conduct their rivalries without violence and terror; and finally,

Third, to make the Religious Society of Friends (or the larger peace constituency, if you will) a significant, ongoing player in the other two struggles. Many operations, endless creative tactics, and many years of labor, will be involved.

As Sun Tzu put this: *In battle, there are not more than two methods of attack - the direct and the indirect; yet these two in combination give rise to an endless series of maneuvers. The direct and the indirect lead on to each other in turn. It is like moving in a circle - you never come to an end. Who can exhaust the possibilities of their combination?*

This was the nub of the strategic outline for peace work Fager presented first to Illinois Yearly Meeting in July 2004. It was refined and presented to dozens of other groups over the next four years, under the heading of "The Hundred-Year Lamb's War."

As hard as Fager worked to develop and advocate for this schema, building on his experience and the proximity to Fort Bragg and the military machine, a rich vein of historical irony underlay it. Undoubtedly, if Carolina Quakers had gathered in 1969 and considered weightily where a long-term peace project could be most shrewdly located for maximum strategic impact, Fayetteville-Fort Bragg would surely have been high on the list of possible targets.

But of course, they did no such thing. Quaker House, in Friendly parlance, was an idea which "did not occur to Friends" in Chapel Hill, or anywhere else. They had to be prodded and pestered into starting it, by an outsider. Then, as earlier chapters have shown, the project often stumbled, unable to find or keep staff, scrambling to pay the bills, and with only an improvised agenda.

As conditions changed, the Board had no plan beyond an almost indefinable "peace testimony." They repeatedly questioned the value and wisdom of what they were doing in Fayetteville, and whether they should keep it up.

In short, the actual development of Quaker House was a prime example of almost the exact opposite of the kind of "long-term, big picture" thinking its latest Director was advocating.

Even so, the project had survived, and was busier than ever. The stress of the second year of war, with the surge of Hotline calls and peace work it had brought, made these cavils largely moot. Such highfalutin musings might be diverting; but there was work to do.

Too much work, it seemed; Fager's reports in the fall of 2004 included pleas to the Board for part-time office help, as he felt increasingly swamped by the combination of program work, plus administration. This latter was more clerical than managerial: donation income had experienced a large, welcome increase. But for each contribution, the single resident staffer had to open the envelope, process the check, send out a thank you note and receipt, then add it to a bank deposit.

When he arrived, there were around 200 of these transactions in a year. By 2004, the total was over 500. The growing mailing list also needed frequent updates; bills needed to be paid and house maintenance issues, both minor and major, to deal with; not to mention all the effort involved in attracting the flow of donations.

And all this was in addition to actual program work: a steady trickle of GI counseling cases which came directly to the house; planning peace protests and conferences; responding to a stream of media inquiries; visiting Friends Meetings and other groups for workshops and presentations; and writing not only newsletters, but also materials about recruiting, the threat of a return to conscription, and related issues in the rapidly-changing conditions of the war.

The Board took this appeal under advisement. It was another year before a regular office assistant, Susan Lees, was brought on to provide the much-needed help.

Speaking of conditions in the war, September brought a grim milestone: 1000 US casualties in Iraq, which were marked with another peace vigil, at which the number of signboards bearing their names had increased to fourteen.

And on September 23, the *Fayetteville Observer* sounded a loud echo of another persisting, little-noticed cost of the war: it reported on a study by the North Carolina Child Advocacy Center of homicidal abuse of children by parents in the state. Over the sixteen years of data surveyed, the incidence of such parental violence against children was steady across the state – except in two counties, where it was persistently twice as high.

The two counties were Cumberland, where Fort Bragg was located, and Onslow, home to Camp Lejeune. Professor Marcia Herman-Giddens of NC State University in Raleigh, who oversaw the study, said that the patterns between child abuse and the military are not a coincidence but "suggest problems in and around North Carolina military families and military communities." She called for a nationwide study of the incidence of such violence around military bases.

The report evoked a quick damage control response from Fort Bragg, with referrals to Pentagon spokesmen, praise for the family support programs at Fort Bragg, and platitudes about how the military is a "tough business." The report was kept to a three-day story, trailing off in quibbles about numbers and the prospect of little concrete change.

Another milestone was soon to be upon Quaker House, in that Fager's three-year term of employment would expire at the end of November 2004. Both he and the Board were ready to continue, and agreement was soon reached on another three year "hitch." There would be no lapse in staffing for Quaker House this time around.

And later that month came the first signs of the "Hundred Year Lamb's War" concept having impact. Four thousand miles from Fayetteville, in Fairbanks, Alaska, at the invitation of the Chena Ridge Friends Meeting, Fager laid out this strategic approach in detail. The response was enthusiastic, and helped give impetus to the founding of the Alaska Peace Center, a regionally-supported project along the lines suggested, which was still operating at the end of 2008.

Final figures for the GI Rights Hotline for 2004 showed that calls to this counseling network totaled 30,487. It was another new high, exceeding the 2003 total of 28,822 by 1665 calls. Quaker House counselors handled 5925 Hotline calls, or 19.4 per cent. This total was down from 2003, due mainly to Steve Woolford and Lenore Yarger taking family leave in late summer when their first child, Geneva Magdalena, was born on July 30. While they were offline, the Quaker House calls were re-routed to other network groups.

167

In the election of November 2004, the administration that started the war retained power, after a campaign that left many on the losing side convinced that chicanery and fraud had provided the margin. Progressive and antiwar forces fell into a deep slough of despond and confusion.

Quaker House had carefully stayed out of electoral politics, but its attitude was not much more upbeat. As the Newsletter put it,

> It feels a bit odd, but the fact is that none of our plans here at Quaker House have been much changed by the results of Nov. 2. We will still take our counseling calls, which are expected to keep growing; we are still planning local and regional peace actions; and we're still thinking about how to help put peace witness on a sound long-term, strategic basis.
>
> For that matter, on reflection it seems unlikely we would have made big changes had the voting turned out differently. It isn't that elections are meaningless or the choices irrelevant. Rather, it's our sense that most of the forces, institutions and persons who are driving the machinery of militarism were not on the ballot this year; they would have still been in place in any event. That's how pervasive and "non-partisan" militarism has become in our culture.
>
> One other thing that hasn't changed is our need for your continuing support–spiritual as well as material. Keep us in your prayers; and keep up your own efforts too. Red, blue, and the other rainbow colors, we're all in this together.

Quaker House and others in the local progressive network also had the calming benefit of a visit by a Quaker healer, John Calvi, who visited shortly after the election to lead workshops in deep relaxation. Calvi had had many years of experience in working with trauma victims, including victims of torture, serious crimes, and sexual battery.

But Calvi, it turned out, had more than relaxation on his mind. During the visit, he told Fager that he was, in Quaker terms, "under the weight" of a very deep concern about the US war machine's use of torture, not only in Iraq and the special US base at Guantanamo, Cuba, but at other sites. He felt Quakers needed to get involved in work to stop this torture program, and asked if Fager would join a group he hoped to form to start such work.

Like others, Fager had seen reports and pictures from the notorious Abu Ghraib prison in Iraq, where many prisoners had been abused and some killed. The abuse had come to light early in 2004, and investigation and prosecutions of mostly low-level Army personnel were still underway.

Fager said he was already very busy, but he would do what he could. Over the next several months, Fager talked with Calvi regularly about ideas for anti-torture work, in particular a plan for holding a Quaker conference on the issue, probably in 2006. He also began to educate himself about the issue.

At that point administration officials were still saying that abuses at

Abu Ghraib were the work of a "few bad apples." Persistent journalists were pursuing contradictions in these explanations, including leads suggesting that the torture had not been a lark or the work of a few deviates, but were based on orders from much higher up. And many of the trails these probes were following pointed them, not only toward Guantanamo and Abu Ghraib, but also in the direction of Fort Bragg and the surrounding region

Fager's tactical instincts were stirred when the Army announced that the court martial of Private Lynndie England, one of the most visible figures in the Abu Ghraib scandal, would take place at Ft. Bragg, probably early in 2005. Given how familiar the post was to mass media, such a trial would likely become a major public event, one around which antiwar and anti-torture protests could be planned. There were a lot of oppostunities there.

In December, however, England's trial was abruptly moved to Fort Hood, Texas, a much more isolated post, where protesters were unlikely to gather and press access was much easier to limit.

But the opportunity lost by this shift would soon be replaced with another that was in many ways better.

16. 2005: Action On All Fronts

Early in 2005, an umbrella peace group selected Fayetteville as the site for its "national" protest to mark the Iraq invasion's second anniversary.

While this could be considered recognition of the importance of Fort Bragg, and the ongoing peace witness of Quaker House and its allies, in fact it was neither. The group, United for Peace and Justice (UFPJ), was still reeling from the 2004 election defeat, and its coalition reflected the widespread state of depression and disorganization in antiwar circles. From all across the country, the reports were dismal: low turnout at antiwar actions, lower morale, little sense of what to do next, and no energy to do it.

Except in North Carolina, that is. At the UFPJ national assembly in St. Louis, a handful of Tarheel activists vigorously sang a different tune. Sure, they too were disheartened by the election results. But not paralyzed: in November they had settled on a plan for a major rally that March, a sequel to the 2004 gathering, in Fayetteville. They were already busy building for it – and y'all come. The assembly also saw Fager elected to the UFPJ Steering Committee, where he repeated the invitation.

As UFPJ surveyed its coalition, nobody seemed to have a real alternative. Thus Fayetteville got the nod as the official "national" protest destination for March 2005.

There was plenty of preparatory work to do, and Quaker House was in the thick of it: again negotiating with the police, obtaining the necessary permits, and fending off their attempts to prevent a march, and impose huge fees for police "services."

Meanwhile, Fager had two unique and revealing assignments in February 2005. One involved a surprising journey about twenty miles up US Highway 401, into Harnett County, just a few miles north of Cumberland County and Fayetteville. As part of Black History Month, Fager was invited to visit Harnett Central High School to speak to a student assembly about some of his experiences working under Dr. Martin Luther King Jr. In Selma, Alabama in 1965.

He didn't know much about Harnett County, except from driving through it that it was mainly rural, less than prosperous, and that cotton and tobacco still ripened there in the autumn, along with collard greens in the winter. But he had read that not so many years ago it had been a stronghold of the Ku Klux Klan, which had mounted fierce resistance to local school desegregation.

That dismal heritage was not visible as students filled the rows of seats: black, white and Hispanic all crowded into the auditorium, with no visible signs of tension or anything remarkable; just another day in integrated America.

This recruiting tractor trailer pulled up at a community college in Fayetteville in 2004. Inside were portable arcade booths, all geared to drawing in potential recruits, especially from young and minority populations. They did a good job too.

That was one surprise. The other was that, surveying the group, the visitor could see several adults in uniform among them. A quiet query to the principal disclosed that these were recruiters, there every day, who were also working as teachers and coaches. They were helping with slots that the financially-strapped school district had trouble keeping filled. And as a measure of their impact, to start the program a student color guard appeared, in full junior ROTC regalia, with dummy rifles and a large US and state flags. Everyone stood as these were marched onto the stage, to be saluted and hailed with the Pledge of Allegiance, before the speaker was introduced to tell his anecdotes.

Fager came away shaking his head. He had read about how pervasive military recruiting efforts were becoming, especially in less than affluent areas. Increasing casualties meant increased demand for new recruits, and the military was massively pursuing new cannon fodder. As the Quaker House Newsletter noted in late 2004:

> How big a force is military recruiting in our culture? The short answer: huge. The longer answer is in a report by the Government Accountability Office: "By fiscal year 2003, DOD's total recruiting budget was approaching $4 billion annually. . . . DOD's total advertising funding increased 98 per cent in constant dollars from

fiscal year 1998 through fiscal year 2003–from $299 million to $592 million. The advertising cost per enlisted recruit has nearly tripled and is now almost $1,900."

Here it was, laid out right before his eyes, in a completely matter-of-fact style. But this was more than charts and tables in a government report: the integration of recruiters into the life of these students was something to reflect on. They were respected by the students; many saw them as role models; many had family members who wore similar uniforms. And the recruiters also showed what large numbers of students could only see as a way up and out of their depressed area, in a state from which industrial jobs had been fleeing by the hundreds of thousands all through their youth.

This setting made Fager increasingly doubtful about the "counter-recruiting" label he and other activists had been putting on their uphill efforts to roll back this tide. Repeatedly, he had seen and heard this campaign target recruiters themselves, and he had sometimes done so himself. Others had taken the idea farther: just weeks before, on January 20, 2005, inauguration day, a group of anti-administration protesters at a Seattle community college surrounded a group of recruiters, snatched and ripped up their literature and heckled them til they were escorted off the campus by security.

Fager had since been on conference calls with student radicals from Seattle and heard them crowing about their great victory in chasing the recruiters away. But particularly after visiting the Harnett County school, he felt increasingly uneasy with that kind of targeting. It seemed too reflective of the military-civilian divide, which he saw overlapping with parallel cleavages of class and ethnicity: activists with more opportunities, and less contact with soldiers or sailors, sneering at those less "advantaged."

This was troubling. If "counter-recruiting" was a problem, what was the alternative? The phrase, he noted ruefully, was all over the Quaker House website, and in its printed materials. This needed attention, but no resolution came into view right away.

While mulling over this and other action items, Fager was also making frequent visits to Camp Lejeune, to counsel Marines who had made CO applications. One of them, Joel Klimkewicz, was already in the brig, serving several months for refusing to obey orders to attend weapons training.

He was a convert to the Seventh Day Adventist church, which in its early years had had something of a "peace testimony," under which members were advised to avoid war and military service. If they did don a uniform, they were urged to find a non-combatant role, in keeping with the church's understanding of Jesus' teachings about being peacemakers and turning the other cheek to evil.

By the time of the Vietnam War, the church had effectively abandoned this policy under pressure from members who were nationalistic-minded veterans. Nevertheless, it remained in their teachings as an acceptable option; and Klimkewicz found it persuasive. He applied for non-combatant

172

conscientious objector status. Then, as he told an interviewer later:

> After 18 months I was denied status and ordered to take my weapon to kill human life. Obviously, I had to follow my conscience and told my commander that I respectfully could not obey. I even explained that I would be willing to do any combat oriented task without a weapon, such as clear landmines, a job I was trained to do. Clearing landmines generally does not require a weapon due to the danger of it falling on a mine or setting one off magnetically. My higher ups yelled at me and threatened different things, but I felt that the judgment that God would give me would be worse than what the military could give.

Marine CO Joel Klimkewicz and his family, shortly after he was released from the brig, April 2005.

Klimkewicz's case highlighted the 'Catch-22" situation many CO applicants found themselves forced into. If he followed the weapons order, higher-ups could then say, "See, you were only kidding about this CO business." But to refuse was a violation of military law. He respectfully declined the order, an infraction which usually merited no more than a fine or a demotion. Instead, he was sent to a full court martial, and was slapped with a lengthy sentence and a Bad Conduct Discharge, an outcome usually reserved for violent felons. After his conviction, the guards literally ripped his uniform off, a humiliating symbol of utter disgrace in military culture.

In the brig, however, his local church members turned out in sizeable numbers, along with his wife and young daughter, for visiting hours on Saturday, his church's sabbath.

Besides arranging additional visits, Quaker House again asked for letters, not only to him, but to officials at Marine headquarters in Quantico,

Virginia as well, appealing for clemency. Church officials also worked on his behalf, and he was finally released in April, two months early. In 2006, he won an upgrade of his discharge to General, "under honorable conditions," a substantial vindication.

Klimkewicz was both atypical and typical of the Iraq "GI Resistance." He was not involved in any of the self-designated "resistance" groups. He even disclaimed the term "pacifist" for the simpler label of "Christian." His primary identification was with his church and family; he was much more interested in the books of Daniel and Revelation than in tomes by Chomsky or other leftists, or joining politically-oriented activist groups.

Likewise, most of the other soldiers who came to public notice for refusing service in the Iraq War were similarly motivated by individual moral or religious concerns. Whatever connections they made with activist groups in the course of their witness, they mainly wanted to get on with their lives.

In an October 2008 blog interview, Klimkewicz, then studying for the Adventist ministry, added a telling postscript to his story:

> A few weeks ago a high ranking leader from my former command gave me a late night unexpected phone call. He wanted to apologize for standing against me and explained that he wishes he had made the same choice. He now suffers from Post Traumatic Stress Disorder as a result of the things he saw and did in combat. He is looking for a way to rid himself of that guilt and looking to the Lord for that peace.
>
> To this an old Japanese Proverb with profound truth applies, "Kokai saki ni tatasu." Simply stated, "Regret is in the past not in the future." The choices we make today determine our future, hence the reason to submit your choices to the approval of God (Prov. 16:9).

During his visits to Camp Lejeune, Fager became quite taken with a custom unknown at Fort Bragg: when Marine units returned to Lejeune, families were encouraged to make "welcome home" banners for them, mainly on sheets, which were hung on fences along NC Highway 24, which the troops passed by as they returned to the base. Thereafter, the sheets often hung on the chain-link wires for weeks, til wind and weather brought them down.

Many of the banners voiced colorful but straightforward messages of greeting: "Welcome Home Sgt. Smith, We Missed You." But other vivid outliers expressed more insistent and often poignant sentiments: "Yay! We Can Finally Get Hitched!" "Welcome Home from Iraq - *Again,* Sgt. Belinski." "You And Me Against The World. I ❤U Corporal George!" "Sgt. Vinnie - Ya Big Stud - Come Home to Momma." And even racier endearments.

Frequent changes were rung on the long-running series of MasterCard credit card commercials:
"Packages Sent - 20; Nights Spent Alone - 210; Tears cried - TONS; 2 weeks

w/cpl Ham - PRICELESS". Or: "Months Gone - 7; Months Pregnant - 9 ½; Hours of Labor - 18; Healthy Baby Girl - 1; Lilly Finally Meeting Daddy - PRICELESS."

Banners at Camp Lejeune . . .

And some were simply stunning, like the one quoting Psalm 144: "'Blessed Be the Lord My Rock, Who Trained My Hands for War and My Fingers to Fight' – Welcome Home Capt. Anzevino." Or: "I'd Give Up Forever, But It's Been Long Enough, Lcpl Jeffy." Marines from Lejeune have paid a heavy price in dead and wounded in Iraq, underlining the relief each of these flapping homemade billboards made visible.

Other vivid events that season were not so esthetically pleasing. As the war ground on, it took a toll that included many more than the names of the dead on the red and green display boards.

In February, there was another soldier shooting

. . . speaking of what credit cards can't buy.

involving Fort Bragg, which left one dead, two wounded. On February 3, Specialist Richard Corcoran shot his estranged wife Michelle, and another soldier whom he found with her, then killed himself. Corcoran and the other soldier were members of Special Forces units at the post, and Corcoran had served a tour in Afghanistan. Both the other victims survived. The Corcorans' seven-month old daughter was in the house at the time, but was unhurt.

Was such a crime war-related? No. And yes. And what could be done about the growing number of similar cases? This was another set of questions which had no answers, and was not even on the Quaker House program agenda – but which refused to go away.

At least there was more welcome in coming home to Quaker House in early 2005. For most of a year, Fager had been dating Wendy Michener, a recent midlife architecture grad and Quaker from Raleigh by way of Oregon. In January 2005 she moved into the house on Hillside, and was soon looking for work at local firms.

Fager was worried about where she would find a job in her field there. A few months later, however, Michener submitted her portfolio to the LSV Partnership, a local firm. At the interview, the lead architect looked up from her resume, eyebrows raised, and commented, "You live at 223 Hillside? That's Quaker House."

Some in this military town might have been nervous to admit such a pacifist connection, but she did. The interviewer, architect Walter Vick, then said, "I met my wife Peggy there." That had been thirty years earlier, at one of the community potlucks overseen by the Wenbergs, where the younger Vick was known for bringing ice cream. After a long talk, Vick hired her. What goes around comes around.

One of the first tasks Michener helped Fager with at Quaker House was intense preparations for a TV interview on the "O'Reilly Factor," a popular right-wing program hosted by Bill O'Reilly, one of the more vocal conservative pundits on Fox News, an overtly right-wing network. O'Reilly's producer had called asking if Fager would agree to come on the show to talk about the situation of GI exile Jeremy Hinzman, whose application for refugee status in Canada was expected to be acted on soon.

At first Fager was dubious about the offer. For one thing, O'Reilly had been vitriolic in his denunciations of Hinzman as a deserter, who deserved only to be sent back to Fort Bragg in manacles, to face prison. For another, O'Reilly was well-known for being macho, manipulative and unfair with guests, talking over and shouting them down. He seemed especially to like having genteel liberals on, especially academics used to being in charge of compliant classrooms, and then mopping the floor with them rhetorically.

So the playing field would not be level. But Fager admitted to Michener and others that he too had his macho fantasies, and one of them was of going toe to toe with a media bully like O'Reilly and coming out in one piece. And here was his chance. He accepted.

But if he was going to step into the ring, he had better prepare. He found resources through the web, and some email contacts, about the basics of such media combat. Major points: always call O'Reilly "sir"; the word was a weapon in such conflicts. And learn how to interrupt and talk over him, as he would interrupt and talk over a guest. Then, very important: fix on a few short talking points that summed up your message and repeat them at every opportunity, whether they were responsive to a question or not.

For several days, Fager worked on these combative techniques, and settled on two talking points: first, standing up for Hinzman's integrity and courage, and second, calling the Iraq war "immoral and un-Christian."

On the day of the interview, February 23, Fox sent a long limousine to pick Fager up. Unfortunately for the driver, Hillside Avenue is a dead-end street, and the vehicle had to come down it in reverse, robbing the scene of its air of momentary opulence. And as was true for most of the guests, Fager was not to be physically in O'Reilly's presence, but in a remote hookup from a studio in Raleigh.

Fager had to sit in a chair on a small dais, in front of a shelf of fake book covers, for more than half an hour, staring into the beady black eye of a TV camera, sweating under the kleig lights and listening through an earphone while O'Reilly berated other guests.

After all the buildup, the interview was very short, less than four minutes in all. Yet Fager managed to get in his talking points, interrupting O'Reilly's effort to paint Hinzman as a coward and a traitor, and repeating the "immoral and un-Christian war" mantra four times.

On reflection, the brevity of the exchange seemed telling. O'Reilly's producer had evidently done some background research at the last minute, and had second thoughts. Of course, the Quaker was a rank amateur up against O'Reilly's practiced media streetfighting skills. But neither was he a cosseted professor, or a green young radical – not the pushover he was expected to be, so the host got him off quickly, to turn to an easier target.

Fager rode the limo back to Fayetteville feeling he had come through the encounter in reasonable shape. The *Fayetteville Observer* reported on the joust, and observed that, "Fager held his own against the fast-talking, sharp-tongued O'Reilly . . . ." And emails were waiting to back him up, including one with a startling revelation: on the O'Reilly show's webpage, the advance headline for the segment had read, "Then, a Quaker institution in North Carolina is helping US soldiers desert... We'll have a report."

The headline included a double falsehood: first, Quaker House did not help soldiers desert; it gave information, and helped soldiers clarify and follow their conscience. And second, despite the teaser headline, O'Reilly made no such allegation in the interview, not even indirectly. In fact, he acknowledged that, "Quakers historically are pacifist and don't like war. And we understand that, everybody understands that, and I think it's respected."

Not by everybody, though; hate mail also came in. One voice mail message called Fager a "fat ineffective dumbass." An email said, "You guys are idiots. Stay out of the military."

Unfortunately, all this talk did little for Hinzman, whose application for refugee status was rejected in March by a Canadian immigration official. The decision was announced on the same day that the Canadian Prime Minister visited with the US president at the latter's Crawford, Texas ranch. This was certainly a setback, but Hinzman planned a series of appeals, all the way to Canada's Supreme court if necessary, and these could take years. And meantime, the war he had refused to join passed its second anniversary, and protests against it were renewed, especially in Fayetteville.

Many middle class antiwar activists across the country preferred to keep their protests abstract, about policies and high officials in Washington, largely ignoring actual soldiers and their families. But on March 19, 2005, many stepped outside their comfort zone. And when they did, they landed

Symbolic coffins carried in the March 2005 peace rally. Longtime Quaker House supporter and Board member Bill Jeffries is at left center.

right in downtown Fayetteville.

The sky over the city on Saturday, March 19, 2005 was a somber grey. That morning, among a large crowd, a hundred people carrying empty cardboard coffins draped with American flags slowly wound their way from the parking lot behind the county health department, a half mile to Rowan Park. The number of mock coffins in the procession did not nearly approach the number of US war casualties, but they were a silently vivid reminder of some of the costs of two years of fighting in Iraq.

Jean Chapman, a North Carolina resident, carried one of the coffins that morning. "The moment I picked one up it became so real," she said. "To me it's very solemn. This is what it's about...broken bodies, dead children, families devastated. When all the rhetoric is gone, it comes down to death and destruction."

Ahead of the coffins, thousands of people sang, chanted and played drums—each with their own way of bearing witness to loved ones serving abroad, soldiers who never came back from the war, and to a God that heals nations without destroying them. Huge white doves perched atop tall poles operated by puppeteers hovered above the crowd along with peace signs adorned with colorful tissue paper. Even a group of anarchists from Greensboro was on hand, dressed in ragtag motley.

But this tendency, the source of so much anxiety among the hundreds of police and deputies surrounding the park, turned out to be an anti-authoritarian drum corps, called Cakalak Thunder, and making use of such impromptu percussion instruments as empty five-gallon plastic water jugs, and – counterintuitively, given their politics – playing in tight, disciplined rhythms. They were a hit of the march.

Contingents of Veterans for Peace and the newly-formed Iraq Veterans Against the War (IVAW) marched together at the head of the column. Among them was Stephen Funk, who flew in from California to join in. The front rank carried a banner that said, "Honor the Warriors, Not the War," and doing their own versions of the military sound-off chants in their deep voices:

> *Tell 'em what we're marchin' for*
> *Peace and justice no more war!*
> *Am I right or wrong? You're right!*
> *Sound off...*

Police officers from across the state and South Carolina gathered at the entrance to Rowan Park where they searched people and their bags with metal detectors. The time consuming process and huge crowd brought marchers to a halt long before they reached the park.

While police officers estimated 2,500 protesters attended the rally, which went on for much of the afternoon, organizers thought the turnout was closer to 4,800. Compared to the millions who marched in early 2003, these were paltry numbers. But they were the best the movement could do at that point, and it was undoubtedly the largest peace rally in this military city's history.

"People say out-of-towners are descending on Fayetteville," said Kara Hollingsworth, a Fayetteville resident whose husband was serving his second combat tour in Iraq. "I'm one of those military families, and I invited these people to come here."

Many of the groups supporting the protest were unused to being in a small, southern town saturated with military culture. Therefore, the national groups abandoned their more comfortable position at the forefront of the show, to allow organizations of veterans and military families to dominate the stage and present the message of support for the troops loud and clear. The organizing committee even had a hospitality committee ready to welcome the arriving out-of-towners to the South.

The focus of the day's events was the band shell stage at the center of Rowan Park. One of the speakers who stepped to the kicrophone was a mom named Cindy Sheehan. Her son Casey was killed in April 2003, shortly after being deployed to Iraq. In a few months, Sheehan was to attract global media attention when she camped out in a tent near the President's Texas ranch to voice her opposition to the war.

Her voice trembled as she told the crowd in Rowan Park, "Today is the second anniversary of the so-called 'shock and awe.' Today is also the first anniversary of when my son's deployment began in Iraq." Sheehan set a serious, emotional tone for the event—for many peace protesters who are also military families, this is about life and death.

Kelly Dougherty, one of the founders of IVAW, took the stage in a camouflage Army jacket with unit patches on the shoulders. She spoke candidly about how she and her military company protected wasteful construction projects run by American companies while all around them Iraqi people suffered from escalating violence and a lack of security. Back at home, she said, the media and the government were telling people that US troops were there to promote liberty and freedom.

"The occupation is the problem, it is not the solution," she said.

In the open spaces beneath the tall pine trees in Rowan Park, the mock coffins were displayed in mutely eloquent tricolor ranks, across the grass from a colorfully varied assortment of umbrellas, part of the Peace Parasols project. Vendors selling buttons and bumper stickers, veterans groups, advocacy groups as well as politicians were set up in tents like a street fair in one corner of the park.

Hollingsworth, of Fayetteville, tried to put the crowd in the shoes of a soldier returning to America from Iraq. "You went to Iraq to find the weapons they said could reach the shores of your nation where your children sleep only to find they never existed. And you come home frustrated, to tell your story to a nation who tells you, 'you volunteered, so stop whining,'" she said.

"I can't remain silent on these issues, slap a yellow ribbon on my car and call it supporting my troops," she concluded to a big round of applause.

Pro-war counter-protesters were again assembled across the street from Rowan Park, with a line of police keeping them at a distance. There were at most 200, from groups such as Free Republic and Rolling Thunder. They dubbed their stretch of grass the "American Zone." Their jeers and heckling, including shouts of "Swim to Cuba!" provided a sometimes intrusive counterpoint while the soldiers and military family members on the stage across the street gave their impassioned testimonies.

The counter-demonstrators doubted that anyone on the other side of the street supported the troops and claimed that the peace protesters were merely nostalgic for the 1960's. Ed Fisher, of Fayetteville, was among them. His wife was deployed to Iraq with the 1st Corps Support Command. "I am here to support the troops," Fisher said.

Scott Kerr, of Greensboro, North Carolina was also among the counter-demonstrators. He held a sign that said "Stop Global Whining." Although he conceded that the people in the park had a right to voice their opposition to the war, "It's disheartening that they would go to a military base," he said. "It is totally disrespectful to the people who have their necks out there right now."

Other Views, Peace Rally March 2005.

Although Lou Plummer was in a position to argue against those who say that vocal opposition to the war has no place in an Army town, he was with the protesters in the park. A veteran and a resident of Fayetteville with a son in the Navy, he explained that the US government failed to plan for what had happened in Iraq since the invasion and "that lack of planning affects our communities more so than most."

"Why pick a military town as the site for an antiwar rally?" asked Plummer, co-founder of Fayetteville Peace with Justice. "As a veteran and a resident of Fayetteville, NC... I can think of at least 50 reasons. Each of those reasons has a name and each were members of our community prior to their deaths in Iraq."

Debbie Liebers was another person accustomed to raising her voice against war in Fayetteville. She moved there in the late 1960's and got involved with the anti-Vietnam protesters. Once something of a hippy and a stalwart in the local progressive community, she had taken acid on Fort Bragg and been friendly to many soldiers back from Vietnam. In May of 1970 she had accompanied Jane Fonda to Rowan Park where thousands of GIs and supporters had gathered for an antiwar rally.

In 2005 Liebers was a respectable grandmother, churchgoer, and "Yellow Dog Democrat," with a special devotion to Hillary Clinton. But she was also a regular at the Market House peace vigils. Surveying the crowd at Rowan Park, she noted that unlike the earlier generation of peace protests, when the activists were united by age and a common lifestyle, Liebers said she was struck by the diversity of people gathered at Rowan Park in 2005. "The people looked so much more ordinary than we did back in the 60's," she remembered. "They were just ordinary people, could be a doctor or a banker."

The presence of so many from the national antiwar community, including peace commandos like Code Pink, brought out liberal media groups like Democracy Now and Pacifica Radio, both of which broadcast live from Fayetteville that day, gave many local activists, including Liebers, a sense of vindication. After the letdown of the election, it was also a sign of hope for renewed energy for work to end the war, and tackle the militarism that made it possible.

17. 2005, cont.: Hello, America: Here Is Your War

The national character of the 2005 Fayetteville rally was not merely rhetorical. Besides the rally, meetings were held at local hotels for Military Families Speak Out, IVAW, and Veterans for Peace. It was the city's moment in the protest spotlight.

The 2005 rally was also a success for Quaker House and the peace constituency of North Carolina. When letters to the editor of the *Observer* called it an insult to the troops and a waste of the taxpayer money spent on the heavy police presence, Fager argued forcefully that to the contrary, it was an asset to the city.

In an OpEd for the *Observer,* he urged readers to,

"... Consider a bit of background:

Since early 2002, when I moved here, the city has mounted several elaborate and expensive projects aimed at revamping the local image, trying to banish the gloomy specter of "Fayette-nam."

But these efforts have not succeeded very well. Perhaps the most spectacular fiasco was the big-ticket makeover program of spring 2002, which was just about to roll out when – well, when the city was hit with a barrage of national publicity of a very different and painful sort. Other efforts have resulted in disappointing crowds, unpaid bills, and pleas for bailouts.

Now consider the peace rally in this light. Not only did it bring in as much, or more, spending than it might have cost, but more important, it brought scads of media to town as well, international as well as national and regional press. And these reporters and cameras dutifully spread the news of what they saw and heard here.

And what was that? Here's a clue: it was 99-plus percent positive. A peaceful, colorful march and rally, respectful of the troops in a military town, gathered in a lovely park, watched by police who were professional and courteous.

In the home of Fort Bragg, the world saw freedom being exercised, and not only defended.

Checking Google a few days later, I found 290 news articles listed about the Fayetteville rally, reports in papers from the *Washington Post* to Japan.

What project or event in recent memory has brought Fayetteville 290 favorable reports in the world press? And how much is that kind of good press worth? My guess: a bundle.

Sure – a peace march and rally might not be quite what city boosters had in mind when planning and yearning for a municipal image makeover. But surprise! It was the peaceniks who got the job done.

There may be similar peace marches in Fayetteville's future. As they come, I hope fans of the city could regard them not as a burdensome intrusion, but as an asset, because that's what they really are.

Fayetteville: *Where freedom is exercised, and not only defended.*

It kind of has a ring to it, don't you think?

In May, there was another murder/suicide. "Slain soldier just returned from Iraq," was the headline buried inside the May 23 *Observer*:

> A woman who was shot to death in an apparent murder-suicide Saturday was a Fort Bragg soldier who had returned from Iraq just hours earlier, a Fayetteville police official said.
>
> The 29-year-old woman was in Headquarters and Headquarters Company, 327th Signal Battalion of the 35th Signal Brigade, said Tom Bergamine, an assistant police chief.
>
> The identities of the woman and her husband, who lived at Cambridge Arms Apartments off McPherson Church Road, had not been released Sunday. . . .
>
> "From what we've been able to find out, (the husband) picked her up about 12:50 p.m. yesterday," Bergamine said.
>
> Neighbors told police the two, who were having marital problems, argued that afternoon, Bergamine said.
>
> One neighbor heard two gunshots, Bergamine said, followed by another shot later.
>
> Police were headed to the apartment for a "well-being check," Bergamine said, when the man called emergency dispatchers at 4:18 p.m.
>
> "He said he had killed his wife, to send the police and said he wouldn't be alive when police got there," Bergamine said.
>
> Officers found the couple's bodies in the living room with a 12-gauge shotgun nearby, he said. The woman had been shot twice, he said.

The next day the names were released: James and Ronna Valentine.

> Jamie Smith, spokeswoman for the Fayetteville Police Department, said investigators have not determined a motive for the shootings.
>
> A large plank of plywood was propped against the couple's front door Monday.

A neighbor said mostly military families live in the area.

This continuing string of fatal incidents was the bloody tip of a very large iceberg of stress and distress. This pain was voiced every day in calls to the GI Hotline. "The war on terror has kept us busy," said Hotline counselor Steve Woolford. On average he estimated that call volume had tripled since he and Lenore Yarger began.

"When we started, there were months when we didn't even get a hundred calls, whereas last year we were averaging 200 a month." There were many more calls where people simply hung up or left messages but didn't respond when Steve called back. That spring calls came from soldiers at 25 different bases, National Guard units in ten different states and overseas stations in Kuwait, Qatar, Iraq, Germany and Korea.

By 2007, more calls had come in to Quaker House by the end of May (4320) than in the entire year of 2001 (3128). The increase in calls was despite the fact that many more agencies were answering calls on the Hotline than in 2000, when the couple started. Then there were only seven or eight groups, and by 2005 there were over twenty.

Lenore Yarger said that the most difficult cases for her were the ones involving a soldier with post traumatic stress disorder (PTSD), a problem that was fast becoming the hallmark of the Iraq conflict. Returning soldiers with PTSD called the Hotline looking for help in getting the support and medical care they were entitled to, but quite often had to fight for. "Someone with PTSD is so weakened by what they've been through that they are afraid to challenge the military, and we can't do that for them," Lenore said sadly. "Those are painful cases."

Polly Coe, a Quaker therapist and social worker whose practice was located near Ft. Campbell, Kentucky, home of the 101st Airborne Division, a large Army base, reported for the Newsletter in early 2005: "Many soldiers I've seen have PTSD symptoms due to the inhuman things they had to do in this war." One was forced by his superior officer to run over a woman and child trying to stop a convoy on a road where many convoys were attacked. Another shot into a crowd that contained women and children and saw children die. These things haunted them, gave them nightmares, flashbacks, disturbed sleep and hypervigilance. Ultimately, the violence of war fed back into violence at home.

Fager agreed. While he took only occasional counseling calls, he also dealt with the occasional walk-in case at Quaker House. Perhaps his most agonizing counseling sessions in 2005 were with a GI from Fort Bragg who had already been to Iraq twice, and had orders for a third tour:

"He was clearly suffering from an intense case of PTSD," Fager reported, "and at the second session, just a few days before he was due to leave, his wife came along. She announced that if he returned to Iraq she would move out and undertake to "meet new people" once he was gone.

185

I haven't heard from him since, and I think that means he got on the plane for Iraq.

For Steve Woolford too, trying to help strangers with such difficult problems could be emotionally draining. "I've had many calls when I've got off the phone in tears," he said. When that happened, he prayed for a quiet moment. But more often than not, thirty seconds later the phone rang again. "It's a roller coaster," he sighed.

But he added, "I've been grateful for the opportunity to work with people in the military, to know what they experience. We feel it is really a gift to us to be able to do this work."

In May 2005, Fager took a counseling call that stuck in his memory. It came from a soldier at Fort Bragg who didn't want to give his full name. "Freddy," had recently returned from a tour in Iraq, and wanted to know if he was crazy.

In Iraq, he had been a tactical interrogator. That meant he interviewed detainees right after they had been taken into custody, before they were sent on to detention camps like, and including, Abu Ghraib.

What he learned from these interviews was that in ninety per cent or more of the cases, there was no reason to hold the detainees– they had simply been in the wrong place at the wrong time. He said this to his superiors frequently; the response was, in effect, shut up and just do your job. He'd seen other things too, needless death and destruction.

When he came back, "Freddy" was expected to train other GIs to be tactical interrogators, and he'd likely be headed back to Iraq with them before long.

But that was a problem for "Freddy. He didn't think any of it was right. Not anymore. As he put it later:

> But going into Iraq–it was a reality shock. For 21 years, thought my country stood for these values, but then to see it firsthand, made my whole foundation crumble – what in the world? What am I supporting with my actions? For the last 21 years, what I've been holding onto, it's not the reality. We don't like to go deep and really look– because it shatters our whole values, what we stand for. We're satisfied to stay at the surface.
>
> Almost like a religious experience. Wasn't reading books, just exposed to this stuff. Can't take credit, it was just stuff that happened to me.
>
> But it does change every fiber of your being.

So far, so good, Fager told him; I'm not a therapist, but you don't sound crazy to me.

Another important part of this was that "Freddy" was a Christian, of a pretty conservative "born again" variety. And he couldn't reconcile what he'd seen with what he understood of Jesus' teachings. He asked a chaplain about this, but the guy didn't take him or his doubts seriously. Instead, he told "Freddy" that if he really wanted out of the service, he should just tell his superiors he was gay.

"Freddy" found that insulting. He didn't really want "out." He wanted to do what was right, what was God's will.

You're not a heretic for asking these questions, Fager told him. Jesus challenged authority too. The fact that Jesus got in trouble for it doesn't mean he was wrong.

But, "Freddy" asked, was there any other option?

This was tricky. GI Hotline counselors are trained not to tell people what to do. So Fager parried with a question: What do you think you ought to do?

"Freddy" didn't know. He couldn't really see himself going back to Iraq. But he was no deserter.

What about applying for Conscientious Objector status? Fager suggested. "Freddy" didn't know much about that, so Fager went over the concept and the procedures.

"Freddy" was interested, but he wasn't sure. Fager didn't press him, except to repeat his reassurances that no, "Freddy," it doesn't sound crazy —or un-christian – to ask the questions you're asking.

It was a long conversation and a disturbing one. "I don't have these kinds of probing discussions about moral and religious issues very often," Fager told a reporter later. Its unfinished character was particularly troublesome. What would happen to a young man of conscience like that? How could Quaker House be of any more assistance to him? Fager didn't even know his name.

But in contrast to many such unfinished contacts, this one had a second chapter. In late June, Fager received an email, and recognized it as from "Freddy." It, and *his response*, said in part:

> *Freddy-- Thanks for getting back in touch; I've been wondering and worrying about you.*

> « Chuck, thank you for the info on my situation. It was really encouraging to talk with you as well. I know that I'm not alone and some crazy person with these feelings and ideas.»

> *Definitely not, on either score: you're not crazy, and you're not alone.*

> « It's been a while since we talked, I spoke with my command about options on getting out and they presented me with one: being a CO. But after looking at the regulations that cover that option and looking over the criteria I felt that it wasn't for me. »

> *I'm not surprised, or dismayed by this. There are plenty of people who don't have CO convictions who nonetheless are deeply opposed to the Iraq War and all*

that goes with it. No matter what the regs say, their consciences (and yours) are as authentic and worthy of respect as anyone else's.

« I know this is different than what you believe, and I respect your stance and especially the support you offer soldiers coming back and dealing with these things, but I felt that I didn't fall into that category. In my heart, after praying and getting in the Word, I felt that God justifies the taking of life in certain situations, Even in certain conflicts (ie. WWII etc.), but definately not this one.»

Maybe sometime when this is over with we can talk about all this. Meantime, just stay safe and know there's no judgment on this end.

« I do, however, feel that my feelings and stance is completely valid and legitimate. »

Yep.

« A few sundays ago, during worship, I was praying about things and felt a real peace about leaving. So, last week I packed my stuff up and left leaving a note that explained my feelings and that I wouldn't manipulate my emotions to categorize myself into qualifying for CO. »

Okay. I'll certainly stand behind your choice .

« I have contacted GI Rights Hotline and they are helping me, but please pray for guidance and protection if you would. Only time will tell what will happen, but I wanted to thank you and let you know your help is definately appreciated. God bless and stay real. »

I'll do my best. . . . .If you need to talk, give me a call anytime . . . . Just be careful about where you're calling from, as we assume that somebody else (other than God) could be listening.
Let me know how your situation resolves itself.

There was to be more to this story, but it was many months before the next chapter opened.

While "Freddy felt alone, in fact many more like him were having deepening doubts, in and out of uniform. By mid-2005, public support for the Iraq occupation had begun to ebb. Although the White House refused to let the press see or photograph returning coffins of dead soldiers, their numbers could not be suppressed. Added to this was the fact that after two years of searching, there was no sign of the weapons of mass destruction that had been one of the main pretexts for the invasion. And besides the abuses of Abu Ghraib, reports of incompetence and corruption in the occupation itself were piling up.

In response, the White House undertook to reverse the slide by sending the president out to make a series of stirring speeches, aimed at rallying the flagging public spirit. In late June, the eyes of the tour's planners turned toward a locale in North Carolina, where the chief executive could be guaranteed a loyal, captive audience.

Friday June 24 was already a busy day at Quaker House. Chuck Fager was feverishly preparing for a whirl of activity at the Gathering of Friends General Conference, or FGC. It was the largest annual Quaker assembly, a centerpiece of his summer visiting rounds, and was due to open in Blacksburg, Virginia in barely a week.

Then the phone rang. It was an area radio reporter: "The president is coming to Fort Bragg next Tuesday to give a speech," she said. "He's going to try to regain public support for the Iraq war with this speech. What protests do you all have planned?"

Fager blinked. This visit was complete news to him. "Um, the truth is we don't have *any* plans," he admitted. "But, well – could you call back in a couple of hours?"

The reporter did, and by then, the answer was different.

FGC was forgotten for several days. All through the weekend, national media hyped the coming presidential speech nonstop; it was, they breathlessly reported, to be the president's big push for regaining popular support for the war. One might have thought it was meant to rival the Gettysburg Address. It was the lead story in many national reports.

And by Tuesday, after three days of scrambling and frantic phone calls, Quaker House was ready to be the launching pad of nearly a whole day of local peace action in response.

All that afternoon, reporters and TV crews swarmed around the house, talking to gathering Iraq veterans and military family members. Their message was straightforward, and echoed that of the large banner that had been unfolded and tacked up along the porch:

"Real Support for the Troops: Bring Them Home Now!"

Inside, military moms made posters, surrounded by toddlers with crayons. Display boards bearing the names of US soldiers killed in Iraq were hurriedly updated (250 names had to be added, the sad tally since the boards were last displayed in March). Veterans of Iraq and other wars talked to reporters, and anyone else who would listen.

Then, as the group gathered its motley forces to head downtown to the Market House and an expanded version of the standard peace vigil, it began to rain. Hard.

They were undeterred. The Market House had an open plaza beneath it, and the vigil was moved inside its arches, where all could stay relatively dry. With the display boards in a large irregular circle, the vigil started on time, at 5 PM, with no lengthy speeches. Vigilers began reading the names of the dead aloud, through a makeshift PA system. Veterans, moms, kids, many people took turns at the reading. A few feet away, several dozen luminaries, small candles in translucent paper bags, were arranged in a peace symbol, one that glowed brighter as dusk fell.

Luminaria were a shining part of the hastily-organized peace witness on June 28, 2005 when the president made a speech at Fort Bragg aimed at shoring up declining public support for the Iraq war.

Except for a break for pizza, the reading continued until nine PM, during and after the presidential speech at Fort Bragg.

Despite the protesters' dampened, somewhat bedraggled appearance, the natural solemnity of such a memorial ceremony was evident to all present. Reporters and cameras circled around the

Jacob Liebers of Fayetteville reads some of the names of US soldiers killed in Iraq, at the expanded vigil, June 28, 2005.

group throughout the four-hour proceeding. Besides many US media, crews from the Netherlands and Belgium were there as well.   More than fifty people took part. As the world counts such things, this was a small turnout. But numbers were not the whole story. Among the vigilers were many who had a personal stake in the cost of the war, and the authenticity of their voices and images were spread far and wide.

The next day it was back to "normal" for Quaker House, getting ready for summer conferences. The banner came down from the porch; the names display boards were folded and stowed, to await their next sad round of updating.

As for the speech, the locals didn't listen; but the verdict of the polls and national media seemed unanimous: after all the buildup, it failed to turn public opinion back in support of the war. Not to put too fine a point on it, the whole incursion had been a flop.

Did the hastily-organized vigil help blunt its impact?

Who could tell? But they had done their best.

Yet if local protest sentiment gained momentum from the presidential stopover, another potential visit showed how fragile that advance could be. In late July, Jane Fonda came to a bookstore in Santa Fe, New Mexico, on a tour to promote her recently published autobiography. In answer to a question, she said she was planning a new antiwar bus tour of military bases, focused on ending the Iraq occupation, and hoped to include a stop in Fayetteville and Fort Bragg. She had apologized to veterans for her unwise visit to North Vietnam, she said, and had been forgiven.

Maybe by some. But when a local reporter mentioned this comment in a New Mexico paper, it was picked up by wire services and flashed across the country within hours. In Fayetteville, angry reactions were as predictable as sunrise.

The *Observer*'s editors harrumphed on July 28 that "If the goal of peace seekers is to attract news cameras, the way to make that happen is to invite Jane Fonda and her tour.

"But if the goal of people who seek peace is to inspire reasoned and reflective national debate about

All Is *NOT* Forgiven: a Fayetteville tavern-keeper voices his view about a Jane Fonda return, 2005.

191

the wars against terrorism and in Iraq, the way to make sure it never happens is to invite Jane Fonda."

"I don't see any good she can do by coming here," added the head of the local Retired Military Association. "All she's doing now is continuing the same old crap she's done back then."

"Just like we don't forget the people we left behind over there," he said, "we don't forget the people who betrayed us over there."

Outside the Gaslight Lounge, on Fort Bragg Road, the owner made his sentiments clear on the marquee, which in short order added: "NO Jane Fonda" to its offer of "Free Pool" on Tuesdays.

Quaker House had heard the talk of a tour, and passed along the public reactions to antiwar bigwigs in New York who were helping with the idea. For that matter, even its Board members were divided over the wisdom of being involved with such a controversial incursion. Fortunately, Fonda thought better of the idea and no tour took place.

Sgt. Abe, The Honest Recruiter

The brouhaha over the Fonda tour-that wasn't showed how close to the surface these old unhealed divisions remained. It fed into the concerns about how to frame recruiting work, which had been simmering ever since the visit to the Harnett County high school the previous February. These finally bore fruit late that summer.

A student intern, John Stephens, spent two weeks at Quaker House in August 2005, mostly hunched over his Apple computer. Stephens was a very talented comic book artist, who had come highly-recommended by a mutual friend, Tom Fox, a Virginia Quaker. But Stephens did not draw comics with pen and ink; instead, his palette was a gray electronic slate attached to the laptop, and he mulled over ideas with Fager and turned them into sketches.

Out of this intensive

collaboration two important innovations emerged: one was a fictional character, "Sgt. Abe, the Honest Recruiter." In his initial strips, such as "Sgt. Abe Explains the Enlistment Document" and "Sgt. Abe Speaks to Parents," the Honest Recruiter pointed out the potential pitfalls of the enlistment process and the tricks recruiters used. His severe expression matched his straightforward motto: "Somebody Has To Tell It Like It Is."

Recruiting is demanding, often frustrating work, which many GIs take on only reluctantly. This 2004 cover image from *Army Times* expresses this ambivalence.

The other important outcome of the work was the new name for Sgt. Abe's mission, to replace "counter-recruiting": instead, it was to be "Truth In Recruiting."

That sounded better: it focused not on recruiters themselves but on their behavior, which under the pressures of high quotas too often fell short of veracity. Moreover, across class and culture "truth" was honored, and deceit disapproved.

The phrase had first emerged earlier that summer, after the *Fayetteville Observer* ran a major article describing the journey of one Fayetteville youth through the recruiting process. The piece was no expose, yet it recounted how the recruiter gave him and other recruits demonstrably false information, then candidly acknowledged its falsity to the visiting reporter.

Shocked by the shameless, acknowledged misrepresentation, and seeing an opening, Fager quickly sent a rebuttal which the paper published as an OpEd column:

> In the July 24 [2005] article, "He's in the Army now," Justin Willett reports blatantly illegal and abusive behavior by recruiters. Specifically, he wrote:

"The last stop at MEPS (Military Entrance Processing Station) is the swearing in. It's official, yet not official. All new recruits who go through MEPS must return a second time before shipping out to basic training or boot camp.

"The second swearing in is the one that really counts, MEPS officials said. Recruits are not prosecuted if they have a change of heart and fail to return for the second oath, the officials said."

This was said to Willett, accurately, because these recruits are formally in a delayed enlistment status.

But what the recruits were told was starkly different, and dishonest:

According to the article, a new recruit entered the "carpeted room with the military seals on the wall," and received a briefing on the Uniform Code of Military Justice, "in particular the sections titled absent without leave and desertion."

Recruits are told they could be court martialed, which could result in the death penalty.

There are several levels of untruth and abuse here:

The first is flagrant exaggeration: The death penalty is on the books for desertion, but only two soldiers have been executed for it since 1864, and the last one was in World War Two, 60 years ago. Typical sentences for desertion in recent years have been about a year, often less.

A second is that, as the recruiter admitted to Willett, these regulations do not yet apply to the recruits who were thus threatened.

A third is that this procedure clearly violates the Army's own rules – specifically, an Army regulation (USAREC Reg 601-95), which states: "At no time will any (recruiter) tell a Delayed Enlistment Program enlistee he or she must 'go in the Army or he or she will go to jail,' or that 'failure to enlist will result in a black mark on his or her credit record,' or any other statement indicating adverse action will occur if the applicant fails to enlist."

In our military counseling at Quaker House, we often hear of such recruiter abuse. But seldom is it conducted so brazenly in the presence of a careful reporter.

I call on the Army to immediately cease this deceptive practice, and to discipline the recruiters involved.

Persons considering enlistment deserve truth in recruiting. The recruits in this case definitely did not get it.

For shame.

There was no rejoinder to the column from the military; but what could they say? The bogus "death penalty for desertion" briefing was clearly wrong; but it was just as clearly a routine technique for these recruiters, who were among the most successful in the nation.

This report showed how common recruiter abuse was, and what an uphill climb faced those who wanted to bring more truth into it. John Stephens later expanded his original drawings into a 41-second animation, uploaded to YouTube, in which Sgt. Abe warned a young recruit about one of the most disturbing features of the military enlistment "agreement"–the buried language which permits enlistments to be extended indefinitely.

Sgt. Abe was "launched" that fall, online and in brochures given out at a large peace rally in Washington DC where Quaker House rented a booth. Fager also went into the website and changed "counter-recruiting" to "Truth In Recruiting" wherever it occurred, and he advocated for the new name in discussions with other recruiting activists. Over the next two years, the name began to catch on; it was adopted by, among others, the new Iraq Veterans Against the War.

When the peace vigilers gathered at Fayetteville's Market House on October 26, 2005, their signs showed why recruiters were having to work harder. The US official death toll in Iraq had just passed another melancholy milestone: "2000 = Too Many," read some signs. "Honor the Dead. Spare the Living. Stop the War," was on others.

Recruiting quotas were high because the US military was stretched much too thin, not only in Iraq, but elsewhere around the world. Further, beyond the spiraling casualty figures, the toll of combat veterans returning wounded in body and soul was likewise climbing rapidly. With it, resistance to recruiters' blandishments was spreading widely in many areas where they had previously enjoyed much success. This was particularly true of those the military marketers termed "influentials," the respected parents, grandparents, aunts and uncles who had previously regarded service as a way out and up for disadvantaged youths. That sentiment, and recruiting results in communities of color, were both declining sharply in these years.

The GI Hotline's continued growth may also have reflected this growing unease. By the end of October 2005, total GI counseling calls to Quaker House had surpassed the total of 5925 for the entire year of 2004. By the end of November, they had exceeded all previous tallies. For the full year of 2005, calls totaled 7050, another record.

The appearance and distribution of the Sgt. Abe materials were part of the effort to make Quaker House a resource to wider peace and activist constituencies. This thrust was further developed by co-sponsorship with the North Carolina Council of Churches of a statewide church peace conference in November 2005, held at Fayetteville's First Baptist Church. Rev. Cureton Johnson, the pastor of this large, historically black congregation, was the only local clergyman who was willing to take any visible step in support of a peace witness or Quaker House. This was in part the legacy of work done by Sandy Sweitzer a decade earlier, after the racial murders of 1995, and Johnson's own history of outspoken activism.

Similarly, Quaker House was now part of the new Quaker Initiative to End Torture (QUIT), which had emerged from John Calvi's conversations over the year since his visit to North Carolina. QUIT made plans for a conference on this troubling topic in June 2006, at nearby Guilford College.

For Quaker House, 2005 was an epic year. The historic peace protest in March had attracted over 4,000 participants and international media attention. Their GI Rights counselors recorded the most calls ever for a year, 7050, a 19 per cent increase over the previous year. Sgt. Abe the Honest Recruiter became the first "virtual staff member," to support truth-in-recruiting efforts. When a president came to town in June to stem the slippage of war support, Quaker House was the crux of an effort that gave voice to the growing dissent. In November, international news media reported that resister-exile Jeremy Hinzman had been granted the right to appeal the Canadian government's initial rejection of his application for refugee status.

As the end of the year approached, Fayetteville progressives were mostly amused by the disclosure by NBC News that the March peace rally in Rowan Park had been on a list of "potential threats" of terrorism compiled by the Defense Department, warranting special surveillance. After all, besides the scores of uniformed police and deputies, plenty of anonymous men with dark glasses and large cameras had been visibly monitoring such ominous groups as the Cakalak Thunder anarchist drummers. There had been many more such watchers than were needed for any actual "threats" in evidence at the entirely peaceful affair. But civil liberties groups rightly objected that this list was part of a new form of domestic spying on legal activity.

The Board and Fager had been much more concerned when twice that year, tax authorities questioned their nonprofit status. First a letter came from the Cumberland County tax office in June, questioning whether Quaker House was really exempt from local property taxes. It was indeed, as a local attorney soon helped them understand. But then in early August, Fager heard from a donor's financial advisor that the Internal Revenue Service had told them the project's tax exempt status had been "suspended."

This was serious. Without tax exempt status, Quaker House would likely be doomed, as donors lost tax deductibility for their contributions. After much frenetic FAXing of documents and letters, and with the aid of another volunteer attorney, on September 20, 2005 a letter came from the IRS, advising that all was well, Quaker House's status had been restored.

That was a relief. But the elation was tempered by the hall-of-mirrors character of the experience. Despite specific and repeated questioning, no explanation was forthcoming from the IRS as to *when* it had happened, on *what grounds* Quaker House was suspended, or *why* no one there had been notified of the action. These brief episodes were bloodless but vivid reminders of the potential vulnerability of a small nonprofit organization espousing unpopular causes.

And the vulnerability of a threatened tax deduction was as nothing to a kind that soon hove into view. The day after Thanksgiving, while returning home from a visit with family, Fager received an urgent call from John Stephens in Virginia. The message was stark: their friend Tom Fox had been kidnaped in Iraq, and his captors were threatening to kill him.

18. 2006: Taking Our Own Casualties: Tom Fox & Torture

Tom Fox had gone to Baghdad with the Christian Peacemaker Teams (CPT), an ecumenical organization that sent small groups into dangerous areas to "get in the way," as their motto stated, of warmaking. His own spiritual path had taken him from a place in the Marine band, playing the clarinet for presidents and dignitaries, to a strong sense of calling to do something direct for peace.

Fox and three other CPT volunteers had just visited a mosque when their car was cut off, and they were taken by armed men to a house in a nondescript Baghdad neighborhood, where they were kept chained together, for most of each night and day. Their kidnapers, a previously unknown group, issued a video of the four, and said they would be killed by early December, unless various exorbitant demands were met.

The CPT policy was for no ransom be offered for kidnaped members, and no armed rescue attempts be made on their behalf. Stephens and Fager talked anxiously about what could be done.

This was not only an "issue" for them; it was personal. Stephens had worked closely with Fox in a health food supermarket, and regarded him as a mentor. Fager had been in the same

Tom Fox, as hostage in Iraq, from a video released by his kidnapers in late January 2006.

Friends Meeting with Fox for many years, their children had grown up together. Fager had talked with Fox at a Quaker gathering the previous summer, not long before he returned to Iraq; Fox had spoken candidly, but without fear, of the risks he would face there. And in fact, it had been CPT folks who had brought information about torture and abuse at Abu Ghraib to investigative reporter Seymour Hersh, who helped break the story.

Now, in the hour of their peril, if there was anything that two obscure Quakers could do, how dare they hold back? But what? They consulted other church-based peace workers with experience in hostage negotiations, and were advised that the more public attention that could be brought to the hostages the better, especially with emphasis on their peaceable character and non-missionary intentions.

With that, the pair leaped into action. In a few hours one evening, operating several hundred miles apart, they created a website, www.freethecaptivesnow.org, started an international petition, and sent calls for signatures and similar efforts speeding around the globe. Others were pressing similar efforts, and within only a few days, racing against the clock, more than 50,000 names had been gathered on petitions, Calls for the captives' safe release had come from not only Christian but many Islamic groups, even some of the most militant.

The immediate result of this astonishing international outcry was that the execution deadline passed with no news, and then another video was released showing them alive, and pleading for action to win their freedom.

At this point, the effort by Fager and Stephens shifted from one of mobilization into a kind of vigil. Each night, week after week, one or both scoured international news websites for any shred of information that might be related, then summed it up on their site. The daily reports, though they most often came down to "no news," were followed by friends of the four from around the world. Many other efforts were also being made through both official and unofficial channels to win the CPTers' release.

This nightly discipline of reporting continued until two culminating events had come to pass: on March 10, they sorrowfully posted that Tom Fox's body had been found the day before in a trash-filled Baghdad vacant lot. He had been handcuffed and shot. Then two weeks later, British and US commandos, ignoring the CPT strictures against rescue, broke into the house and freed the remaining three.

No one felt the trauma of this fourteen-week ordeal more keenly than the captives and their families; yet it was also very close to many who were not physically restrained, including Fager and Stephens. "Night after night," Fager recalled, " I lay awake thinking about what Tom and the others were going through, wondering if they were even still alive, while I was home in my bed, safe and warm. And how many thousands of Iraqi families were in much the same position, wondering what had happened to their loved ones who had disappeared? I prayed a lot in those weeks."

In the strict sense, this intense vigil was not part of the work of Quaker House. Yet ties both personal, spiritual, and even professional linked them. Fox had been military; he had worked with a religious peace group. And they shared a focus on the Iraq War in particular, and peacework more generally.

For that matter, searching nightly reports from Iraq that rarely were seen in major US media, Fager learned much about the intense and bloody ethnic-religious civil war underway there, at a time when official Washington was refusing to acknowledge the masses of blood-soaked data that gave the lie to their official line about the occupation's success. Consider, for instance, this excerpt from the report from March 13, 2006, three days after learning of Tom's death:

13 March 2006

Not a "Good Day in Baghdad" . . .

At least 66 people were killed and more than 300 wounded in a series of attacks in Iraq, including 50 dead and 290 injured in a triple car bombing of a Baghdad Shia neighbourhood. Described by US Ambassador Zalmay Khalizad as "a good day in Baghdad", Aljazeera said it was one of the worst days of violence there in recent months.

Sunday's attacks coincided with the announcement that Iraq's parliament would meet on Thursday for the first time since the December elections.

Elsewhere in Baghdad, US forces were fighting a fierce battle with Iraqi fighters in a western neighbourhood. Police said the fighting erupted about 3pm in Khadra.

An AP Television News cameraman reported that a US helicopter landed nearby to evacuate casualties.

It was not known what prompted the fighting or if there were any dead. There was no immediate comment from the US military.

And these blasts came after a night of fierce violence in Baghdad. Officials at Yarmouk Hospital, one of Baghdad's biggest, said they had received at least 20 bodies overnight, all victims of violence. Most had been shot.

Amid the carnage and chaos, there was no news Sunday of the three remaining Christian Peacemaker Team captives.

While this vigil was ongoing, its impact was reinforced in mid-January, when Fager attended a conference on torture at Princeton Theological Seminary. Attenders heard several memorable presentations. One was by journalist Mark Danner, who described how two "suspected terrorists" had been taken at night from an airport in Sweden in December 2001:

An unmarked plane landed. A masked team emerged, dressed in black, and communicated mostly by hand signals. The suspects' clothes were cut from their bodies with special scissors, and then diapers were put on them, complete with narcotic suppositories shoved into their rectums. They were dressed in jumpsuits, hooded, and then strapped to mattresses in the Gulfstream jet. In a few moments, the aircraft was disappearing into the night air. Only much later was it disclosed that the jet was headed for Egypt, where the two suspects were held and tortured; one of them is still in prison at the end of 2008.

The case was not an isolated one, Danner said, and the plane was operated by the CIA as part of a new US program of what was called "extraordinary rendition," or more accurately international kidnaping for torture.

Human rights attorney Scott Horton, right, discussing ways of holding accountable US officials for officially-sanctioned programs of torture. Beside him is Michael Ratner, Director of the Center for Constitutional Rights, a major player in this ongoing effort.

Another speaker, human rights lawyer Scott Horton, made an equally forceful, if more abstract point: legitimized torture was a prime manifestation of a ruler's ability to declare some citizens outside the protection of the laws. And if a ruler could do that with impunity, then that ruler was above the law. And when a ruler or ruling group attained that double capacity: to act *beyond* the law's restraints, and to put citizens *outside* the law's protections, then they had achieved the essence of tyranny.

Horton underlined his point by paraphrasing a main thesis of a German political philosopher Carl Schmitt, an intellectual supporter of the Nazi regime, "Sovereign indeed is he who controls the exception." Legitimizing torture was one of the most important of such "exceptions."

200

This aircraft, a Gulfstream IV, has been used as a "torture taxi" on many occasions. This photo was taken by "plane-spotters" at its home base, Aero Contractors, in Smithfield NC, not far from Fayetteville.

The implication of this charge was that since at least 2001, in many more incidents like the one in Sweden, the rulers of the United States had been acting on it as policy. And to that point at least, they were doing so without hindrance or meaningful legal challenge.

These points, and others, left Fager persuaded that torture was a major issue of the day: the practices, which were supposedly prohibited by both US and international law, were bad enough in themselves. But even worse were the implications of their legitimation for any remaining sense of the United States as a law-abiding country, one where the liberties of anyone, citizen or alien, were safe.

From this gathering was launched the National Religious Campaign

Real Owner: The CIA

Aero Contractors Ltd., has been identified as one of several CIA front companies with torture connections, based in North carolina.

201

Against Torture (NRCAT). Quaker House was a founding member, and not only for reasons of principle. As he delved into the subject, Fager was horrified to learn that Fort Bragg and the surrounding region of North Carolina was one of the major centers of what he came to call the "Torture Industrial Complex."

In fact, the plane that flew the two prisoners from Sweden to Egypt had taken off from Smithfield, North Carolina, less than an hour north of Fayetteville. The plane was operated by a CIA shell company, Aero Contractors Limited, from the small Johnston County Airport. (Was it merely a coincidence that Johnston County was, like adjoining Harnett, a longtime Ku Klux Klan stronghold?) Another clandestine outfit, Centurion Aviation Services, flew from the Fayetteville Regional Airport, where it had its own separate terminal, down a secluded side street off the main terminal roadway.

In several parts of the world, hobbyists called "plane-spotters" had begun noticing these mysterious flights, tracking and cross-checking their flight paths from public records on the Internet. An informal but damning portrait soon emerged of an extensive international torture traffic: most such planes took off from North Carolina, and picked up their operators at Washington's Dulles International, near CIA headquarters. From there they hopped across the Atlantic, refueling at Shannon, Ireland, Prestwick, Scotland or some other airport near the Atlantic coast. Then they often dropped off the international radar for several days at a time, before re-surfacing enroute back to the US.

Where were these planes during these blacked out periods? And why did so many land frequently in Jordan, Afghanistan, Poland and Romania, all places where there were CIA connections with local secret agencies notorious for torture? Over time, more and more accounts of their missions leaked to the surface. The case of the two Egyptian refugees "rendered" from Sweden in 2001, mentioned earlier, was one.

Another involved Khaled El Masri, a German citizen of Lebanese descent, who was kidnaped in Macedonia in late 2003, evidently because his name was similar to that of a terrorist suspect. He spent five awful months in the "Salt Pit," a terrible CIA-run Afghan prison, before Langley realized their mistake and flew him back to Europe, dumping him in rural Albania in the middle of the night. Numerous similar horror stories were verified.

The flight that took El Masri to Afghanistan began in Smithfield, North Carolina at Aero Contractors; but his case did not end when he finally returned to Germany, suffering serious after-effects from his imprisonment. In January 2007, a public prosecutor in Munich issued indictments against thirteen CIA employees for El Masri's kidnaping. The agents had all used false names for their missions, but three of them were later identified, and all are pilots for Aero, residents of North Carolina. The indictments were ignored by the US authorities, but they remain pending as of the end of 2008.

"The subject of whether or not torture was permitted by the Bible was discussed in church [in Smithfield]—and many congregants believed it was," said Trevor Paglen, co-author of *Torture Taxi*, one of the first books to fill in the details of the rendition flight program. "There's nothing random about the CIA using this rural area in North Carolina. If you want to shut up a secret operation, this is where you would do it. It's a God, guns, and guts area."

There was more. Fager found a 2005 article in the *New Yorker* magazine by reporter Jane Mayer, which disclosed that survival strategies taught to Special Forces soldiers at Fort Bragg were being "reverse-engineered" into torture techniques for use at Guantanamo Bay and other US prisons. The secret "Torture Migration Conference" in September 2002 had been a central event in that process.

"It was like waking up one morning in 1938 Germany and discovering that you're right next door to SS headquarters," Fager said of the gathering cloud of disturbing details. "They weren't actually torturing people right here; but much of the key machinery was located nearby, and many of the techniques and plans came out of Fort Bragg. That's why I call the whole mix the 'Torture Industrial Complex,' and there was just no way we could keep quiet about it." Over these months, the issue of torture insistently elbowed its way into a prominent and ongoing spot on the Quaker House agenda.

The first Quaker conference on torture was held in June 2006 at Guilford College, with Quaker House handling much of the logistic work. At that moment, it was a pioneering effort. Yet soon enough, there was an increasing band of allies in this crusade. By the time the second Quaker torture conference convened in June 2007, the 80-plus Quakers on hand were joined by representatives from Evangelicals for Human Rights, NRCAT, NC Stop Torture Now, and an international group, the Paris-based Action by Christians for the Abolition of Torture, or ACAT. Fager got acquainted with the ACAT staffperson on hand, a Quaker named Gretchen Ellis, and the connection was to prove fruitful later.

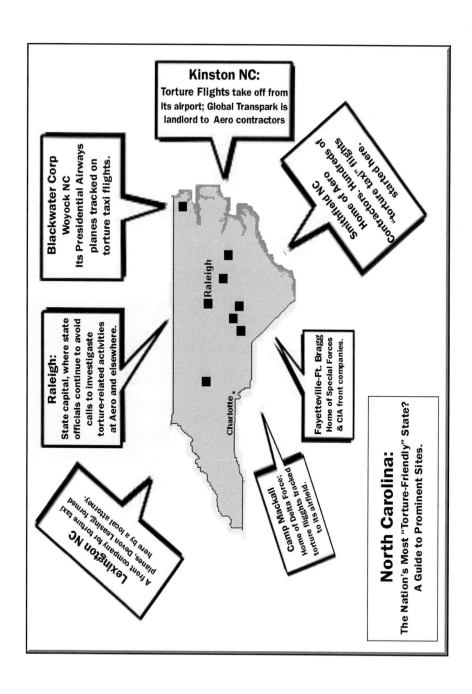

19. 2006, cont.: Epiphany & the Vampire Slayers

In late January, 2006, on an otherwise unremarkable day, there was an epiphany.

A call had come to Quaker House from a soldier at Fort Bragg named Lopez. He was in trouble, he said, because he had gone AWOL to take care of his sick mother, who was mostly alone in Chicago. He had returned after a couple weeks, though – he never meant to desert – but now his company commander was going to give him a summary court martial and send him to the brig. Could somebody from Quaker House come and attend the trial? Maybe that would restrain the commander's wrath.

As cases went, this wasn't exactly big. It wasn't a matter of conscience; Lopez admittedly had violated regulations; and Quaker House couldn't do much in terms of actual intervention. But after explaining this, Fager said, sure, he'd come. An empathetic presence in a hostile situation was at least something. The court martial, Lopez said, was set for 11 AM on January 30, 2006.

But Fager missed the brief trial. The commander moved it up til 9 AM, and when he arrived, Lopez had already been taken into custody, headed for two weeks in the brig at Camp Lejeune, after a stop at the Womack Military Medical Center at Fort Bragg for a doctor's appointment. The first sergeant said that if he hurried, Fager could probably catch up with them and at least speak with Lopez briefly.

That's what happened, and Fager later visited Lopez in the brig, for which he was grateful. But that isn't the point of this story. On the way to the barracks, Fager had driven past the 4th Psychological Operations Group, a large unit at Fort Bragg. Like other units there, its location was marked by a large wooden sign in front of the building. All the signs were of large rectangular planks painted dark brown, with the unit name in white. They were uniform, like what the soldiers wore.

But across the top of this sign was an extra plank, on which was a two-word motto: "Words Conquer."

It wasn't much, yet when Fager saw it, he nearly drove off the road. "Words Conquer." The slogan had an almost physical effect, like the Zen master's slap to induce satori, enlightenment. Suddenly, much, maybe most, of what Fager had seen and heard and learned about the military in four years in Fayetteville seemed to clap together like the report of one of the post's big artillery pieces right next to his ear.

And like a Zen lesson, a koan took shape:

Bullets Kill.

Bombs Destroy. But

Words Conquer.

It summed up so much: "Extraordinary rendition." "Enhanced interrogation techniques." "Collateral damage." "The 'last throes' of the Iraq resistance." There were a thousand examples.

The short motto that said so much.

But it wasn't only the words used that could vanquish, he saw. Equally potent was the ability to *prevent* words from being used, such as "civil war" in Iraq. But it came much closer to home as well: he remembered the Bragg post commander at the public meeting about the seven 2002 domestic *murder-suicides,* stepping so carefully around those words as if they must not be spoken, because they must not.

In the same way, the Pentagon brass skillfully prevented the

The Fayetteville Observer

HOME EDITION   VOL. CXXI-No. 216   TUESDAY, APRIL 24, 2007   www.fayobserver.com

9 Bragg troops killed

20 soldiers are wounded in attack at Iraq base

INSIDE
■ Congress n
President Ann

82ND MOURNS FALLEN SOLDIERS

Blast kills 6 from 82nd

Group was on patrol in vehicles near Samarra

By Kevin Maurer, Staff writer

March 7, 2007 - Six 82nd Airborne Division paratroopers were killed Monday in what was the deadliest single day for the division in the Iraq war.

3 Fort Bragg soldiers killed

2 more soldiers identified

Pair died Monday while serving in Iraq

Troops and families from Fort Bragg paid a heavy price in the war's fourth year, as these headlines from 2007 show.

adoption of a common definition of domestic violence, which in turn prevented any reliable analysis of all the data pointing to an epidemic – another verboten word. All that was left were "flukes," "clusters," or "anomalies," as in that unhappy summer.

The same strategy was operative in the big Airborne Museum only three blocks from Quaker House: almost seventy years of war was depicted there, with meticulous attention to detail of weapons and gear, and a gung-ho saga of heroism – but with no casualty figures anywhere in the big hall.

The truth of the motto of the 4th Psychological Operations (in many of the inside manuals it was called, more candidly, Psychological *Warfare*) Group was on every hand.

And then, another insight: one of the main objects of conquest, perhaps the main one in fact, was not Iraq, or the "Axis of Evil," but us – you and me, Americans. Even when we were not overtly "at war," the citizenry of the US had to be kept persuaded that it was not only necessary but right and good for the world to spend half a trillion dollars and more each year on something called "defense," and to sacrifice sons and daughters in its rites. And this persuasion was carried out primarily through words, and supporting images – psychological operations, in short.

As the 4th Group's commander no doubt knew, even The Master would have approved:

> *Sun Tzu said: In the practical art of war, the best thing of all is to take the enemy's country whole and intact; to shatter and destroy it is not so good . . . .*
>
> *Hence to fight and conquer in all your battles is not supreme excellence; supreme excellence consists in breaking the enemy's resistance without fighting.*

In one sense, this was hardly a new discovery. "Psywar" has been around for decades, nay centuries. Yet it still came home that day with the crash of an old truth newly rediscovered.

Fager often carried a small digital camera with him. When he finished talking with Lopez, he drove back to the building and took several photos of the sign. The image was soon on the wallpaper of his computer, as a sign and a constant reminder: especially within the US, this sign marks the central front of the field of battle. Words Conquer.

The rising concern with torture paralleled a decline in the impact of peace rallies. Quaker House and its allies organized two more annual protests in Rowan Park, in 2006 and 2007. The results were paradoxical. By every measure, the quality of the rally programs improved each year. But attendance dwindled, to about a thousand in 2006, and then only a few hundred in 2007. That year, for the first time, the weather turned against them – it rained the day before, and was near-freezing on the morning of the rally, which felt colder to North Carolinians accustomed to mild winter weather.

Which was a shame. The summer before, Jane Fonda had sent

Quaker House a rare copy of the suppressed documentary FTA, about her traveling anti-Vietnam shows. Watching the film, the staff was struck by the skill and impact of the performances, and decided to try to book singer Holly Near, one of the young members of the cast, for their 2007 rally. Back in Fayetteville after thirty-six years, Near gave a standout performance. There were also riveting testimonies by half a dozen Iraq veterans, stinging satire by emcee-comedian Dave Lippman, and powerful speeches by Rev. William J. Barber, President of the NC NAACP, and retired Col. Ann Wright.

Wright had served at Fort Bragg, where she worked on contingency

Quaker House welcomes a crowd of media and peace pilgrims for Fayetteville's largest ever peace rally, in March 2005. After this year, attendance at the next two annual rallies declined sharply.

plans for invasions of various countries, including Iraq. She later said that she was dismayed at how the carefully-prepared plans were completely ignored for the actual invasion increasing needless destruction and loss of life. In 1987 she joined the diplomatic corps. Wright resigned her government post in March 2003 in protest of the Iraq invasion, and had become an outspoken critic of the war.

But there was more to it than that. Somehow, as overall public opinion turned decisively away from the war (even polls of soldiers showed this), the morale and cohesion of the consciously antiwar constituency seemed to dissipate. At the beginning of 2007 a large and hopeful march had circled the Capitol in Washington, calling on the new Congress, in which the

209

opposition Democrats had gained a narrow margin of control, to cut off funding for the war, to end it and all that went with it.

But the new Congress did no such thing; instead they voted for every dollar of the tens of billions demanded for continued war by the White House, just as obediently as the old Congress done for so long. Calls for impeachment, for investigations into torture, war profiteering and other flagrant abuses were ignored, or fobbed off with token hearings that were little noticed.

The decline in numbers for the rally did not silence objections, however. A Letter in the *Fayetteville Observer* on March 17, 2007 complained:

Why do war protesters think saying, "I support the troops, not the war," gets them a pass at protesting? It escapes me. Please explain how supporting the troops but not the war makes things any better. Does it soothe their guilty consciences by saying that? It sounds like, and is, an old and tired cliche. Stop using it.

If people are against the war, then, by God, be against the war. Just stop trying to qualify it by saying, "I support the troops"!

Fager had a ready reply to such complaints. Polls like the one by *Army Times* had documented the deep disaffection with the war in the uniformed ranks.

"Before this," Fager said at the 2007 rally, I felt we were speaking *for* the troops. This year, though, we're speaking *with* them. They want out of there as much as we want them home."

Wendy Michener responded with an Op-ed piece on April 15, challenging the fallacy,

. . . that it is impossible to support the soldiers in Iraq while opposing the war. Where did this idea come from – when our leader has spoken, only traitors disagree? Doesn't that sound like places where it is illegal to disagree with the government? Is the US military a creature of this administration or is it a professional force pledged to defend our country? Is it not independent of political parties?

The people in our military have chosen an honorable profession. They don't make the major policy decisions and they cannot pick and choose which orders they will obey – if they want to stay in the military. To confuse the person in uniform with the decisions made in Washington dishonors everyone.

Questioning the big policy decisions is our job. It is our job to make sure the commitment of our military service people is never misused for venal or dishonorable reasons. It is our job to stand up and object if we believe their sacrifice is being wasted or being used for any purpose besides the defense of our country.

This war fails on all these counts. . . .

Yet even if much of the public concurred with this sentiment, the urge to express it in large public demonstrations had largely vanished. Disillusionment with the new Congress was quick and deep, and with it a widespread sense of near-paralysis spread like a flu epidemic among peace activists. In 2007, a march in Washington on the same day as the Fayetteville rally was small and ended in frozen disarray. By the following spring of 2008, with a presidential campaign underway, neither Quaker House nor the national peace groups proposed large public gatherings to mark the war's fifth anniversary.

Yet this dissipation of the "peace movement" did not herald any diminution of activity at Quaker House. The GI Hotline was now a constant, which continued to set records. Preparations were also ongoing for Quaker conferences on torture in June of 2006 and 2007 at Guilford College. Sgt. Abe was kept busy as well, while reports of recruiter abuse and folly accumulated.

And then there was that other issue which was so hard to turn into program, but impossible to ignore: the war kept coming home. This kind of "blowback" included more than spousal and domestic violence. As the occupation dragged on and morale sunk with each fruitless month, returning soldiers brought back with them a range of deadly aftereffects, which were as likely to be dangerous to themselves as to family and others.

Warnings had been given as early as 2004. High-level military physicians and psychiatrists spoke out about the mental health toll of the Iraq war. "There's a train coming that's packed with people who are going to need help for the next 35 years," Stephen L. Robinson told the *New York Times* in December of that year. Robinson, a 20-year Army veteran, was now the executive director of the National Gulf War Resource Center, an advocacy group. Dr. Stephen C. Joseph backed him up: "I have a very strong sense that the mental health consequences are going to be the medical story of this war," he said. Joseph served as the Assistant Secretary of Defense for Health Affairs in the mid-1990s.

Many chapters of that story were played out in and around Fort Bragg:

One case was especially heartbreaking: in 2006, the Thanksgiving holiday was November 23. On or around that day, Faye Johnson Vick, the wife of a deployed army colonel, took her two children, Jason, aged two, and Madison, three months, into the garage of their home on the north edge of Fayetteville. She put them into the family car, no doubt strapped them into child seats, climbed in herself, and then turned on the ignition. The car idled in the closed garage until it ran out of gas. Detectives found the bodies on November 28, by which time the three had been dead for several days.

Another remains a mystery: On May 5, 2007, Sgt. Sameer "Sammy" Rateb was scheduled to leave Iraq for some leave time at home near Charleston, South Carolina. There he had family and a wife waiting to greet him. Sammy had been, friends said, a proud member of the 82nd Airborne. He had deployed to Afghanistan before Iraq, and had just re-enlisted for another five-year hitch.

So why was he found hanging in his shelter, his wrists in handcuffs behind him? The army wanted to call it a suicide. But his mother objected, saying that the shackled wrists were very suspicious. So an investigation was launched, which as of this writing, eighteen months later, has not yielded any public conclusions.

Then there was the recurring family horror: in

A Fort Bragg Mystery (one of many): Why was Sgt Sameer "Sammy" Rateb of the 82nd found hanging in Iraq in My 2007? Was it suicide—or something else? And why was the Army still silent about it at the end of 2008?

November of 2007, another 82nd paratrooper, Sgt. Steven D. Lopez, went AWOL from Fort Bragg, and turned up in Lovell, Wyoming, where his wife and their two children were staying with her parents. His wife, Brenda Lee Davila, had recently refused to return with Lopez to Fort Bragg.

His father told a reporter that Lopez, who joined up shortly after September 11, 2001, had deployed to both Afghanistan and Iraq.

> "After that was when he really started having a tough time," Daniel Lopez said.
>
> "He volunteered for a lot of patrols, and he participated in a lot of close combat situations. He told me he had seen a lot of things that he couldn't even talk to me about," he said.
>
> "We knew he would have bouts where he was really depressed, but he would assure us he would be OK."

Except he wasn't. According to the local paper:

> Based on accounts by police and family members, the couple had a dispute around 1:30 p.m. Monday [November 5, 2007], with Davila saying she did not want Lopez to see their toddler children, a boy and girl. Lopez left, but returned shortly before 2 p.m. to confront Davlia, said Amy Lopez, his sister.
>
> Lopez told Davila that if he couldn't see the children, then neither could she. Then he shot her and, without hesitation, shot himself. It all happened in seconds, said Lovell Police Chief Nick Lewis. Lewis said as many as seven people witnessed the event.

Several other cases remain obscure: through 2008, at least seven Fort Bragg GIs committed suicide, died mysteriously or were killed on or near Fort Bragg, with only token press notice being taken.

Then, in December 2007, like a vampire from the coffin, an all-too familiar pattern re-emerged. Between December 2007 and September 2008, three female GIs from Fort Bragg and a fourth from Camp Lejeune were murdered by husbands or boyfriends.

The first was Maria Lauterbach, a Marine who was eight months pregnant, allegedly as the result of a rape by fellow Marine Cpl. Cesar Armando Laurean. Lauterbach disappeared in mid-December; her dismembered and burned remains were found buried in Laurean's backyard in mid-January 2008. Laurean disappeared, and eventually re-surfaced in Mexico, where he was born. He was arrested there, but at the end of 2008 was fighting extradition back to North Carolina, with no conclusion to the case in sight.

Then on June 21, 2008, guests at a busy Fayetteville motel complained about a bad smell coming from a room with a 'Do Not Disturb" sign on the door. When police went in, they found the decomposing body of Army Specialist Megan Touma completely submerged in the full bathtub. She had been strangled, drowned, or both.

Touma, who was also several months pregnant, had missed a formation at Fort Bragg several days earlier, but evidently no notice was taken of her absence. After some bizarre twists in the case, including mysterious typed letters to the newspaper and the police from someone claiming to be the Zodiac serial killer, another soldier, Sgt. Edgar Patino, was arrested and charged on July 29. Touma had told friends that she was involved with Patino when both were stationed in Germany, and Touma thought they were engaged, but then she discovered that he was actually married.

Bumpersticker on a car near Camp Lejeune NC, photo taken December 2006.

By the time Patino was arrested, a third case was making headlines: Second Lieutenant Holley Wimunc, a nurse at Fort Bragg's Womack Medical Center, didn't show up for work on July 10. When a colleague went to check on her, she was gone, and her apartment showed signs of arson. Three days later, a state forest ranger discovered an untended fire in woods near Camp Lejeune, and found that it was burning mutilated human remains. The next day Wimunc's estranged husband John, a Marine stationed at Camp Lejeune, was charged with her murder.

In late 2007, this continuing toll had at length become something more concrete than a source of melancholy for Quaker House. A call came from a woman named Christine Horne, from Florida, asking for help.

She was not in the service, or a veteran. But thirty three years earlier, on December 3, 1974, her mother, Beryl Mitchell, had been brutally murdered by her father, a Special Forces officer and Vietnam veteran, at Fort Bragg. Her father initially denied involvement, but was soon arrested, convicted, and served twelve years in prison for the killing. Christine, then nine years old, was whisked away to live with her paternal grandmother, and endure the loss of her mother.

Horne worked for decades to overcome the trauma of that event. In 2007, as part of that process, she decided to organize a memorial for her mother in Fayetteville. She wanted the event to be as visible as possible to help focus attention on the chronic social sickness of domestic abuse. But the only person Horne knew in Fayetteville, a friend of her family, refused to participate in organizing the event.

Then she read a piece about the 2002 murders on the Quaker House website. "Can we really be surprised when this violence comes home, when what is sown elsewhere is also reaped among the families who live with its professional purveyors?" the piece asked. Although the article was five years old, Horne was moved to call Quaker House: could she find some help there?

Indeed she could. Working in the background, staff aided with arrangements and media contacts, gave Horne a base of operations, and appealed to members of the local chapter of the National Organization of Women (NOW) to join in, which they were eager to do.

One would think that few cities would be more tuned in to the need for public attention to and discussion of domestic violence. But as in so many other areas, this ugly legacy was met mainly with the minimum of visible attention – words, or the lack thereof, were again to conquer.

But not quite, not this time. Christine Horne led a powerful ceremony on October 1, 2007, which also marked the start of Domestic Violence Awareness Month. It was attended by the sheriff, the chief of police and other dignitaries, and heavily covered by regional media. Particularly moving was the appearance at the memorial of numerous women, strangers but themselves survivors of domestic violence, who heard about it and came to share the witness.

"This commemoration, while very personal, was not only about closure in Christine's life," said the report in the Quaker House Newsletter. "Hardly a week goes by here now without someone voicing their apprehension about an expected increase in domestic abuse when the thousands of soldiers from Fort Bragg, now in Iraq, return in the coming months."

A year later, those apprehensions had been realized in eastern North Carolina. With the three brutal murders of female GIs attracting wide attention, a similar idea came up again. This time it was retired Army Colonel Ann Wright, who had been a major speaker at the 2007 Fayetteville peace rally, who contacted Quaker House, in hopes it could help organize some kind of public witness to pressure the military to take this epidemic more seriously.

Again, acting in the background, Quaker House and the NOW chapter went to work. Christine Horne also called, and said she wanted to

Four Carolina Victims of
The War At Home 2007-2008

Cpl. Maria Lauterbach

Spc. Megan Touma

2nd Lt. Holley Wimunc

Sgt. Christina Smith

join in as well. Plans were drawn up for a daylong series of events on October 8, to include a vigil outside the gate at Fort Bragg, a reception and seminar at Quaker House for professionals and others interested, and a closing gathering at Beryl Mitchell's gravesite.

Just as the press releases were being drawn up, however, there came more bad news: on September 30, a fourth female GI, Christina Smith, was murdered, attacked while walking with her husband, stabbed and her throat slashed, left to bleed to death, like Shalamar Franceschi back in 2002.

Within days her husband, Sgt. Richard Smith, and Pfc. Matthew Wayne Kvapil were charged with the crime. Smith was alleged to have solicited Kvapil to wield the knife, for a payment of $30,000. All three worked for the 4th Psychological Operations Group at Fort Bragg.

This new case only spurred on Ann Wright and the others, and once again, Domestic Violence Awareness Month in Fayetteville got a public boost in a place that needed it badly. In describing the vigil to the media beforehand, Quaker House staff were careful to note that it was not to be an antiwar event. A reporter from *People* magazine got the message, as did the *Fayetteville Observer.*

> The crowd hovering outside one of Fort Bragg's gates Wednesday was a protest of sorts.
>
> But it was not the anti-war kind that Fayetteville sometimes sees.
>
> This was a protest with purple ribbons and signs about soldiers killed by their husbands or boyfriends, not by insurgents.
>
> In a way, it was a protest against the military. But not against the people who serve. Against the military culture that, the protesters think, makes it difficult for a woman in the military to tell her commanders that her soldier husband is threatening her. Against the military bureaucracy that, the protesters think, hides sexual assault complaints and brushes victims to the side.

> "It's military killing other military," [Ann] Wright said. "Why are these men feeling like they can kill these women? ... The military has to address this."
>
> Patricia Gregory, who served eight years active-duty National Guard, stood near the sign marking the Fort Bragg line and held a sign about stopping domestic violence in the military.
>
> "There are predators in the military," Gregory said. "And for those predators, young, inexperienced women who are away from home for the first time are very easy to pick out."

The response from Fort Bragg public affairs staff was almost peevish. Following the murders in 2002, they said, Fort Bragg had hired twelve victim advocates, fifteen more psychologists, added anger and stress management programs, and made some important changes to its domestic violence reporting policies. Soldiers were now able to seek help from therapists at Womack Army Medical Center or from chaplains at the Watters Family Life Center. Spouses could receive advice from a victim advocate or medical attention without triggering an investigation of a soldier.

And even if a soldier were to be disciplined, they added, his family would not be left to struggle–a new transitional compensation program entitled them to up to 36 months of support from the Army, including housing and health care.

The *Observer* dutifully reported that "Fort Bragg officials say the military's programs to prevent sexual assault and domestic abuse work."

"Nothing could be further from the truth that we don't attempt to be proactive in reducing domestic violence," a Fort Bragg spokesman insisted. "They can go to our chaplains, Womack Army hospital and to the Army Community Services," McCollum said.

Survivor: Christine Horne, whose mother was murdered in 1974 by her Green Beret father at Fort Bragg, stands by an exhibit at Quaker House honoring the memory of her mother and so many more, October 2008.

"We are sometimes baffled – why would someone do that and especially with all the help that is available? A divorce is so much easier."

These were good questions. More programs were indeed available in 2008 than in 2002. But Ann Wright had tackled these claims in an opinion piece a week earlier in the *Observer*:

> The military claims it is doing more to prevent such violence. I think it's clear the efforts are not enough, and are not taken as seriously as they should be. . . .Such violence happens across society; but the military has a particular problem in these areas.

Veteran Pat Gregory also spoke of this:

> Gregory said she believes that the military promotes a culture of coercion and fear that could prevent young women in the early stages of their military careers from telling anyone if their soldier-husbands are threatening them or if their superiors are harassing them. . . .

> Gregory said she thinks the military sometimes hides victims of abuse or pushes their complaints to the side to avoid damaging a unit's morale.

> "What I would be interested in is what happened two years ago? What has the Army quietly pushed aside?" she asked.

The lack of answers suggested that questions like these would sooner or later be raised again here, and elsewhere in the American military realm.

20. 2006-07: Brilliant Careers That went Wrong – Or Maybe Right

   While major public peace actions dwindled after 2006, considerable interest focused on those few soldiers who stood up against the war. Without mass GI resistance as in the Vietnam years, nevertheless some genuine heroes came forth. Quaker House had worked directly with Stephen Funk and Jeremy Hinzman, and a few other less visible cases.

   Others included Lt. Ehren Watada, at Fort Lewis, all the way across the country in Tacoma, Washington. In the spirit of the Concerned Officers Movement of the Vietnam years, in June 2006, Watada refused to deploy to Iraq with his unit, the Second Infantry Division, on the ground that his study of the war had persuaded him that duty there would make him a party to war crimes. (Unlike those years, however, Watada's witness was not publicly joined by others. Instead, numerous reports showed that young officers were simply leaving the military in droves at the first opportunity.)

   Watada was not, he said, a Conscientious Objector, and was even willing to serve in Afghanistan, which he considered a justifiable war. His statements were what would be expected from an educated officer: thoughtful, well-prepared, and calmly delivered. Yet for his refusal, and his public statements about it, he was charged with "conduct unbecoming an officer and a gentleman," and "missing movement," and faced the possibility of seven years in prison, as well as dismissal from the service.

   Sizeable support vigils were organized on Watada's behalf that summer, including highly visible vigils on an overpass above heavily-traveled Interstate Highway 5, which passed right outside the main gate at Fort Lewis.

   Quaker House made a brief connection with the Watada support effort, through the Gathering of Friends General Conference, which in early July 2006 was held at Pacific Lutheran University, just a few miles away from Fort Lewis. Chuck Fager joined a Watada vigil, met the Lieutenant, and organized a support meeting at the Quaker gathering.

   But another, more significant connection was made in Tacoma. A local attorney, Larry Hildes, sought Fager out and told him he had a client that knew him. "Here?" Fager said. "But I'm from North Carolina."

Hildes said it was somebody Fager had done counseling with awhile back, who had gone AWOL. A bit more discussion identified the mystery GI as the one called "Freddy," the tactical interrogator who had called more than a year earlier, and then emailed that he'd gone AWOL rather than return to Iraq or continue teaching other soldiers to do what he had been doing there.

The GI's name was Ricky Clousing, Hildes said. He had family in the Seattle area, and that's where he'd headed after going AWOL. Clousing planned to surface soon and return to Army custody, Hildes said; in fact, he'd been trying to, with Hildes negotiating for him, but Army officials claimed to be unable to locate Clousing's records. (This was a familiar story, Fager noted, wondering how often it was a dodge, and how often just plain incompetence.)

But Clousing was going to surface soon regardless, Hildes said, and when he did, chances were good that the Army would send him back to Fort Bragg. In theory he could be court martialed at Fort Lewis. But with one vocal and visible resister already on their plate in Lt. Watada, the odds were that Ft. Lewis commanders would want to rid themselves of another one ASAP; so stand by for updates.

Ricky Clousing, aka "Freddie," stopped at Quaker House while returning to Fort Bragg from AWOL, to face a court martial, August 2006.

These were not long in coming. Early the next month, Veterans for Peace held their national conference in Seattle. Lt. Watada spoke there, to cheers and vows of solidarity. And on August 11, a young Ricky Clousing took the podium. He told the group that in Iraq:

> "As an interrogator I spoke to Iraqis each day. This gave me an idea of what local civilians thought of coalition forces . . . I witnessed our baseless incarceration of civilians. I saw civilians

physically harassed. I saw an innocent Iraqi killed before me by US troops. I saw the abuse of power that goes without accountability."

"I stand here before you today about to surrender myself, which was always my intention . . . I stand here before you sharing the same idea as Henry David Thoreau: as a Soldier, as an American, and as a human being, we mustn't lend ourselves to that same evil which we condemn."

Then he drove to Tacoma, and accompanied by Hildes and a retinue of family members, veterans and media, walked across the same bridge where the weekly Watada vigils were held and through the main gate to Ft. Lewis.

Once he was physically on military turf again, Clousing's missing records were suddenly discovered, and he was, as expected, ordered back to Fort Bragg.

Fager met him at the Raleigh airport on August 18, as did several reporters and a TV crew. Clousing, his hair a dark mop and wearing a tee shirt bearing the motto, "Free Speech," made a good interview: he was unassuming, clear in his views, and didn't indulge in sloganeering or ideological rhetoric. And the evident serenity with which he faced the prospect of going to jail was impressive. "I really don't feel nervous. I totally feel at peace," he told a reporter. "My only regret is I couldn't be what my unit wanted me to be."

"He could have had a brilliant military career," Fager wrote in the Newsletter, "if only his faith and conscience hadn't gotten in the way."

Once Clousing was back at Fort Bragg, much of the work of Quaker House on his behalf was familiar: build support, both before the trial, and afterward. Initially he was charged with desertion; but because he had voluntarily returned, everyone knew this was unlikely to stick. Thus there remained AWOL, which would. Ricky had both an army defense lawyer, and a former military defender, David Miner, working with him, to negotiate a plea deal.

The army had two priorities in these talks, it seemed: first, its pound of flesh, which meant jail time. And second, it wanted to prevent the trial from becoming a platform for attacking the Iraq War, and allegations about torture and abuse. Words Conquer – and the fewer words said in public by Clousing or by any witnesses he might call, especially about matters like detainee mistreatment and the morality of the Iraq War, the better.

For his part, Ricky also wanted two things: first, to be able at least to bear his witness as to why he came to leave his post; and second, as short a sentence as possible. The leverage provided by the media attention coordinated by Quaker House was an indirect factor in the bargaining, but a real one. Whatever Ricky's fate, it would not go unnoticed by the outside world.

The ultimate deal came out well for Ricky. The desertion charge went away. From a year, the sentence offered dropped to three months. With reduced time for good behavior, it would decrease another few weeks. In return, the Army insisted that he plead guilty to AWOL. For the Army, a guilty plea would cut short the trial, and prevent the parade of defense witnesses talking about Abu Ghraib and other abuses.

The plea bargaining went on in a manner peculiar to the military justice system. Rather than negotiating with the court, Ricky's lawyers talked to the division commander's office. It was the commander who had the final authority as to the sentence. Their agreement would be kept confidential, however, until the court hearing. The military judge, who would know there was a deal, but not the terms, would also pass sentence. If the judge's sentence was less than the deal, it would stand. But if the judge's sentence was longer, the commander's deal took precedence.

And Ricky still had a card up his sleeve. Even after entering a guilty plea, he was permitted to address the court to explain his actions and present any mitigating factors, in the hope of winning a reduced sentence. This meant he would have the chance to bear his testimony. The trial, now revised to a sentencing hearing, was set for October 12.

When Clousing took the stand that morning, in a small upstairs courtroom on Fort Bragg, the Army judge, Col. Patrick Parrish, looked irritated. For his part, Clousing looked very different than when he had arrived in North Carolina almost two months earlier. He was in a dark green, full dress uniform, with gold sergeant's stripes on the sleeves, a red braided cord through the left shoulder epaulet, the 82nd's maroon beret folded at his side. The bushy hair was gone, as his head was shaved almost bald in the aerodynamic paratrooper style.

As Clousing began to describe the pattern of routine abuse he saw on the streets of occupied Iraq, the judge's irritation seemed to deepen. He interrupted Clousing frequently, and refused to let him read excerpts from his journal detailing his early struggles of conscience in Iraq. Yet no matter how much the judge disliked the fact, Clousing was entitled to speak in his own behalf, officially in hopes of gaining a lighter sentence. Col Parrish's hostile demeanor made clear that there was little chance of that, and everyone in the cramped courtroom knew it. But no matter how pro forma it was as a legal procedure, other audiences were listening to Clousing's testimony:

One was half a dozen other soldiers who had also been AWOL and had shared barracks space with him. They sat in the courtroom, listening closely and rooting quietly for their comrade.

The other audience was a row of reporters, who were closely monitored by a major and a sergeant from Fort Bragg's Public Affairs Office. Through the media, Clousing hoped to have his story heard across the country. Among the scribes was a correspondent from the *New York Times*,

223

which ensured a nationwide readership.

Despite the judge's repeated interference the main elements of a compelling story were told:

How Clousing was a born-again Christian who joined the Army after taking several mission trips with the evangelical group, Youth With a Mission.

How he trained to be an interrogator for Army intelligence, was assigned to the 82nd Airborne at Fort Bragg, and performed well enough to be fast-tracked for promotion to sergeant in less than three years.

How he went on patrols in Baghdad and Mosul, interrogating scores of Iraqi civilians who were swept up in searches and raids, and reports about many more detainees.

How his own interrogations and the records he reviewed showed clearly that upwards of eighty-five percent of the Iraqis who were detained by occupation forces, often for months, with no legal rights and without their families knowing if they were dead or alive, were being held for no reason – they were, as he put it, "just in the wrong place at the wrong time."

And how he could see, and told his superiors, that this treatment of hundreds and thousands of innocent Iraqis, was self-defeating. Worse, it was turning them into supporters of the insurgency, creating much of the resistance that the occupation forces were fighting to eradicate.

How these pleas fell on deaf ears.

How he saw numerous abuses of Iraqis on the streets, including the killing of an unarmed Iraqi youth.

How after his return to Fort Bragg, he sought help from the Army in resolving the questions of conscience that had been haunting him since his deployment – to no avail. A chaplain told him God approved war; a psychologist suggested he say he was gay or mentally ill, so he could get out of the Army.

How Clousing considered filing a Conscientious Objector claim, but ultimately decided against it, because while he was sure the Iraq war was immoral, he wasn't sure all wars were. How he finally decided that he had to separate himself from the Army and the war, by going AWOL for fourteen months. And how many of the church groups of his youth didn't understand or sympathize with what he had been through, seeing the flag and the cross as essentially the same thing.

When the young soldier was finished, the judge mulled over the testimony briefly, then pronounced sentence: eleven months, almost the maximum; looked at another way, Clousing's act of conscience was worth no more than a month's credit in the judge's estimation. But with the plea deal, Clousing hoped to be out of jail in time to get back to Seattle for Christmas.

His GI buddies crowded around to wish him well when the hearing finished and he prepared to head off to confinement.

Then the question was where he would serve the time. Fort Bragg, large as it was, had no brig of its own. Mention had been made of the Fort Leavenworth military penitentiary, though this seemed unlikely because it was mainly for the most serious offenders. More troubling was talk of the Army brig at Fort Lewis. It was close to Seattle, but conditions there for visiting and writing were very restrictive.

Ricky Clousing, at his "Get-out-of-the-brig" fete at Raleigh NC Friends Meeting, December 2006.

Fager was relieved when he heard it was to be Camp Lejeune. Quaker House knew how to handle that. In short order, visits were being lined up, and letters and cards were coming in. In a letter, Clousing passed on a message for Veteran's Day 2006:

> As I sit here with 44 other prisoners counting down individual sentences I'm overwhelmed at the irony of the situation. One month ago I was a Sergeant in the United States Army. One month ago I traded my uniform for an orange jump suit. I'm not the only one. There are a number of soldiers, airmen and marines who had no idea of how to transition once back from Iraq. Some of us, exposed to the unjust occupation and abuse of power in Iraq, went AWOL. Others turned to drugs, confused and perhaps seeking to understand what they had just participated in. Why were we sent to fight? Why were we to watch both sides dying around us?
>
> The guards are yelling now.

Eighteen months ago I was on the other side of this reality, interrogating Iraqi prisoners in their orange jumpsuits. No longer of use to the military now we sit here, disconnected from society in every way possible. Because a soldier who is able to see the humanity of the "enemy" is no longer an effective one. As put in Chris Hedges' *War Is a Force That Gives Us Meaning* – "the tension between those who know combat and thus know the public lie and those who propagate the myth usually ends with the mythmakers working to silence the witness of war."

This Veterans Day let us not forget the families broken by the burden of war and the soldiers sacrificed for those who profit. Not only that it was unnecessary but while those who deceived a nation are still not accountable for their actions, those affected by their war now sit behind bars. For all the education in a society and lesson from hindsight mean nothing unless we translate it into human action.

As planned, he was released on December 23, picked up by several supporters and taken to Raleigh for a celebration, then sent off to Seattle and a hero's welcome.

And a week later, the US death toll in Iraq passed the 3000 mark. On January 3, 2007, Fayetteville peace vigilers unfolded 37 name boards, which now stretched most of the way around the Market House. All the names had been hand-copied onto them from casualty lists by volunteers, who reported that the process was typically an emotionally draining one.

21. 2007-08: Facing Forty–And Just Getting Started

Another set of demands was closing in on Quaker House as 2007 opened, of a more mundane sort. The needs of the house for a major renovation could no longer be put off. The roof and the heating system had already been replaced. A basement storage space under the back corner had been flooded twice, once when a pipe in the crawl space froze and burst, and the other when the water heater next to it sprang a leak. Then there was the matter of old wiring, which in 2004 had almost sent the place up in smoke. The house needed new paint, inside and out. Plus a long list of additional items.

As all these items came to light, some hard facts had to be faced: for one, that for more than thirty years, the house had been maintained mainly by earnest amateurs, staff and Board volunteers, patching and making do, even undertaking additions – a back porch had been enclosed to make another bedroom–without bothering over such things as permits and building codes. Meanwhile, numerous less visible but potentially more hazardous issues, such as dangerously obsolete wiring and rot in the roof of the small garage, had gone unaddressed.

As the scope of these needs became unavoidable, the cost looked daunting: well over $100,000, in a time when costs of materials were rising rapidly. As might be expected, the question was raised in the Board, "Why not just sell it and move to a cheaper place?"

A good question, and a proper one for a project of Quakers, who do not bless or sanctify their buildings. Yet after a more careful look, this option was laid aside, for reasons both negative and positive: many of the more costly repairs would have to be made before a sale anyway, so the house could meet codes, thus drastically reducing the likely net proceeds.

More significant, because of its long tenure, the house was legally able to combine several functions: residence, office, place of worship, and meeting site, which would be very hard to replicate in one place elsewhere, due to updated zoning. The "Quaker House" sign on the front lawn was a good example: strictly speaking it was illegal. But a sign had been there so long it was grandfathered in. Also on the plus side, the inclusion of Quaker

227

House in the historic district gave it a certain patina of respectability—and even, some felt, protection—that its minority pacifist convictions needed in this military community.

But beyond all the specifics, the underlying imperative was that no letup was in sight for the Quaker House workload. So if it was in "right ordering," to use Quaker jargon, for the project to continue for the foreseeable future, then the house needed to be put in order. It was not about luxury, or gentrification. It was about good stewardship for continued service.

But if they were to stay and bite the renovation bullet, where would the money come from? When all was said and done, the price tag could approach $200,000; for Quaker House, that was a daunting figure. After all, only the year before, for the very first time in its nearly four decade history, the Board had approved an annual budget of more than $100,000. Yet daunting or not, they also realized that inaction was not saving money but only adding an inflationary increment to the ultimate cost.

The upshot was a Board agreement that they needed professional help with such an undertaking. But the right help was not easy to find. One Quaker fundraiser who was approached wanted Quaker House to set out to raise at least a million dollars, with half for an endowment. The fundraiser felt confident that the money was out there, and left the impression that $200,000 was hardly worth the effort.

But Fager and others resisted the million dollar idea. "We don't need that much, even if it's 'out there.' It's too easy to end up shaping your program according to what you're told you can raise money for," he argued, "rather than finding the funds to fulfill your mission," adding a repetition of his mantra: "We're not here to build an empire, but to do our work, of which there's plenty. We need the renovation to be better able to do this work in the coming generation."

So they looked for a fundraiser who would help them meet their goal, rather than press them to trade up to someone else's. They found him in Doug Herron, an experienced Quaker fundraiser from the Philadelphia area. At the end of March, 2007, Herron spent two days consulting with theBoardabout planning a campaign for $200,000.

Herron's experience and professionalism was very effective in giving the Board a sense that the goal could be reached. He also helped them break up the daunting total amount into manageable "bite-sized" pieces that individual members could handle. The first step was gathering pledges from theBoardand staff, which to everyone's amazement added up to nearly one-third of the total. This response built confidence.

"This was a real first for us," said Betsy Brinson, a Board member from Richmond, Virginia. "We'd never had a capital campaign before." Brinson grew up on Fort Bragg in a military family, but like so many others, left Fayetteville to go to college and never went back. She joined theBoardin 2002 and agreed to chair the capital campaign.

The plan was to raise the $200,000 in cash and pledges by February 2008, with the work to start as soon thereafter as possible. As the capital campaign kicked off, there were still moments of near-panic when the goal seemed huge, unrealistic. But the response was generous. Board members fanned out to organize events and make personal solicitations. Treasurer Curt Torell, along with the office assistants, Susan Lees and the replacement she trained in mid-2007, Roderick Lewis, kept up with the paperwork. By the November 2007 Board meeting, campaign clerk Betsy Brinson was able to report that the target amount had been surpassed, with a sizeable percentage of pledges already in hand.

At that point, design work for the renovation was far advanced. This effort marked a turn for Quaker House toward using a professional contractor and skilled craftspeople for the bulk of the work. Yet plenty of labor was still contributed by Board volunteers. For instance, the house had to be completely emptied, and temporary quarters rented. Juggling all the elements of the renovation process was an enormous and demanding job, and one Board member, Betsy Johnson of Wilmington NC, was crucial to it getting done.

In addition, Board member and architect Wendy Michener produced and donated the detailed house drawings and design options, several thousand dollars worth. In this she worked closely with Betsy Johnson, who had also worked on two previous historical renovations. Michener then shepherded the plans past the close scrutiny of the city Historical Commission, which had to approve all changes affecting the external appearance of the house – down to and including the use of paint colors considered authentic for a bungalow-style dwelling of its vintage. Another Board member, Steve Newsom, found and donated a number of new appliances, and put his carpentry experience to work as well. Volunteers from the Roanoke, Virginia Meeting contributed building skills for a week. By early April, 2008 the work was underway.

Yet while the staff might be temporarily displaced persons, program work continued. In Iraq, the rate of US casualties had slowed due to what the Pentagon called "the surge." Nevertheless, by the late March 2008 it was about to pass the 4000 mark. The name panels, now more than 45 in number, were put up for a vigil at the Market House, and now went essentially all the way around the building, and had to be held up with nylon cords, since there were not that many vigilers to hold them all up.

As part of the interregnum, and to get away from the physical upheaval at the house, Fager took advantage of an offer that had come from ACAT, the Paris-based anti-torture group, to visit and speak about the work in North Carolina. He spent several weeks in Europe, giving talks to twenty different groups about the need for international cooperation in the effort to hold accountable those responsible for the US torture system.

As part of the journey, Fager made two side trips. On the first, he visited a Swiss official named Dick Marty, in the lovely lakeside city of Lugano, Switzerland. Marty, a former prosecutor, had conducted a pioneering investigation of US torture flights and related clandestine activities in Europe, penetrating layers of denial and untruth in many governments. His reports, though brushed off by the CIA and little noticed in US major media, remain the baseline for future investigations.

"Knowing what he knows," Fager wrote of the

Swiss parliamentarian and former prosecutor Dick Marty, who led a pioneering investigation exposing US torture flights through Europe. His advice for ending this scourge: "Patience and determination."

This book includes Dick Marty's two masterful investigative reports on US torture flights in Europe.

visit, "I asked, is there any way to stop the perpetrators from achieving impunity for their actions?"

Marty's English was limited, but his response was unmistakable: "That's exactly the right question to be asking," he said. But he was not sanguine. The US government, he explained, had extracted pledges of immunity for its operatives from most European governments. Challenges to that complicity would be difficult. But he was not suggesting Fager and other anti-torture advocates simply give up and go home. "This will be a long work," Marty said. "It will require patience and determination."

On his other side trip, Fager flew into Shannon, Ireland, to visit local Quakers and an intrepid Irish planespotter, Edward Horgan. Horgan met him at the airport, and over a glass of soda in the lounge, described how both US military forces and clandestine agencies used the Shannon airport as a regular refueling stop, despite the fact that Ireland was officially a neutral country and not part of the NATO alliance.

Then they walked out toward Horgan's car, and there right behind the airport fence, a stone's throw away, was a large cargo airliner with the name "Evergreen International" on its fuselage. Horgan pointed it out indignantly. Evergreen, he explained (and other sources confirmed), is a charter company that has one client: the CIA. The plane they were looking at was not likely involved in torture flights, but rather carrying a load of the miscellaneous cargo that any ongoing American military operation demands. In less than an hour it was gone. "These kinds of planes are in and out of here all the time," Horgan complained, while the government compliantly looked the other way. Planespotting in Shannon was easy, it seemed; sometimes even effortless.

Meanwhile, back home calls to the GI Hotline had continued at record levels all through 2007, reaching a total of 9496 for the year. This was an overload level for Steve and Lenore, who had their second child, Charles Quinn Yarger, in May 2007. There was experimentation with adding a third part-time Hotline counselor during this period, but no long-term arrangement had yet worked out.

While internal issues in the Hotline network made total call figures unavailable, there were signs by mid-2008 that call volume increase might be leveling off, after fourteen years of continual increase. Steve and Lenore

Retired Irish Army officer and veteran planespotter Edward Horgan at work at the Shannon International Airport, May 2008. Inset at upper right is a reputed cargo plane for the CIA he had spotted the day before. Horgan has been arrested several times for protesting torture flights and military stopovers at Shannon, which flagrantly violate Irish neutrality.

231

could only speculate about what was happening. Most callers said they had found the Hotline via the Internet. Could awareness by that medium be reaching a saturation level within the military population at its present level? Could the recent slower casualty rate be easing anxieties among some GIs and family members? Or was this just a statistical blip? Whatever it was, the call level was still near historic highs.

At the same time, the issue of torture remained salient. For one thing, there was no sign of recession in the Carolina "Torture Industrial Complex." To the contrary, in mid-2008, at the Fayetteville airport, the secretive Centurion Aviation Services was building a new hangar, doubling the size of its facility. To the north, Aero Contractors was expanding in Smithfield NC. Elsewhere the economy might be troubled; presidential candidates might be proclaiming their abhorrence of torture; but for the Carolina "torture taxi" companies, business still seemed to be booming.

But anti-torture work continued as well. Quaker House was integrally involved in planning two Quaker conferences on the subject, in June of 2006 and 2007. It was part of the religious coalition NRCAT. Chuck Fager was also active with the group North Carolina Stop Torture Now, which focused on exposing what was happening around Smithfield and Aero. Further, as investigations into the torture system continued, the extensive role of Fort Bragg in hatching it, through the Special Forces center there, came increasingly to the light.

Admittedly, this was a subject which still gave many people shudders of aversion. "The accounts of actual torture carried out by agents of 'our' government were very difficult to sit through," Fager reported in the Quaker House Newsletter, describing his own reactions to facing up to what was happening. "Contemplating their implications for me as a person, a citizen and a Quaker, was intensely painful." Such reactions make torture hard to organize around. But it was something that Quaker House, given its location, could not avoid.

The project's role as a catalyst and resource likewise continued. Besides the support work on domestic violence, it was a source of ideas that other groups adopted and turned into concrete events: A church peace conference in Greensboro; an anti-torture gathering at Duke University; a major protest at Smithfield. All grew out of ideas generated from Quaker House, but without its name on them. In addition, its "Truth In Recruiting" slogan was adopted by more groups in the field, usually without credit.

From April through June, the renovation work went well. It was finished on time, in mid-July, and within budget, facts which homeowners will know are often amazing accomplishments. Completion was timely in another way, in that the larger economic collapse was setting in, but Quaker House was fixed up and the work paid for, just in time.

From the outside, as the Historical Commission hoped, the house looked just the same, except with a fresh coat of historically accurate dark green paint, set off with smart mustard and cream trim, with red accents. But there had also been much repair and even reconstruction on the brickwork and wall supports. Inside, some of the changes, like the new wiring, were largely invisible. But the office and office space was reconfigured to be more useful and efficient, and a much needed second bathroom was installed.

In the dining room, where the GI Resistance exhibit had been hung on the wall with tape, exhibit board now covered most of the walls, to create a dedicated display area. (The first exhibit went up in early October, as part of the domestic violence event with Ann Wright and Christine Horne.) The garage was almost all new.

When the Board met in the "new" house on October 25, the impact was complex: certainly there was pleasure at the makeover, plus pride in the collective accomplishment it represented. Yet the very quality of the renovation, combined with the fact that its completion came on the cusp of the project's fortieth year, turned the Board reflective. Given that we have put Quaker House physically in shape for a long period of additional service, they asked themselves, how can we best build on what has been done and do the most to meet the needs and opportunities that are coming?

Board members Curt Torell, left, and Betsy Johnson at work on renovating the Quaker House garage.

This could have sounded like an echo of the indecisive fretting over the years, loudest when there were long intervals without staff, questioning whether there was still a need for Quaker House or value in keeping it going. It could have, but it didn't. This Board was not struggling to find a purpose, but looking to build on strength and achievement.

Moreover, the timing was right for such a rethinking of strategy and priorities: in Washington, a new administration would soon take office. This brought hope, but also a pledge to expand the military and the war in Afghanistan. Such expansion meant even more recruiting, aimed especially

The renovated look of Quaker House: forty years of witness, and just getting started.

at those with fewer other opportunities. Plus there was recurrent talk of "national service" proposals that sounded a lot like a new draft. Militarism remained alive and well, in the US and elsewhere. The torture taxi companies in NC were growing. The plague of violence within the military culture, so evident around Fort Bragg and Camp Lejeune, seemed unchecked by the Army's showcase programs. There was also the problem of "war Christianity," which identified America with a divinely-mandated mission to remake the world. The evidence of this outlook, and the hazards it posed, was all around, and Fager felt keenly both the need to find a way to challenge it, and the lack of such an effort so far in his tenure.

And that's not to mention that the overall economy was facing big shocks, which were sure to impact small nonprofits like Quaker House.

Looking further ahead, the prospect of change within could be seen: Chuck Fager was soon to be the longest-serving Director. Even so, his contract would end no later than 2012, and one of its goals was to oversee an orderly transition, without another damaging gap in staffing. That had been a rare occurrence in Quaker House history; could it be made to happen?

The Board resolved to consider these issues and opportunities in a strategy retreat early in 2008. Anticipation and morale were high: the house was now in "fighting tri"; the staff had a unique body of experience; there was much in the way of resources to share; and the pervasive militarism of our society offered an abundance of targets.

As its fortieth year of witness opened, the Board, staff and supporters of Quaker House could rightly conclude that even with all that has gone before, they are indeed just getting started.

A Note On Sources & References

Both the author and the editor spent considerable time in research for this book, and labored long and hard to make it as factual as possible. However, there was neither time nor resources for making it into a scholarly treatise. Those who want to check detailed sources for many items in the account above can expect to do checking on their own, retracing some of our footsteps. The list of references below suggests where we went for information.

Above all, we made use of the Quaker House archives, which are held in the Friends Historical Collection of the Hege Library at Guilford College, in Greensboro NC. Under the skillful care of College Archivist (and Quaker House alumna) Gwen Gosney Erickson, these encompass minutes of board meetings, newsletters, correspondence and memos, many new clippings from various papers, and other documents.

The archives also include Bruce Pulliam's incomparable collection of *Bragg Briefs* and other "ephemera" of the GI resistance around Fort Bragg during the Vietnam years, as well as a sheaf of Military Intelligence and other surveillance reports, pried loose from government filing cabinets by Director Bill Sholar in the late 1970s.

All in all, the Quaker House archives is a compact gold mine of information, not only about this project, but about a very contentious era in American cultural and social history. It will be of much use to historians astute enough to make use of it.

Likewise, the archives of the *Fayetteville Observer* were a constant resource. These are available online back through 1988; but consulting them involves user fees. The *Observer* is a remarkable enterprise, independently owned, serious about journalistic professionalism, and able to balance a strong pro-military orientation with a commitment to fairness. It has been a pleasure to read it and interact with its staff; in recent years, it has been equally agonizing to watch its roster and coverage contract as the foundations of print journalism collapsed under it.

In addition, we conducted many interviews with former Quaker

236

House staff and Board members. Among these (our apologies to anyone we forgot) were:

Kenn Arning	Bill Jeffries
Ann Ashford	Mac Legerton
Wood Bouldin	Debbie Liebers
Judy (Hamrick) Dixon	Dick Marty
Alex Doty	Anne Matthysse
Virginia Driscoll	Bruce Pulliam
Gwen Gosney Erickson	Harry "Scotty" Scott
Bob & Barbara Gosney	Greg Sommers
Bob Gwyn	Sandy Sweitzer
J.C. Honeycutt	John Wenberg

For the account of the years since 2001, current Director Chuck Fager drew extensively on his own memories and personal notes, as well as minutes, newsletters, emails, clippings, and related sources. Much of this too will eventually find its way into the Quaker House archives. A fuller exposition of his adaptation of Sun Tzu and military strategy for peace work can be found in a booklet, *A Quaker Declaration of War,* and on the Quaker House website: quakerhouse.org . We also made use of the more than twenty issues of the Quaker House Newsletter n this decade, which are available online at the website.

Books

We relied less on books as sources, but several were very valuable. For background about Fayetteville-Fort Bragg, one could do no better than Catherine Lutz's *Homefront: A Military City and the American Twentieth Century* (Beacon Press 2001). Besides drawing an in-depth portrait of the areas's history and development, Lutz draws from this story a revealing analysis of the growth of US militarism since the 1920s.

For some of the most important recent information about Fort Bragg and its role in the so-called war on terror, two books have been eye-opening and sobering: first is Jane Mayer's *The Dark Side* (Doubleday 2008). She deals primarily with what we have called here the "Torture Industrial Complex," at its Washington nucleus and hatchery; but along the way, this intrepid reporter for *The New Yorker* lifts the curtain on the key events in the creation of a torture regime that took place at or "migrated" from Fort Bragg.

The other basic volume is Alfred McCoy's *A Question of Torture* (Holt 2006), which brings out the sordid and shocking decades-long history of the developing US torture system, a story which many of us still have difficulty facing.

More compact, but pioneering in its journalism, was *Torture Taxi: On the Trail of the CIA's Rendition Flights,* by Trevor Paglen and A.C. Thompson. These writers essentially discovered the network of amateur planespotters who helped connect the dots of the international torture flight system.

There are numerous other books related to this topic, and their number increases monthly; they are worth keeping up with, as this matter is far from played out.

Concerning the epidemic of violence within the military, which encompasses not only domestic assaults, but suicides/homicides and sexual assaults as well, there is to our knowledge no comprehensive or reliable study as yet. In large part this is a result of the military's skillful application of the dictum, "Words Conquer," by means of ongoing resistance to accurate information gathering or reliable analysis. Yet we do not shrink from declaring that such an epidemic exists, is ongoing, and service-wide, and urgently needs such close attention.

Likewise, the central role of religion as a pillar of US militarism is a fact that cannot be gainsaid. Yet it is only recently that a scholar from this background, Charles Marsh of the University of Virginia, published his *Wayward Christian Soldiers* (Oxford 2007) and began the long overdue critique of this dangerous cult.

Likewise, we are still waiting for a full and informed account of the penetration of the US military by extremely conservative, pro-war Christian fundamentalist groups. This phenomenon too is undeniable, but still seen only in glimpses, and evidently beyond the grasp of most military reporters. Two recent books, however, show from radically different angles its importance and danger:

The first, *With God on Our Side: One Man's War Against an Evangelical Coup in America's Military* (St. Martin's 2008), by Michael (Mikey) Weinstein, tells how the author, a Jewish Republican lawyer and very loyal graduate of the Air Force Academy discovered the evangelical infiltration and indoctrination entrenched there, which left him horrified and radicalized. Besides writing this book, Weinstein has founded the Military Religious Freedom Foundation, which has filed lawsuits challenging this infiltration, with impact that it only beginning to be felt.

The second could be a doppleganger for Weinstein: it is *Never*

Surrender (Faithwords 2008), by retired general William "Jerry" Boykin, who was commander of the super-secret Delta Force, and is a prime specimen of the current crop of warriors who see America as God's chosen Christian nation to smite (literally) the terrorist infidels. His book is a brief for crusaders; and by the way, he considers Mikey Weinstein's work "demonic."

Online Sources

The Defense Domestic Violence Task Force whose executive director, Deborah Tucker, visited Fayetteville in 2002 after the seven-homicide outbreak, issued several reports. There was much of value in them, from which the interested reader could learn much. Search for them at: http://www.dtic.mil/dtic/ .

There were other online sources which were quite useful to us. An amazing documentary film of the Vietnam era GI Resistance, *"Sir! NoSir!"* was released by Displaced Films in late 2006. It tells many jaw-dropping and inspiring stories of the insurgency that drove the late Col. Robert Heinl to distraction. Our only complaint about it is that it shamefully neglects Fort Bragg; but there was so much great material, and only 90 minutes to cram it into, so they had to make cuts somewhere. At their website, however, there is a detailed and highly informative timeline of the GI resistance, which does include numerous events in Fayetteville as described in this book. Find the timeline here: http://www.sirnosir.com/timeline/timeline.html

Additional Online sources: Chuck Fager read both Sun Tzu's, *The Art of War* and the *Marine Corps Doctrinal Publication 1-1: Strategy* handbook online, where they are available in multiple locations. And both author and editor shamelessly admit that they frequently consulted that burgeoning font of practically all knowledge, Wikipedia.

1969-2009: 40 Years of Front-Line Peace Witness ...
... And Just Getting Started.
www.quakerhouse.org